Within these pages we are afforded a rare privilege. Each of these narratives represents an opportunity to sit down with a Cherokee National Treasure for a visit. Each artist, craftsman, linguist, each keeper of our traditional ways, has graciously allowed us into their kitchen, their living room, their studio, or onto their porch to share with us their story—the story of what motivates, inspires, and drives them to create, build, teach, and to carry on the traditions and the language of our Cherokee people.

Those of us who worked on this project, and those of you who will be reading these narratives are not reading essays or articles. We are not studying theses or dissertations. We are being allowed to step into the lives of our Treasures and to hear their stories in their own words. The stories and the words are theirs, and not yours or mine. The voices are their voices. We would no sooner change or alter this than we would correct a host who invited us to sit in front of the fire and have a friendly chat.

It is their choice to share their stories with us in their own words. It is our privilege to listen and to learn.

Gayle Parnell Samuels

LOST
ARTS
ORAL HISTORY PROJECT

PROJECT DESCRIPTION

What is it that makes us Indian?

It is not the color of our skins or the blood in our veins. Being Indian is a way of life, living and remembering our past.

Today it is painfully clear that certain aspects of our past are in danger of being lost forever. Areas of our culture, our ancient skills, our traditions, our arts are dying. They die each time one of our elders dies without passing along the arts and skills that their parents taught them.

If conditions remain the same, the logical conclusion is that many of our traditions will be lost forever. This does not have to be the case.

We are at a very important time in our history. We can sit back and allow important parts of our culture to be lost or we can take actions to preserve it for many future generations to come.

If we are to attempt to save our "lost arts", we must act now. The CHEROKEE NATION OF OKLAHOMA, NORTHEASTERN STATE UNIVERSITY and the CHEROKEE NATIONAL HISTORICAL SOCIETY are making that attempt through a project entitled, "Lost Arts" Project.

We are interested in preserving certain areas of our culture by combining oral history interviews with elders still practicing the dying skills, video taping those skills and developing an elementary curriculum program for area schools.

ORGANIZATIONS

This is a joint effort of the Cherokee Nation Department of Planning and Development, the Northeastern State University Bilingual Education Center, and the Cherokee National Historical Society.

These three organizations have a common goal, the preservation of these "Lost Arts." The project will involve the utilization of each of these organization's special skills. It is our hope that the organizational cooperation will lead to further joint efforts.

We invite interested individuals and organizations to become involved in this unique education and historic preservation project.

CHEROKEE NATION OF OKLAHOMA
Julie Moss

CHEROKEE NATIONAL HISTORICAL SOCIETY
Jacqueline Greb

NORTHEASTERN STATE UNIVERSITY
BILINGUAL EDUCATION CENTER
Dennis Snell

COMMUNITY ADVISOR
Hastings Shade

cherokee national treasures 2011 medallion ceremony

(Front) Lucille Hair, Betty Jo Smith, Lena Blackbird, Dorothy Ice, Lizzie Whitekiller, Anna Mitchell, (middle) Anna Sixkiller, Bessie Russell, Margaret Wilson, Kathy Vanbuskirk, Sue Thompson, Betty Christie Frogg, Ruth England, Thelma Forrest, Vivian Cotrell, Kathryn Kelley, Shawna Cain, Edith Catcher Knight, (back) Roger Cain, John Ketcher, Ed Fields, Al Herrin, Thomas Muskrat, David Scott, Jess Oosahwee, Noel Timothy Grayson, Knokovtee Scott, Toby Hughes, and Perry Vanbuskirk. On-screen in background behind group is Lorene Drywater.

CHEROKEE NATIONAL TREASURES

in their own words

by the Cherokee National Treasures
- in their own words
edited by Shawna Morton Cain
and Pamela Jumper Thurman

published by Cherokee Nation

ISBN: 978-1-934397-18-3

Published by Cherokee Nation

PO Box 948
Tahlequah, Oklahoma 74464

Distributed by
The University of Oklahoma Press
2800 Venture Drive
Norman, Oklahoma 73069
www.oupress.com

Edited by
Shawna Morton Cain, PhD
Pamela Jumper Thurman, PhD
Betty Christie Frogg

Copy-Edited by
Lead Copy Editor Gayle Parnell Samuels

Back Dust Jacket Photography by Thomas Muskrat

Publishing Supervision by
Quaid Publishing LLC
10 Cosmos Court
Santa Fe, New Mexico 87508
800 335-9208
tom@tomquaid.com
Tom Quaid
800 335-9208
Gloria Quaid, Project Manager
Shelli Clemenceau, Design Supervision
Tom Quaid, Publishing and Printing Supervision

Archival material and photographs provided by
Cherokee National Treasures and family members

Printed in the Unites States of America

CHEROKEE NATIONAL TREASURE

table of contents

categories

cherokee national treasures book review board

These individual Cherokee National Treasures have demonstrated commitment to the original mission and goals of the Lost Arts Project founded in 1987, which was the impetus of what became the Cherokee Living National Treasures -Master Craftsman Series of the Lost Arts Program (Resolution No. 74-88) that was unanimously certified by Tribal Council on August 15, 1988.

The original purpose of this legislation was to ensure that the Cherokee Nation would continue to "preserve those Cherokee art forms that otherwise may be lost through the passage of time." As traditional Cherokee artisans who live and continue to create in a contemporary world, these individuals have worked well together to perpetuate traditional art forms and the knowledge that informs Cherokee artistic traditions. All have dedicated their lives to ensuring that our unique Cherokee artistic past is not forgotten or lost. As a group, these individuals making up the Cherokee National Treasures Book Review Board have proven through time that they hold and respect the values of those Elders and culture bearers who came before us. As each continues to teach, support and preserve our traditional and ancient art forms, they represent and understand the wisdom of our cultural artistic expression through time immemorial.

Kathryn Kelley,

Born December 6, 1930
Grove, Oklahoma

Cherokee National Treasure
Traditional Basketry—Awarded 2003

Cherokee National Treasures Association
Elders Advisory Board Member

Betty Jo Smith,

Born March 26, 1931
Lost City Community

Cherokee National Treasure
Traditional Foods—Awarded 1991

Cherokee Nation Tribal Council Member, 1979-1983

Cherokee National Treasures Association
Elders Advisory Board Member

Lorene Drywater,

Born June 19, 1932
Steely Hollow Community

Cherokee National Treasure
Traditional Clothing—Awarded 1990

Cherokee Native Art & Plant Society
Elders Advisory Board

Cherokee National Treasures Association
Elders Advisory Board

Dorothy Ice,

Born December 26, 1935
Briggs Community

Cherokee National Treasure
Traditional Loom Weaving—Awarded 1991

United Keetoowah Band—Tradition Keeper—Awarded 2013

Cherokee National Treasure Association
Executive Board Member

Al Herrin,

Born March 13, 1936
Tahlequah, Oklahoma

Cherokee National Treasure
Bow Making—Awarded 1991

Cherokee National Treasure
Advisory Board and Selection Committee, 1988-Present

Bessie Rackleff Russel,

Born June 22, 1938
Rocky Ford Community

Cherokee National Treasure
Traditional Basketry—Awarded 1999

Cherokee Native Art & Plant Society
Elders Advisory Board Member

Cherokee National Treasure Association
Elders Advisory Board Member

Edith Catcher Knight,

Born December 6, 1939
England Hollow Community

Cherokee National Treasure
Traditional Clothing—Awarded 1992

Cherokee National Treasure Association
Executive Board Member

Thelma Vann Forrest,

Born February 9, 1940
Tahlequah, Oklahoma

Cherokee National Treasure
Traditional Basketry—Awarded 1992

Cherokee Native Art & Plant Society
Board Member

Durbin Feeling,

Born April 2, 1946
Tahlequah, Oklahoma

Cherokee National Treasure
Cherokee Language—Awarded 2011

Cherokee National Treasure Association
Elders Advisory Board Member

Donald Vann,

Born October 22, 1949
Tahlequah, Oklahoma

Cherokee National Treasure
Painting—Awarded 2013

Cherokee Medal of Patriotism—Awarded 2013

Cherokee National Treasure Association
Elders Advisory Board

Betty Christie Frogg,

Born August 7, 1955
Wauhilla Community

Cherokee National Treasure
Traditional Basketry—Awarded 2010

Cherokee National Treasure Association
President

SEAL OF THE CHEROKEE NATION
ᏣᎳᎩ ᎠᏰᎵ
SEPT. 6, 1839

Osiyo.

I am honored to introduce you to a new book coordinated by my friends Roger and Shawna Cain that profiles Cherokee National Treasures, the prestigious citizens who actively work to preserve and revive Cherokee cultural practices that might otherwise be lost from one generation to the next.

The profiles and photos within this book are compelling and you will come to better understand how our tribal National Treasures represent the very best values of our tribe. Their efforts collectively make us all better, stronger and more beautiful.
The Cherokee National Treasure Award was created in 1988 and is given annually to a select few during the Cherokee National Holiday. Since its inception, about 100 Cherokee Nation citizens have been recognized for their artistic and preservation work.

Our community, our culture and our commitment as Cherokees have taught us to leave the world a better place for today, tomorrow and the generations ahead. I can tell you that all of these citizens in their own, humble way have done that. Each of these Treasures possesses a true gift. Those talents help shape the Cherokee Nation today, while protecting our unique culture and lifeways.

Honorees are selected based on their skill and cultural and historical knowledge, and each of them is committed to education and cultural preservation. They are all actively involved with the preservation and continuation of traditional practices.

These men and women preserve different aspects of our Cherokee culture for future generations, including craft-making, language, graphic arts, contemporary arts, storytelling, music and other art forms. Because of their love and commitment to their respective discipline, the spirit and heritage of the Cherokee Nation remain as vibrant today as ever.
It speaks volumes about our tribal government that we strive to honor the people who are keeping our traditional ways alive. These individuals exemplify the values that we hold dear as a people and sovereign government.

I am honored to know most of our Cherokee National Treasures. I thoroughly admire them all and respect their talents. They all deserve our deepest respect and gratitude because they are role models for young and old alike, and their positive influence propels us all, as Cherokee people, forward.

I would also like to extend a special thank you to Cherokee Nation citizens Pamela Jumper Thurman and Gayle Parnell Samuels, along with all of the National Treasures, families and friends who contributed to this outstanding project.

To each and every one of them I say a heartfelt *Wado.*

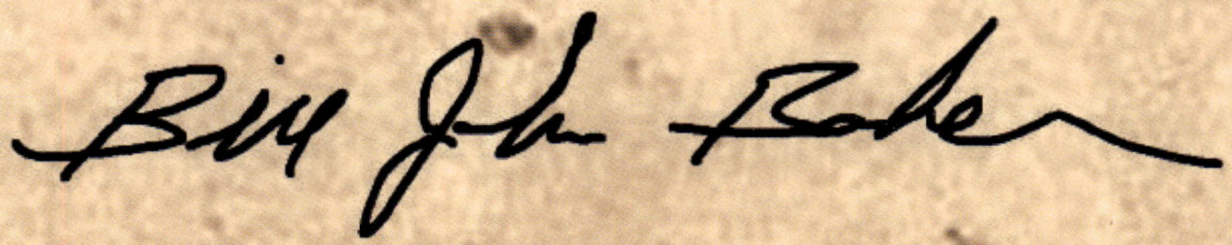

Bill John Baker
Principal Chief, Cherokee Nation

Acknowledgements

We would like to express our deepest appreciation to the many individuals who contributed to the completion of this book.

Chief Bill John Baker
Deputy Chief S. Joe Crittenden
Chuck Hoskin, Jr.
Bryan Shade
Gayle Parnell Samuels
Betty Frogg
Cherokee Nation
Cherokee Nation Businesses

To the following people who gave their time and effort in helping to locate and identify families and friends of our Cherokee Treasures, we say thank you. Also to those who provided access to and shared their collections of Cherokee National Treasures art for photographs.

Cherokee Advocate
Cherokee Heritage Center
Cherokee National Historical Society
Cherokee Phoenix
Diligwa 1710 Cherokee Village
Five Civilized Tribes Museum
Fred Jones Museum
Gilcrease Museum
Greenleaf State Park
Murrell Home
National Public Radio
Philbrook Museum

Wesley Chuculate
Shelli Clemenceau
Jim Cosby
Karen Coody Cooper
David Cornsilk
Bill Davis
Phyllis Edwards
Phyllis Fife
Jodi Fishinghawk
Kenneth Foster
David Fowler
Peggy Webster Fredrick

Susan Gilliland
Jackie Grebb
Sequoyah Guess
Aaron Lamar Hair
Roy Hamilton
January Hoskin
Sam Jones, KJRH-TV
Owen Knight
Brendalee Lassiter
Dick Lay
Annie Loy

Pamm Martin
Linda Martin
Nancy Oosahwee
Brenda Lawrence Partain
Barbara Plested
Gloria Quaid
Tom Quaid
Margaret Raymond
Madonna Ritchie
Dawni Saloli
Anna Sixkiller
Sandy Smith
Mr. and Mrs. Rex Earl Starr
Stephanie Stick
Sammy Still
Rennard Strickland
Emily Thompson
Susie Thompson
Gary Thurman
Linda Vann
Kathy White
Sue Wolfe

We must acknowledge the family members and friends for their contribution in telling the stories about those Treasures who have left us. Because of their valuable assistance, this book is richer in context and every story is told.

And finally, never-ending gratitude to the Cherokee Treasures for sharing their stories, for perpetuating our Cherokee culture through the practice of their art, time spent demonstrating, educating the public, and unselfishly mentoring and teaching other artists.

Wado!

Shawna Morton Cain Pamela Jumper Thurman

Introduction

Cherokee National Treasures Book Project

Cherokee History is the story of our ancestors—our story—and the stories that Cherokees will look back upon in the future. It is through the voices of our Elders and ancestors that we learn to understand our past, present, and future as Cherokee people.

As Cherokee, we know that our history is not only well documented, but very rich. We also know that much of our history has been passed down through oral traditions from ancient times to today. This book evolved from a commitment to honor the tradition of sharing stories, stories that are passed from one generation to the next by Cherokee people. These stories teach us lessons, remind us of earlier times, and often provide a unique history of who we are and how we came to be. Our art plays a very vital and tangible role in those stories. The timeless tradition of listening to the stories of those who came before us is cherished. It is from these stories that we continue to explore Cherokee history through the voices of Cherokees in the twenty-first century.

Our Cherokee National Treasures are those Cherokees who have been distinguished by the Cherokee Nation and the Cherokee National Historical Society as Master Artisans and Craftspeople in producing and preserving Cherokee art forms that might otherwise be lost through the passage of time. Since 1988, Cherokee National Treasures have been honored for preserving the traditional art forms of bow making, gig making, pottery, blowgun and darts, basketry, carving, loom weaving, clothing, bow and arrow, flint-knapping, turtle shell shakers, traditional foods, doll making, marble making, stick ball sticks, quilting, mask making, Cherokee language, painting, sculpture, storytelling, and metalsmithing.

Hastings Shade, a Cherokee from Hulbert, first approached tribal officials about concerns that as traditional Cherokee craftsmen died, so did their crafts. Shade had tried to find artisans to teach him some of the old ways and learned how few traditional craftsmen are left. (*Cherokee Advocate*, 1988) At the same time, Cherokee Elders stressed to the Cherokee Nation that too many traditional art forms were being lost. As a result, the Lost Arts Project was initiated with the assistance of Northeastern State University and the Oklahoma Foundation for Humanities. The thirty-sixth annual Cherokee National Holiday exhibit, "Discovering the Lost Arts," was displayed in the W.W. Keeler Tribal Complex. This was the first time that traditional Cherokee artisans were honored as Living Treasures, demonstrating Cherokee traditions involved in making bows, gigs, marbles, blowguns and darts, and also including the Cornstalk Shoot.

Since its inception, Cherokee Nation has honored ninety-four Cherokees as Cherokee National Treasures. *Cherokee National Treasures: In Their Own Words* is a compilation of personal narratives as told by each living Cherokee National Treasure, as well as by friends and family of those Cherokee National Treasures who have passed on but live with us today in spirit.

This project would not have been possible without the involvement and guidance of the Cherokee National Treasure Book Review Board. This board, comprised only of Cherokee National Treasure Elders, set guidelines to ensure that all Cherokee National Treasures—living and deceased—would be well represented. These Elders discussed and came to a consensus as to the methodology and how to best represent the Cherokee National Treasure program, its historical significance and Cherokee art as it enters into the twenty-first century.

The book is organized with the recognition of each category in the order that it was added, while the artists are presented by birthdate to honor the Elders first. Though the artist may not appear in the category for which he or she was recognized, the book follows a logical chronology and evenly distributes the stories.

We are grateful beyond words for the generosity of those who shared their stories and to their family members and friends, each of who have been essential to the success of this project. Their dedication has been a significant contribution to this project and has gone far in corroborating just how important it is that Cherokee practices and art traditions continue today and in the future. It is only through the sharing and passing on of our peoples' stories, arts, knowledge, and cultural practices that we continue to record and preserve the beautiful tapestry that is our Cherokee history.

Making of Medallions

Making of the Medallions

Since the Cherokee Nation and the Cherokee National Historical Society officially established the Cherokee National Living Treasure program on August 15, 1988, individual Cherokees have been distinguished as Master Craftspeople and Artisans at each Cherokee National Holiday. They were honored as Treasures for their contributions in perpetuating the Lost Arts and later, for their creation of the more contemporary art of the Cherokee.

Twenty-three years after the program was initiated, a group of Cherokee National Treasures who were working together to build a Cherokee National Treasure Mentoring project began to realize that we were losing track of our living National Treasures. Recognizing the impact of this loss, this group of Cherokee National Treasures began to meet at a local nonprofit organization located on Main Street in Tahlequah, Oklahoma. Led by an Elder's advisory board—Lorene Drywater, Thelma Forrest, Dorothy Ice, Kathryn Kelley, John Ketcher and Betty Smith—the group decided to begin teaching and mentoring projects in the Cherokee arts as well as researching and archiving stories, pictures, and artwork of Cherokee National Treasures.

After locating the families of both living and deceased Cherokee National Treasures, the group approached the Cherokee Nation to celebrate both the program and all Cherokee National Treasures with a commemorative, handmade copper medallion. The medallion was designed by the Cherokee Elders Advisory Committee and Mike Teehee, student of artist Toneh Chuleewah. Toneh volunteered his time to mentor Cherokee National Treasures Roger Cain and David Scott to produce handmade copper medallions to honor all of our living and deceased National Treasure master artisans.

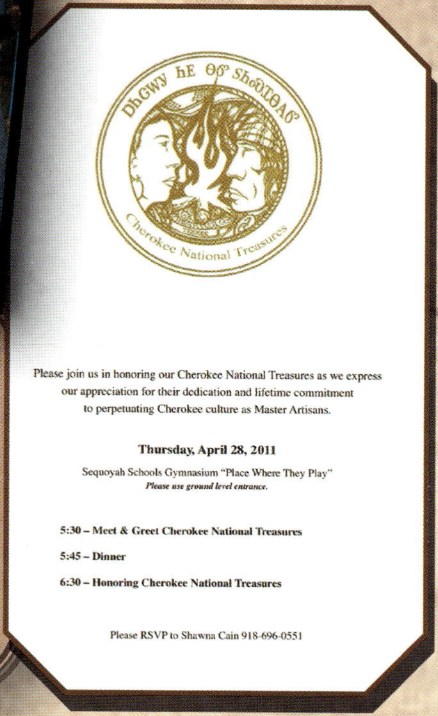
Please join us in honoring our Cherokee National Treasures as we express our appreciation for their dedication and lifetime commitment to perpetuating Cherokee culture as Master Artisans.

Thursday, April 28, 2011

Sequoyah Schools Gymnasium "Place Where They Play"
Please use ground level entrance.

5:30 – Meet & Greet Cherokee National Treasures

5:45 – Dinner

6:30 – Honoring Cherokee National Treasures

Please RSVP to Shawna Cain 918-696-0551

On April 28, 2011, the Cherokee Nation, the Cherokee Native Art & Plant Society and Cherokee Nation Entertainment sponsored the Cherokee National Treasure Medallion banquet and celebration at Sequoyah Schools Gymnasium Place Where They Play and the medallions were presented.

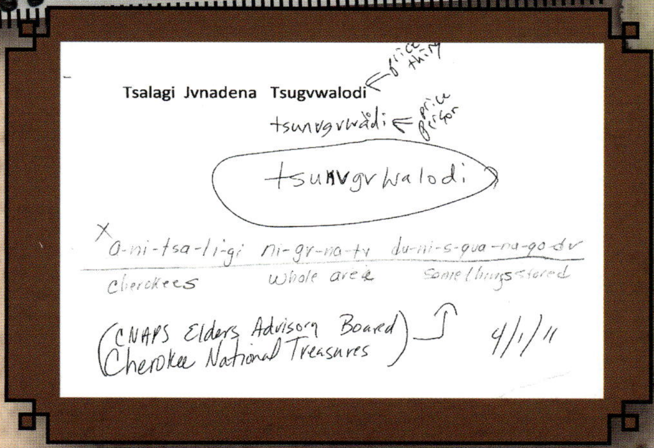
Tsalagi Jvnadena Tsugvwalodi

Description of the Medallion

The Elder's Advisory Board chose copper as the medium for the commemorative medallions because Cherokees have used copper as a medium of artistic expression for thousands of years. Mike Teehee drew the illustration to depict the Elder Advisory Board's concept for a design incorporating a Cherokee woman facing a Cherokee man with the sacred fire connecting them. Coming up with a phrase to be etched in Cherokee atop the medallion that would encapsulate the English language title for "Cherokee National Treasure" required the guidance of many Cherokee National Treasure first speakers. The Cherokee phrase *A-ni-tsa-la-gi Ni-gv-na-tv Du-ni-s-qu-a-na-go-dv* which may be translated from Cherokee to English as "Cherokees who are repositories of important and treasured objects." This medallion, and all that it embraces, continues to serve as an object of honor for Cherokee National Treasures, past, present, and future.

Cherokee National Treasures

1988
Alex England
Bow Making

1988
Todum Hair
Gig Making

1988
Anna Belle Mitchell
Pottery

1988
Lyman Vann
Bow Making

1989
William Cabbagehead
Blowgun/Darts

1990
Ella Mae Blackbear
Basketry

1990
Clarence Downing
Carving

1990]
Mattie Drum
Loom Weaving

1990
Lorene Drywater
Traditional Clothing

1990
Ruth England
Traditional Clothing

1990
Mary Foreman
Basketry

1990
Hester Guess
Loom Weaving

1990
Lucille Hair
Loom Weaving

1990
Sally Lacy
Basketry

1990
Stella Livers
Basketry

1990
Rogers McLemore
Loom Weaving

1990
Thomas Muskrat
Carving

1990
Jennie Sapp
Basketry

1990
Knokovtee Scott
Carving

1990
Maxine Stick
Basketry

1991
Wendell Cochran
Traditional Clothing

1991
Alan Herrin
Bow and Arrow

1991
Dorothy Ice
Loom Weaving

1991
Eunice O'Field
Basketry

1991
Scott Rackliff
Flintknapping/Carving

1991
Hastings Shade
Carving / Gig Making

1991
Anna Sixkiller
Basketry

1991
Nancy Smith
Turtle Shell Shakers

1991
Eva Mae Smith
Turtle Shell Shakers

1991
Betty Jo Smith
Traditional Foods

1992
Thelma Forrest
Basketry

1992
George Fourkiller
Basketry

1992
Minnie Jumper-Handle
Doll Making

1992
John A. Ketcher
Loom Weaving

1992
Edith Catcher Knight
Traditional Clothing

1993
Vivian Leaf Bush
Turtle Shell Shakers

1993
Betty Garner
Basketry

1993
Jess Oosahwee
Blowgun/Darts

1994
Luther "Toby" Hughes
Carving

1994
David Neugin
Bow Making

1995
Vivian Elaine Cottrell
Basketry

1995
Tom Webber Wildcat
Turtle Shell Shakers

1996
Lena Blackbird
Basketry

1996
Richard Rowe
Carving

1997
William Foster
Bow Making

1997
Nadine Wilbourn
Basketry

1998
Noel Timothy Grayson
Bow Making/Flintknapping

1999
Lee Foreman
Marble Making

Cherokee National Treasures

1999
Mildred Justice Ketcher
Basketry

1999
Bessie Russell
Basketry

1999
Albert Wofford
Gig Making/Carving

2000
Wynona Dreadfulwater
Loom Weaving

2000
Marie A. Proctor
Basketry

2001
Willie Jumper
Stickball Sticks

2001
Richard Shade
Bow Making

2001
Polly J. Whitekiller
Quilting

2001
Margaret Wilson
Quilting

2002
Wanna Lou Barton
Turtle Shell Shakers

2002
Jim Buckhorn
Bow Making

2002
Linda Mouse-Hansen
Basketry

2002
Sam Lee Still
Carving

2002
Lizzie Jane Whitekiller
Quilting

2003
Rosie Chewie
Basketry

2003
Kathryn Kelley
Basketry

2004
Perry Vanbuskirk
Ball Sticks

2004
Kathy Vanbuskirk
Basketry

2005
Jane Osti
Pottery

2006
Shawna Morton Cain
Basketry

2006
Rachel Dew
Basketry

2007
Roger Cain
Mask Making

2008
David Scott
Cherokee Language

2009
Bill Glass Jr.
Pottery

2010
Ed Fields
Cherokee Language

2010
Betty Christie Frogg
Basketry

2010
Sue Thompson
Cherokee Language

2011
Durbin Feeling
Cherokee Language

2011
Bill Rabbit
Painting

2011
Lisa Smith
Turtle Shell Shakers

2012
Cecil Dick
Painting

2012
Victoria Mitchell Vasquez
Pottery

2012
Tonia Weavel
Clothing

2013
Tommy Wildcat
Flute making

2013
Donald Vann
Painting

2013
Martha Berry
Beadwork

2014
David Comingdeer
Stickball Stick Making

2014
Clesta Manley
Painting

2014
Eddie Morrison
Sculpture

2014
John Ross
Language

2015
Dan Mink
Digital Design

2015
Dennis Sixkiller
Language

2015
Robert Lewis
Storytelling

2016
Demos Glass
Metalsmithing

2016
Richard Fields
Bowery

2016
Vyrl Keeter
Flint Knapping

bow and arrow

The traditional arrow-making material of the Cherokee, back in the East, was cane. As a matter of fact, there is one species of cane that was used for arrows. In Cherokee, the name for that cane is the name for arrow (i-hi-ya). *Cane shoots were used for arrows, and I doubt the arrows I make today out of cane—and I use this—is called giant cane, that we have here. It is what makes these cane brakes. I cut the small sprouts and use it to make arrows. And you can straighten it with heat.*

—Al Herrin

Pictured left: Alan Herrin arrows , photo by David Fitzgerald; This page, clockwise from top left: Noel Grayson bow arrow, photo by Jeremy Charles; Jim Buckhorn, photo by David Fitzgerald; Al Herrin, Richard Fields, Jim Buckhorn, photo by Jeremy Charles

alex england

September 3, 1903
Peavine, Oklahoma

BOW *Making*

You look for the heart of the Bois D'arc wood; that is the yellow part. The way to test your bow is by pulling it back thirty-six inches to see if it will break. Usually, the bow is drawn twenty-seven to twenty-eight inches in cornstalk shooting. Two to three months (are) needed to season wood after it has been cut from its trunk. The time to cut wood is in the winter—December, January, February, or March before the sap rises. (The) old timers say to cut Bois D'arc in December in the dark of the moon..." Usually, the young ones couldn't wait." Select a tree that is about six to ten inches in diameter, six feet high with no knots. The one log is split in four. Each quarter may end up being suitable for a bow, but sometimes only one-fourth is usable. Wait one to two months before you cut it in four. Put coal oil (kerosene) on the ends to keep it from splitting. Take bark off it and let it age for three to five months. It is hard to find a good six-foot tree of Bois D'arc. Good places to look are on the side of Wild Horse Mountain or on creek bottom. Knots on a log will make the bow weak.

Making a Bow String

Take the fur off the hide. Cut hide into string by starting on the outer edge and cutting in a spiral line about one-eighth to one-sixteenth inch wide. Put the string in water for two days and one night. It will be soft and can be twisted any way. Hang up one end of the string by a nail. Put a bucket of water on the other end of the string so it is hanging. After a day, it can be strung on the bow. To tie it to a bow, open the end and run it through. Cowhide is the best. One hide can make four to five strings. When using squirrel, about four squirrel hides are needed. Soak squirrel hide the same length of time. Or use four groundhog skins. It weakens the hide if you use ash to take the fur off. Just scrape the fur off. You can use beeswax on the bow string. And for the bow, you can use hog lard. Put it on there to shine, to keep it from cracking. Also you can use beef tallow.

(Excerpt from Interview with Al Herrin)

Mr. England told me a lot of stories of Cornstalk Shooting. He said that the long time ago when he was just a young man, it would be a guy in the community who would go out and set up matches with other communities. Maybe one guy from (the) Tahlequah area would go over around Stilwell and set up a shoot. OK, and they would meet some place—an open field long enough to shoot. Some (participants) shot 110 yards. They'd set cornstalks up and a lot of people would come from all around, (by) wagon and on horseback and all this kind of thing. The cornstalk shooting would last all day. (There would be) two teams. And when they started shooting, the best shooters would always shoot first. (The best shooter) set the pattern for the rest of the shooters. Then everybody would shoot. And then everybody would walk down there, just like they do today, and get their arrows. And you count the number of cornstalks.

So, you can raise up the cornstalk pile and look and you can see which cornstalks the arrows have penetrated, and you can count them. So, you keep a count. And back in those days, whichever team got the most stalks would get one point. And they went to, I believe, it was twenty-one points that they would go to and whoever won that would win (something like) a set in tennis or something. That was just part of the game. That wasn't the whole game. And all the time this was going on, the spectators and family would be under the shade tree and watching this and

Continued on page 260

Photo courtesy of Cherokee National Historical Society

lyman vann

May 22, 1907
Tahlequah, Oklahoma

OK, I gotta tell ya a little about Lyman Vann! He's another one I knew very well. Lyman, he was a master craftsman—that's what we called it back then—in bows and arrows. But I never did see Lyman make a bow, myself. So, the bow that he shot all the time? I'm not sure if he made it or not. But he was the most remarkable archer—one of the most remarkable archers I have ever seen, instinctive, just as natural as breathing. He was a deadly shot.

He and I would go rabbit hunting, and we would go up around Bald Hill and in there, south of the Sequoyah Training School. We'd hunt rabbits with bows and arrows. We'd always get a bunch of rabbits. Some of them he hit running. And that's pretty hard to do—to hit a rabbit running with bows and arrows. But, anyway, we used to have a lot of fun.

At the cornstalk shoots, Lyman had a unique way of shooting. He would start out like the cornstalk shoot was down there. He would start out like this, and he would come up and swing around—now he would do this in fast motion—and then as he came around right here, he would break his draw.

He would draw and release, like that. He wouldn't hold. It was that smooth! He'd go up and draw and shoot. He was deadly. Of course, if we were hunting rabbits, he didn't go through all of that, he just up and shot. He had a certain way that was very distinctive. He had a kind of a windup, like a pitcher.

Now Lyman's son, Pete, is the main one that holds the cornstalk shoots that they are having by the Cherokee Nation Complex. I think they have them one Saturday a month. They have a pretty good bunch. I've gone out there and shot with them a few times. But, different ones had their own styles. Lyman's style of shooting was one of the most unique I ever saw. (He was) probably one of the most natural bow shooters I ever saw.

—By Al Herrin,
Cherokee National Treasure
Interviewed by Shawna Cain

From top: Cornstalk Shoot Counting Stalks, photo courtesy of the Cherokee National Historical Society; Lyman Vann competing in bow shooting competition; Lyman Vann Korean War Veteran, Fort Gibson National Cemetery, photo by Jeremy Charles

george fourkiller

December 8, 1907
Mulberry, Oklahoma

Photo courtesy of The Cherokee Advocate

He showed me different talents at various times. I didn't really know anything about him making baskets until later in his life, but I did know he worked with other wood 'cause I would see him working on different things. He was good at making those wood splints for baskets. There was an elderly woman I took him to, and she bought some of his shavings for her to make her baskets. He helped people with materials for their baskets. He would sell his baskets to Mrs. Starr in Stilwell. She was the main person that would buy them around here. You know, Earl Starr? She would get old chairs and have Dad redo them. She would put (them in) a showcase room, and she would not let them use them after he finished them. He would do oak rocking chairs and dining room chairs with hickory. He did a lot of chair bottoms.

They notified us about a month ahead that they were going to make him a Cherokee National Treasure, and we gathered up all his baskets to take. After getting the award, he sold out of all his baskets right there.

He was originally from Peavine Community. Then the last place I remember was in Wauhillau. But he was mostly brought up in Peavine and, later in life, Wauhillau. But (I) guess you can say he is from Mulberry 'cause it has always been his home. He has been a member of the church for a number of years. I remember walking all the way from Wauhillau to go to Mulberry Tree Baptist Church. He cared a lot about the church and made a collection basket for them. Don't know if they are still using it. He would ring

Clockwise from top left: George Fourkiller receiving Cherokee National Treasure with Chief Wilma Mankiller, photo courtesy of Cherokee Phoenix; White Oak Basket and tool for shaving white oak splints, photo by David Fitzgerald; Hickory Chair with white oak woven seat by George Fourkiller, photo by David Fitzgerald

in every year with the church bell. He was very active in the church.

When I moved back here, I would go out and get his white oak for him. It had to be a certain size and diameter with no knots in it. One time I went down to cut a tree, and I always start splitting from the other end. After I got through splitting, Dad come down there and saw how I was getting wood and told me, "I told you to start on this end," pointing to the top of the log. And it stuck with me 'cause I had been doing it the hard way until he told me how to do it easier. Around here, it was getting to where it was hard to find any white oak that suited him. Around the house here, there wasn't any good enough for him. The only power tool he used was (a) chain saw to cut the tree down.

He used a homemade vise. He had two types of vises. He would get that wood down to what he wanted, then put it in the other vise made of wood and bolts. He would set it down in to make his shavings. It was a homemade vise, and to put pressure on it, you had to press with your feet on it

Continued on page 260

stella gonzales livers

April 20, 1911
Dahlonegah, OKlahoma

Photo courtesy of family

Stella Gonzales Livers was born April 20, 1911, in Adair County, Oklahoma, and died at the age of 83. Her parents, Spencer Gonzales and Sarah Feathers Gonzaless, were original enrollees of the Dawes Act. Cherokee was her first language, but she could speak English to her children and her grandchildren. She had one brother, John, and three sisters—Jacqueline, Ollie, and Annie. They were raised on Dahlonegah Mountain in Adair County. Keeping with family tradition, Stella learned to weave baskets from her mother and her sister, Jacqueline. Stella married Joe Livers and had a daughter, Carol Livers Sanders, and from a previous marriage, Stella had a daughter, Lizzie Sawney Duncan, and two sons, Billy Fay Sawney and Johnny Ray Sawney. They resided in the Cherry Tree district where they were very active in church activities. They would walk to church to Cherry Tree Baptist, only three miles down the road.

When Stella was ready to make her baskets, she would go out with her husband and daughters, Carol and Lizzie, in October, to harvest buckbrush and honeysuckle. She enjoyed going out in the woods to look for them. She called them "runners." She didn't use a pattern or ruler, just her know-how. She always thought it was easy to strip the bark, but her husband would smooth the nubs with his pocketknife for her. She would start with sixteen runners and do the bottom first. If it

Right, Stella Livers, courtesy of family. Far right, Stella Livers' daughter, Carol Sanders, holding "Pedestal Cake Stand" with cover made of buckbrush by Stella; Below: Stella Livers at home, photo courtesy of family

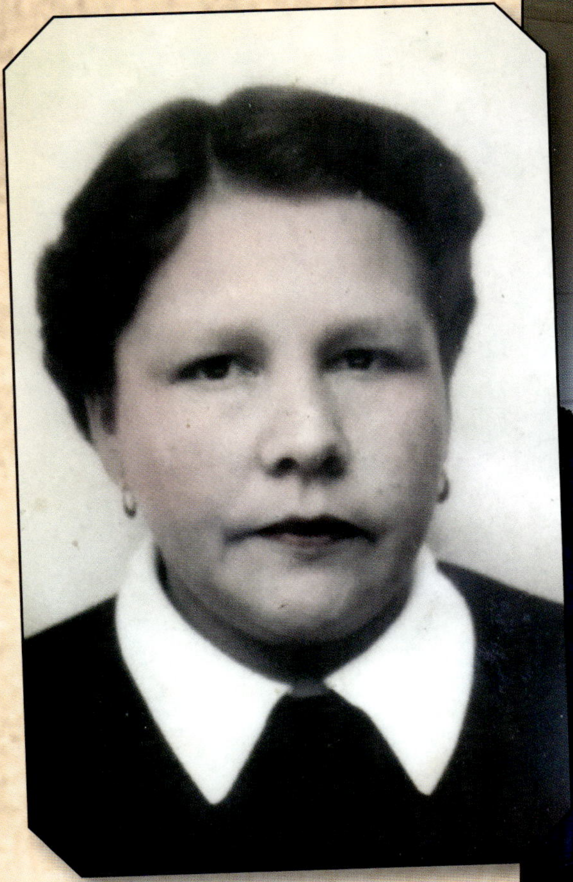

didn't turn out the way she wanted it, she would do it over. She took great pride in her work. She used natural colors in strands of her baskets. She boiled blackberries for purple color, the cover of a walnut for a green color, beet juice for a red color, or cherry bark for a brown shade. She then boiled the runners in the pot of dye to color them. One of her favorite award-winning baskets was a covered cake-serving dish shown above, at far right.

When Stella was seventy-four, she was interviewed by the *Muskogee Phoenix* paper, and her interview has several quotes that need to be shared. She was such a tiny woman—less than five feet tall —but she was a go-getter with an attitude. Some of her quotes include, "I ain't got no education, but I can do anything. I can read a little. I can write a little, not much." The interviewer, Leilani Roberts, thought Stella looked tired but her response was sweet, as she was making a basket while Leilani was there. "I'm not tired. I don't have to concentrate. I just do it. I've been doing it all my life, I guess. My eyes are bothering me a little. I like to work baskets. When I get tired, I go outside."

Stella was a very active lady, even to the end of her life. The year she died she had two gardens. When her daughter, Carol Sanders, was asked what she wanted people to know about her mother, she said, "She was always busy. She'd go all day long, and she never got tired. In the evening she would say, 'What we gonna do now?' She enjoyed her church work and her baskets. She canned a lot, and she cooked for people. Daddy had a strawberry patch out here and used to hire workers, and she'd cook for

Continued on page 261

gig making

1988

"The best time for gigging is late at night. Lanterns are used near the front of the boat to help spot the fish. Once the fish has been found, the gigger will force the spear into the water, piercing the fish. Barbs on each fork of the gig keeps the fish secured."

—*Todum Hair*

"In Oklahoma, gigging season in the Illinois River opens, I believe, the first of November, and it stays open until about the end of March or something like that. So, it is during the winter months. The reason for that is that the water is clearer in the winter time. Usually, there is not as much wind. You're only supposed to gig rough fish.

You don't gig bass or any kind of game fish. But, you gig things like carp and suckers, and Red Horse are suckers and Drum—different kinds of rough fish.

That whole water in there was very deep. It was like fourteen—or probably a few places there even twenty—feet deep in those days. We would build a big fire out on the gravel bar and we'd have a pot—black pot down there with lard in it and get to boil it. And we'd bring these fish in, and the women would bring cornbread from home, and there'd always be a big pot of coffee. And we would bring those fish in and clean them. And then you get that out and cornbread and potatoes—frying potatoes. But anyway, we used to gig, and these gigs right here, no telling how many hundreds of fish they've killed.

—*Al Herrin*

Pictured left: Todum Hair and Hastings Shade gigs, photo by David Fitzgerald, photo by Sammy Still.; This page, left to right: Hastings Shade, courtesy of NPR; Hastings Shade Gigs, photo by Sammy Still; Todum Hair, photo by David Fitzgerald

willie jumper sr.

March 31, 1911
Barber, Oklahoma

Willie Jumper Sr. was born on March 31, 1911, in Delaware County, Oklahoma, and, at an early age, moved to the community of Barber with his mother and father. Willie was quite the artisan when it came to tradition. He had mastered the art of making *kvnvchi* bowls, *kvnvchi* pounders, and stickball sticks as well as the ball you use when playing stickball.

Needless to say, the years that Willie spent on this craft and handiwork were short-lived. Suffice it to say that it was probably within the last ten years of his life. Hollowing out a *kvnvchi* bowl with nothing more than a rasp file and a small hatchet and whittling a *kvnvchi* pounder with some makeshift knife (required tedious hours). When it came to making the stickball sticks, he always chose the choicest hickory trees that he could find. The younger the tree, the better it was for him to work it. He would cut the sticks and save one end; then he would wet them down in a creek or in some large container of water—usually overnight.

The following day, he would take the sticks and would put the shaved end over a hot fire until it reached the desired curvature. (That) made it easy when it came to stringing the leather that would form the pocket for the stick ball. The ball he made with deerskin, and (he) stuffed the inside with whatever would take on a cylindrical shape. Then he would sew the ball up with deer sinew or plain old thread—usually the twine variety for longevity purposes. Willie was more fond of making the stickballs (than he was of) the other two forms of art that are mentioned.

Willie Jumper Sr. passed away in August 1977. However, his legacy will live on through his wife and their fourteen children, ten of which are still living. I nominate Willie Jumper Sr. for the title of Master Craftsmen for the year 2001 during the 49th annual Cherokee National Holiday.

— Nomination letter for Master Craftsmen 2001
49th Cherokee National Holiday

Continued on page 261

From top: Willie Jumper holding his hickory Stickball Sticks; Willie Jumper, age 43; Minnie and Willie Jumper, Cloth Doll by Minnie Jumper, Stickball Sticks by Willie Jumper, photo courtesy of Alice Jumper Wilder

rogers mclemore

September 18, 1912
Tahlequah, Oklahoma

Photo courtesy of family

"A Dying Art
Indian Weaver Last of Craftsmen:
There's More Money Elsewhere"

Tahlequah: For hours, he labors before the old oak loom as sunlight from a curtainless window casts a glare upon his work. Silence in the huge room is broken by the sound of a squeaky foot peddle which separates the threads. A tug on a cotton rope sends a fly shuttle filled with pale yellow yarn whistling between the strands. He pulls the comblike part called a reed toward him to tighten the yarn together. He repeats the rocking motion over and over—step on the foot peddle, tug the rope, pull the reed. An Indian pattern with tiny diamond shapes slowly begins to appear. In two more hours, Rogers McLemore will complete this blanket and start on another one. By the end of the day, he will have completed three.

The stout 66-year-old man, wearing his customary Big Smith overalls, flannel shirt, and cap, is a craftsman of a dying art—the art of hand-woven Indian blankets, rugs, and shawls. He cocks his head back and lets out a high-pitched giggle at the thought of himself as an artist. Rogers speaks better Cherokee than he does English. Answers to questions come after periods of silence and a nod of the head.

For the past sixteen years, Rogers has been working for the Sequoyah Indian Weavers Association, located five miles east of Tahlequah in the predominantly Indian community of Briggs. Members of the community changed the sign on the front of the building to read "Cherokee Indian Weavers" after tourists thought the name Sequoyah was referring to the tribe, according to Lucille Hair, manager of the weavers. "We're Cherokees, not Sequoyahs," she remarks, with a laugh at the ignorance of some who do not know the name of the Father of the Cherokee syllabary.

The weavers' name originated because of the association with Sequoyah High School and the Bureau of Indian Affairs. The weavers started with the help of the Bureau of Indian Affairs, in the late 1940s, with one loom located in a church. It was one of several projects started by the BIA to relieve unemployment among Indians, according to John Ketcher, a BIA official who worked with another official, Bill Ames, in getting the program on its feet.

Carpentry students from Sequoyah High School dismantled an Army barracks at Camp Gruber, a World War II post, and transported it to Briggs in 1948. Three decades of wear, weather, and neglect of the building are obvious at once. Inside, the sheet rock ceiling has pulled away from the nails and hangs down. Three different colors of linoleum tile are marked by worn pathways from loom to loom. Rogers has tried to repair the outside steps, but they are still rickety. The white paint has chipped away from the outside walls.

The looms were handmade by students from the Chilocco Indian School about the same year the operation began. Five of the seven looms are left, but only one or two are in operation. The Briggs project and a program in Jay, Oak Hill Weavers, are the only operations still in existence. "Most of them just folded up," says Ketcher. The BIA discontinued the projects in 1954 and turned the businesses over to the communities.

The post-war economy caused prices to inflate, and the demand dropped. Interest of the people dropped, and the people can make more money working elsewhere than they can weaving blankets. Rogers sells a blanket for forty-five dollars. He keeps twenty dollars, and the rest goes to a fund to pay bills and expenses. "He could work someplace else for a lot more money," says Ketcher. Money is not his main concern. He started out as a janitor and handyman for the weavers. While sweeping the

Continued on page 261

Top: Sara Wofford, daughter, (at right) with Susie Thompson displaying George Fourkiller loom weaving, from the Collection of Susie Thompson, photo by Emily Thompson; Below: Pictures of Roger McLemore from the original article, "A Dying Art—Indian Weaver Last of Craftsmen: There's More Money Elsewhere," photos by Mary Urech

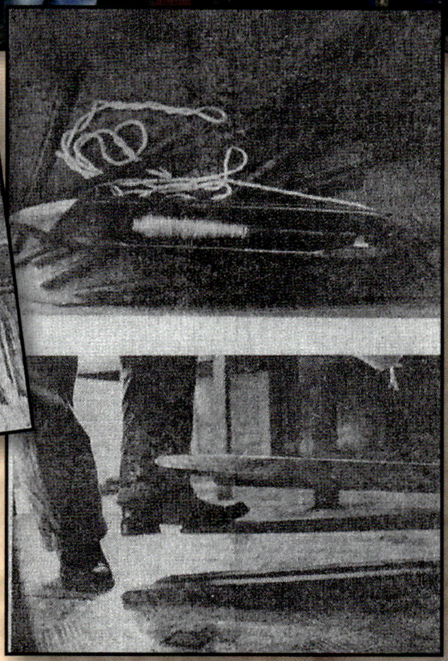

cecil dick

September 13, 1915
Tahlequah, Oklahoma

Photo courtesy of Cherokee National Historical Society

In the painting, the light and dark man is a wizard or a shaman. The light and dark are symbols of his power. The light denotes an ability for curing disease, casting off witch's spells from people, love charms, good fortune in hunting or war, finding things or people lost or seeing into the future. If displeased, the dark is meaningful of his ability to cast spells of a dark nature over people. In the painting, the shaman is curing the woman of a fever. In his hand is a gourd dipper containing an ember which has been quenched by the water in the dipper. The objective is to cause the fever to leave the body by calling down seven degrees of cold. Seven is a symbolic number to the Cherokees—a magic number. A lesser number to four beings prowled the darkness and would fly a great distance to especially disturb people who were sick or to destroy parts of newly dead so that the complete spirit body could not go where Cherokees went after death. The greatest and most powerful is the raven, or as some say, the raven mocker. This being is depicted as a ball of fire and, while flying through the air, makes a noise as of a rushing wind. The second in power takes the form of the great horned owl, then the hoot owl, and last, the screech owl.

The men at the corners of the shelter are smoking sacred tobacco. That is tobacco prepared by a powerful medicine man. One is blowing smoke toward the symbolic raven which is seen flying away in the upper left of the painting. The man at the opposite corner is blowing smoke toward the owl still in the tree. This is for the protection of the woman with the fever. The other figures are friends and relatives waiting for the woman to be cured of her fever. The small boy has eel skins tied around his wrists. This is to make him strong and wiry as an eel when he is grown. One woman has a woman's pipe in her hand. The medicine man is wearing a raven skin on his head to give him the raven's power. The woman under the shelter is the Beloved Woman of the tribe. She has seven feathers in her wand, and this is the number of clans in the tribe. She also wears a feathered cloak made from the feathers of black birds, ravens, or turkeys. Her word can be final in settling disputes, whether or not war can be declared, or the fate of captives.

The fellow on the platform, who has been so startled at seeing the raven, is waving his skin blanket, is a living scarecrow. He sits on his platform and keeps the birds scared away from the plants. Every tobacco plant has been blessed by the medicine man for curing and making into the tobacco—sacred tobacco—for smoking at ceremonials. The figures going into the council house are going in for a booger dance, a fun dance. It is, or was, a dance for entertainment. The dancers—clowns—wear masks and do funny things in their dance. The houses are made of bent and woven poles covered with mud, then overlaid with chestnut bark so the mud will not be washed away by the rain and snow. The little domed house in the background is a Cherokee sauna. Stones are placed inside, heated, and water poured over them to make steam.

The Curing of the Fever

Commissioned by Dr. Ed Pointer in 1960s. Donated to Cherokee Nation by Doctors Bryce Bliss, Jim Brixey, Richard Deed, Coy Edwards, Shelly Lee, Herb Littleton, Danny Minor, Ed Pointer, Tom Ward, and Steven Younger.

The painting itself is a mixture of influences from the studio painter of Santa Fe to Bacone, but mostly, the ideas of Cecil Dick. I am persuaded that, since the Cherokees were woodland Indians, there must be a woodland accent. I have tried to keep a certain amount of "primitivity" in the painting as I felt I was painting a semi-primitive people—their culture and beliefs. Only you can decide whether I have succeeded or failed."

— Cecil Dick

Excerpt from *Spirit Red* by Rennard Strickland

Story set in 1972:

. . . One morning about a week later, Cecil said,

"Chooch, I've got to go back home. I've got to drink some sassafras tea—got to thin my blood!"

Continued on page 262

"Booger Dancers," photo by David Fitzgerald

Cecil Dick in Tsa-la-gi Village, photo courtesy of the Cherokee National Historical Society

hester chair guess

September 9, 1915
Briggs, Oklahoma

Photo courtesy of family

Hester Mae Chair was born to Reverend Jim and Lizzie Wilson Chair and lived her early life in Briggs, Oklahoma. Hester was a full-blood Cherokee who was fluent in the language. Hester and her sister, Lucille Hair, were both recognized as Cherokee Living Treasures in 1990 for loom weaving.

Like her sister, Lucille, Hester became a Sequoyah Indian weaver and wove wall hangings and blankets. Hester married Dick Guess, and they had three daughters—Jimmie Triplett, Margaret Guess, and the late Liz Littledave.

Granddaughter Jalana Ellis recalled that her favorite memory of her grandma is how funny she was. "She had a great sense of humor and smiled all the time. What made her so special was the fact that no matter what any of us grandkids, or even her kids, did, she loved us anyway. She made me feel loved no matter what. Her love was unconditional for sure. She was the glue that kept the family together."

Hester loved playing marbles. "Every time we had a family get together,

Clockwise from top: Hester and her sister, Lucille "Winnie" Hair, photo provided by the family; Hester receiving her Master Craftsman award beside her sister, Lucille. Photo courtesy of Cherokee Advocate. Hester Guess photo courtesy of family

PLAQUES WERE presented to the 1990 Master Artists during the 38th Cherokee National Holiday. Pictured l-r are Principal Chief Wilma P. Mankiller, Mattie Drum, Hester Guess, Lucille Hair, Edwin McLemore accepting for Rogers McClemore and Deputy Chief John Ketcher.

she made sure we all played a game of marbles and dominoes. We all wanted Granny on our team because she was really good at both of those games."

Even as a young girl, Hester was a strong Christian and active in church activities. When she was a mother herself, she made sure that her entire family attended church, too. Nothing made her happier than seeing all of her family at church every Sunday.

—Jalana Ellis, granddaughter
Interviewed by Pamela Jumper Thurman

pottery

1988

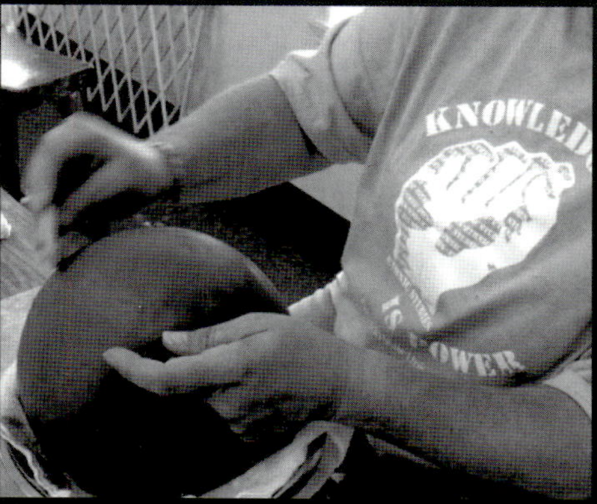

"Last night, I sifted seven cups of clay as fine as possible with a fine screen—as fine as that of a tea strainer. I also sifted one and one-eighth cups of sand as temper. I then worked kneading and pounding for about an hour. And then, in the clay, I saw an Indian sitting, and I began to form him, with head bowed and feather fan in the right hand. I added a blanket around him and when I finally finished, I called the piece 'Meditation.'"

—Anna Belle Mitchell

"I was the first contemporary living Treasure. What I hope that has done is open the door for other contemporary artists to have the chance to become Cherokee Treasures, too. I hope there's not any restrictions on art. It's still a creative process, no matter how you approach it. If we're going to call it art, it's got to be open. I'm for everybody."

—Bill Glass Jr.

"Pottery has been the path of a passion. It is something that I am passionate about, want to do, love to do. So for me, it's been a real path to a passion, I've enjoyed the whole journey. I will always be making pottery, painting, and doing sculpture. I am grateful to the Creator for all the blessings that this journey in art has brought to me. I will be passing it on, as it was passed to me. **Wado***"*

—Jane Osti

"There was just such pride in being named a Cherokee National Treasure. But at the same time, I really feel like it is something that I share with Mom and Dad and their spirits knowing that I received this honor. It also changed me a little bit. I feel a responsibility—even more so now—to share and teach and guide and mentor others, especially other Cherokees. I also feel a deep responsibility to really know what I'm talking about. I feel as though I am an ambassador for our people, for Oklahoma, for our tribe, and for what I've learned from my mom—to share her knowledge and keep traditional pottery alive. It's such an honor to carry it forward."

—Victoria Mitchell Vazquez

Pictured left: Pottery by Victoria Mitchell Vazquez, photo by Pamela Jumper Thurman; This page, left to right: Pottery Class, photo by Pamela Jumper Thurman; Pine Needle firing pots, photo by Pamela Jumper Thurman; Pots by Anna Belle Mitchell and daughter, Victoria Mitchell Vazquez, photo by Roger Cain

lizzie whitekiller

with ella clark

November 18, 1916
Lost City, Oklahoma

Photo by David Fitzgerald

Margaret Raymond: How long have you been quilting?

Lizzie Whitekiller: My mother taught me when I was a girl. Her name was Patsy Ketcher and she taught all of her girls. There were seven girls and four boys. I learned from Mama and my sister-in-law, Doris Batt. They had quilting at church every Wednesday for W-youth. From then on, I was quilting at my house and I taught Ella Mae (Lizzie's daughter)—and Rose, wasn't it? My oldest daughter—to quilt. I tried to teach all of them but some of them can't learn fast.

We charged three dollars a quilt. Nowadays, you can't get one for that. The money went for missionaries and our pastor and Sunday School Association. It also went to support the church. We had all the old patterns. Each one made a block of whatever you wanted. We went to sell that for the church. (If) anyone wanted to buy it, maybe $10 a quilt.

I'm ninety years old and three months, and I been making quilts since I was thirteen year old. I quilted for the church about twenty-five year and from there, I quilted at the house, too.

I made about five quilts (each) for my boys and girls—that's ten of them and I just got two quilts of my own—that's about fifty. Some (quilts) were donations for the buildings and whatever quilt I had, I'd take it for the benefit for that family in need or for donation.

Ella Clark: I started quilting around 1980. I moved to Wagoner in '80. And I called Mom and said, "I don't have anything to do."

"Well," she said, "Get you a sewing machine and start sewing." So I'd come over here, and she'd show me how to do it. She really, really wanted me to learn how to hand quilt. I'd make the tops, and she showed me how to flat-quilt because I didn't have anything else but a machine. I started lap-quilting and she gave me a hoop, and I started hoop quilting.

Then, I got this place out at Taylor Ferry, and she said, "Hang it from the ceiling." She'd come over there and show me how to tack it on the frame and how to roll it and get those little cookie things and roll it up. When she was going down there (church), I went when I was a teenager. They tried to teach me, but I wasn't interested in quilting. But, you know, as a teenager, you are not interested in doing all that? I liked to listen to them and eat their cake and pies and lunch.

Designs and Patterns

My mother started me out with the "Crazy Quilt" 'cause I wasn't into patterns and I was using scraps. Then she got me into "Card Tricks." She would never do appliqué because she didn't like appliqué but we had the "Bear Paw," "Caesar's Crown," and "Mirror, Mirror." She had old books.

Lizzie: Well, I got some of my ideas and books at garage sales. My daughter-in-law, she bought me two, three of them. I got the "Eight-Pointed Star," "Card Trick," and "Mirror, Mirror" from the paper. I don't know where my "Mirror-Mirror" went to. I made two of them. I gave it to somebody, I guess. We also made "Double Wedding Ring."

Ella: Remember when the old sale barn used to be out there? In town? Well, Mama told me they had scraps over there. I still have some of them left. Then we graduated into buying fabric-store stuff. We got to where we couldn't hang the quilts anymore, so we'd do the hoops and, of course, you know people couldn't come and help us roll every time we needed it. So we ended up getting a four-frame and now, we can make quilts as big as we want them or as small as we want them. She's got one up in there. That's how I learned. Mom taught me just everything.

Mama used to say, "Now, those stitches are kind of getting long now and you need to take it out that far." So I'd take them out and start again. She told me don't make big stitches 'cause you'll get your toenails caught in it.

Lizzie: My mama and my sister, Lillie Roach, sold at the booth (at Swimmer's). My daddy used to make log—cut the log, cut a hole in it—and grind the hominy and *kvnvchi.* That's what he used to do. Well, you get a rock and you pound on the hickory nuts as much as you can. You have a colander and we used to take all the goodies out of the hull and put it in there. The kids done that. When we got through with that, and then he pounded it. There was a little hulls in there yet. They just roll it up and make that *kvnvchi.* You put that *kvnvchi* in hot water and check on it and get all the hulls out of it and use that liquid and usually hominy grits.

Corn-Husk Dolls

Lizzie: My father was Rev. Jack Batt. My mama was Elsie Ketcher. At a family reunion, we make a basket one time. We make baskets for the kids.

Ella: We just go out; it's not natural. It's more like commercial reed. We just bring it over and put them in tubs and get them all softened up. We make them like a certain length. The six bottoms, we start making them, and then you cross them and get your weaver and go around and kind of stretch it out as you go around. The kids really like to do that with us. That's one way we can get the basketry for the smaller kids. I was Director of Indian Education when I retired at Wagoner Public Schools.

Contest for Quilts

Lizzie: Well we had one (contest). I'm going to tell you a story. My son—that one that stay with me but he down fishing now—bought four of them (quilts). And his wife is an American Airline lady and she works at Douglas. She put all them quilts in the show down there and she won first prize for all them quilts—my quilts. She put her name on it.

Ella: We enter the Cherokee Quilt Show—the Holiday Quilt Show. We got one of mine a $100 gift certificate and I got that. We got first place, second place and ribbons. Then we went to Wagoner County Fair and got ribbons there. We enter those two—Wagoner and the Holidays. I just recently started keeping pictures of them.

Quilt With Your Family

Lizzie: Well, I thought of my daughter, Sherrie. She made the pictures in there and got my box out with all the kids' pictures and she put them on a white piece. And we had that material we got from Arkansas, and I just put them right there with all our pictures. The people brought them down to see. My grandson and daughters and my great-grandson and daughters—all of them, every one of my family pictures is in there. It's got two five-generations.

Continued on page 262

From top: Lizzie Whitekiller displaying quilt, courtesy of family; Lizzie Whitekiller making fry bread early 1970s; Lizzie Whitekiller, courtesy of Cherokee National Archives

Photo by David Fitzgerald

todum hair

February 1, 1917
Wickliffe, Oklahoma

A few years back I was asked by an elderly Cherokee lady to go visit a medicine man named Todum Hair in Wicliffe, Oklahoma, to get some medicine for her surgical wound that wouldn't heal. I had heard and read about Todum but had never met him before. When we left that day, I was excited to meet the legend!

Surprisingly, we found his house easily, and we were welcomed into his house to discuss our problem. We sat and visited a while before Todum rose up and said, "Let's go get that medicine for you!"

I stood up and said, "Let's go." So we headed to town!

I had no idea "getting medicine" was going to involve so many stops. I thought we were going out into the woods. I was just happy to be hanging out and chauffeuring the great Todum Hair.

The first stop he directed me to was a small diner in Salina. The waitress obviously knew Todum well and knew what he wanted to order. She took us to his "usual seat," as she put it. As I sat there with Todum, I began to notice pictures on the wall of an Indian man—wearing colorful clothes and a Plain's headdress—walking in parades and riding horses and parade floats. I guess Todum saw me looking around at all these pictures on the café wall, and he humorously said, "Yeah, those are me."

The waitress came back by and said, "Yep, our Todum is famous!"

Top: (filmstrip) Todum Hair; Gig photo by David Fitzgerald; Todum hair in parade, photo courtesy of Cherokee National Archives

I couldn't get over how many pictures there were of him on the walls and he was in all sorts of parades! I had always thought Todum would be a quiet man. He was pretty quiet during our visit. But, in town, Todum was known. He greeted everyone on the street and in the café as if he knew them. Todum sat there proud and told us how a person in the past had gotten him one of those Sequoyah outfits to wear in a parade.

Todum told everyone there how someone had made a "traditional costume" for him to wear in an upcoming Cherokee Holiday parade, but when the time came he wore his favorite "parade clothes" for the parade instead of the one specially made for him. When the person asked him why he hadn't worn the new clothing, Todum simply replied, "It didn't fit." (He laughed.)

We left the place after a delicious meal and headed to Pryor so he could do some banking. He invited me to go inside with him because he was asking the lady if we could go collect a couple plants from her family's land. We headed to the place where we could get the plants needed for my friend's wound. The people there were perplexed about why we were there to collect a plant for medicine. They knew who Todum was but didn't understand why we were there to collect some catnip. Turned out catnip—the whole plant—is what we were looking for. That's what we needed for this woman's wound. On the drive back, Todum explained how to prepare the plant for use and apply it so that the wound would heal. When I asked the lady later if it had worked, she said that it had. I will always remember that about catnip now and know that it is good to use when I have a wound that isn't healing well.

When we got back to his home Todum invited all of us out back to look at his "parade clothes." We felt honored! From a storage room, he pulled his outfit from this box and

Continued on page 263

Photo by David Fitzgerald

lucille hair

April 2, 1917
Briggs, Oklahoma

When I think of my grandma, the community of Briggs automatically comes to mind. The two are inseparably linked. She was born, lived her entire life, and died there. We have had over six generations live in the home that her father, the Rev. Jim Chair, built on the allotment of her mother, Lizzie Wilson Chair. The house was a one-room log cabin that members of the community helped build when the original home burned to the ground. Her grandfather, Stout Chair, also died there. He emigrated from the Qualla Boundry, North Carolina, in the 1870s. Over the years, parts of the allotment were sold to the church she loved, Cedar Tree. She sold land to Briggs School for the track and football field. Grandma also gave each of her children land to build their own homes on, making them promise to never sell it outside the family. Her home was surrounded by her children, the school where she received her eighth-grade education, and her church. If she wasn't sitting outside in the yard, she was at church, and if she wasn't at either one, she was up at the weaving shop. She loved to weave.

One of my favorite memories is waking up in the morning to the smell of coffee and

From top: James Lamar Hair with his mother, Lucille Hair; Lucille Hair at loom; Lucille Hair at loom. Photos courtesy of Aaron Lamar Hair

bacon. Grandma would come in and wake me by my Cherokee name. *"Ha-di-da, O-ga-n."*

She would say, "Get up, *Ogan*, I'm going up shop."

From the kitchen window, I would watch her walk across the yard. Sometimes, she would have one or both of the little girls with her. Often, she would pull them in a wagon across the yard and up the highway to the weaving shop. She would be up there for hours, rain or shine, putting up her warp, threading her loom, and finally weaving her blanket or wall hanging.

Sometimes, I would go up and check on her. Her loom was at one end of the building, and Rogers McClemore's was at the other end. They would be up there talking Cherokee and listening to country music on a very old radio. If they hadn't had lunch, Grandma would send me down to Earl's Store to get sandwiches, pop, and chips on credit. When she would finish a blanket, she would walk home, sit around the kitchen table, and tie it off. I miss those days.

Back in the day, she would weave her blankets not so much for cultural preservation, but for a financial supplement. She had a skill, and she used it selflessly to help others and her family. She donated many blankets—to different organizations and to people—for raffles and fundraisers. All the chiefs I have ever known have come to her for blankets to give as gifts to other officials, visitors, and dignitaries. Whenever one of the kids or grandkids needed anything—such as books, shoes, school clothes, money for a trip, gas, etc.—she would say, "Guess I better go up shop," and off she would go.

I used to get onto her for letting her blankets go so cheap. When I was a kid, she would sell them to a man for $75 who would turn around and sell them for $225. That never bothered her as much as it did me. That $75 was a lot to her.

Continued on page 263

polly jane whitekiller

September 18, 1917
Hulbert, Oklahoma

Polly Jane Harry Whitekiller was born in Delaware County near Jay, Oklahoma to her parents, Taylor and Sallie Mouse Harry. The youngest of five children, she attended Sequoyah Orphan Training School and was a graduate of the Sequoyah Indian School. She married Birdchopper "Amos" Whitekiller, and they had one son, Billy Whitekiller. They had two grandchildren, Denise Whitekiller-Rooster and Billy Whitekiller Jr. She also had two great-grandchildren, Joshua and Jorden Rooster.

Polly was a longtime, devoted member of the New Hope Baptist Indian Church where she taught Sunday school for more than forty years and held many other offices in the church. She enjoyed teaching the Cherokee language and the Cherokee Bible to the many children whom she cared for. A kind and caring woman, she opened her home many times to friends and whoever was in need. Another of her God-given talents was the art of quilting.

"My grandmother has been hand quilting since she was twelve years old. She has told me stories of how they used to sew quilts with my aunt and the other ladies at the church. She said that when you first began quilting, the younger girls worked on baby quilts for women who had a baby in their community. The older ladies worked on quilts for sick or elderly.

"She made quilts for family and friends. Most of the quilts were given to her to be quilted. The materials included the quilting top, batting, and lining.

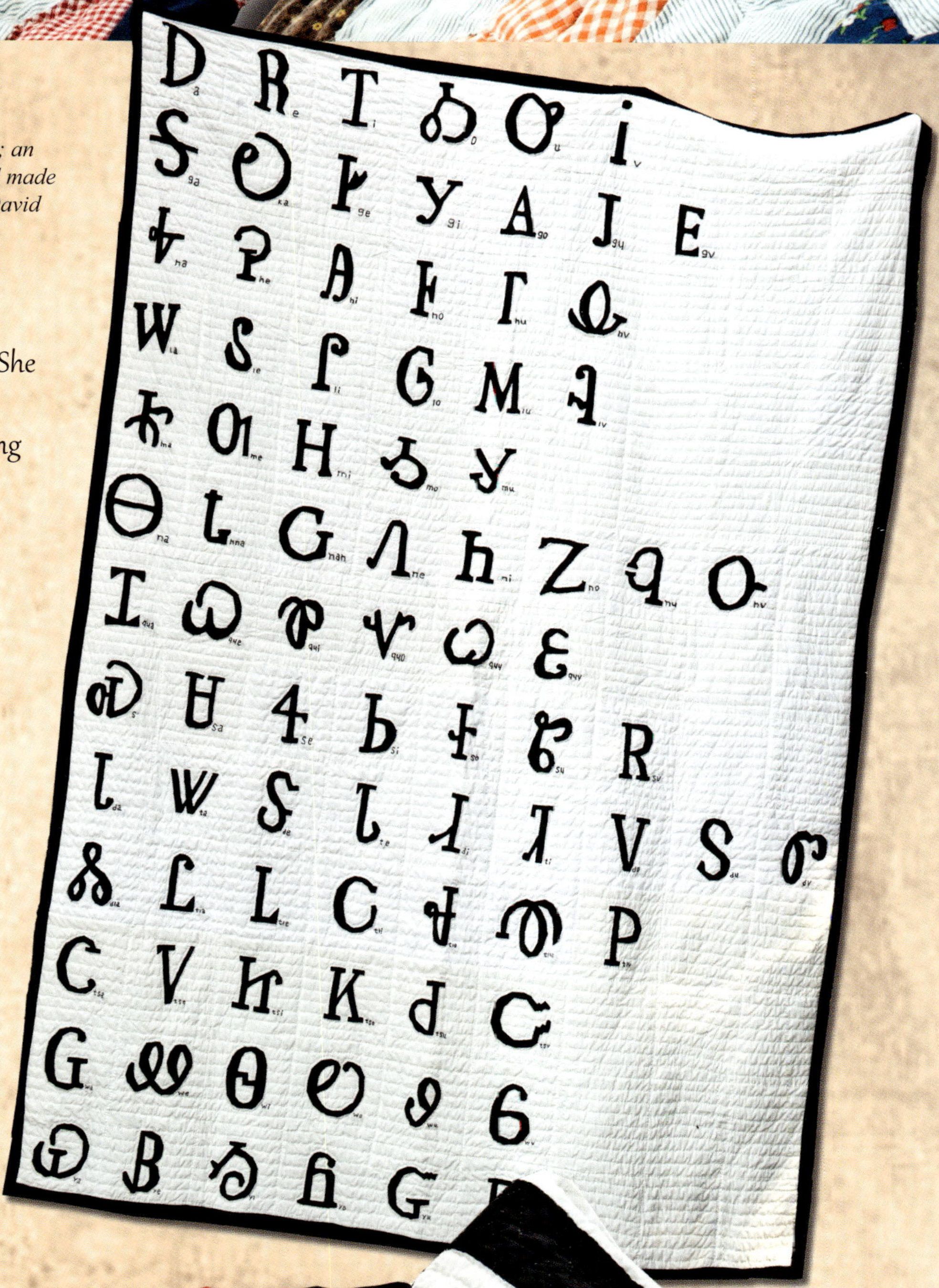

Clockwise from top: A Syllabary quilt; an Indian Maiden quilt;and a fan quilt—all made by Polly Jane Whitekiller. Photos by David Fitzgerald

My grandmother put them together and quilted. She developed her own personal style in quilting and improvised with each quilt top. She made a quilting pattern from my brother's hands when he was younger.

"I remember growing up, and I was tall enough to walk under her quilting frame and play with it. My grandmother would get on to me because she thought that I would get stuck with a needle or pins. The other day, I was watching my son, and he did the exact same thing I used to do when I was little. I always remember her quilting every day, except on Saturday, when she would work on quilt tops, and Sunday, (when) she rested.

"Quilting kept her busy; my grandmother had strong hands and indentions on her thumbs and fingers from the needles. I wanted my grandmother to be recognized for her talent and art. I'm very proud of my grandmother and wanted to nominate her because she is a living treasure to me. "

(From Polly Jane Whitekiller's nomination form for Cherokee National Treasure, her obituary, and the obituary published by Mallett Funeral Home, Wagoner, Oklahoma.) Compiled by Pamela Jumper Thurman

blow guns

1989

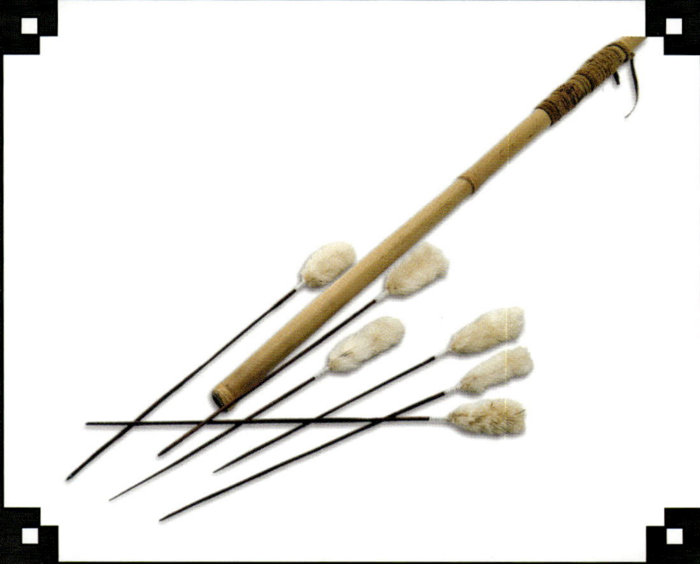

Photo courtesy of The Cherokee Advocate

mattie drum

February 26, 1920
Greenleaf Lake State Park, Oklahoma

Mattie Drum was designated a Cherokee National Treasure in 1990 for weaving, specifically for her hand-woven belts worn by men at stomp dances. Her daughter, Corinna Drum Neal, said former Principal Chief Wilma Mankiller presented her mother with the Cherokee National Treasure award. "Mom was pretty intelligent. She just saw something one time and she just did it, you know. She always told us she was smarter than any of us going to school because she could speak three languages—Muscogee (Creek), Cherokee, and English."

She learned how to crochet. She just looked at something crocheted and she learned to crochet. Neal said her mother's belts were hand-woven using different colors of yarn. At the end of her six-foot belts, Drum attached balls or bells of yarn that she would give a special cut with scissors to give the bells fringes. "These are really easy to make. What she would do is get some yarn and go around her hand, and then she would cut it and then fold them over, tie yarn around it and that would make the balls," Neal said.

Muscogee (Creek) men wore the belts at ceremonial grounds during stomp dances. The belts were tied around the waist, and men would let the bells hang to one side. People would come to Drum to request her belts for stomp dances and would request certain colors. "They would tell her what color they wanted and she would fix them up for them. If she bought the yarn for them, she would charge them for it, and if they brought the yarn, she would charge them half-price just for fixing it," she said. "I saw her work on one, and if she worked on it steady, it would take her three or four days."

Neal said her mother didn't place her belts in area art shows, choosing just to make them for people. Neal is in possession of two of her mother's belts and another, unfinished belt that she cherishes. She said she plans to finish the belt for her mother. Her mother showed her "one time" how to make her belts, and Neal said she now wishes she had paid more attention at the time.

Drum was a lifelong member of the Stokes Ceremonial Grounds near Vian about twenty miles from Drum's home near Greenleaf Lake. When she was younger, Drum danced in stomp dances at Stokes. She shook turtle-shell shackles that contained small pebbles to help keep the rhythm during stomp dances. The shells were tied around her calves and worn under a traditional skirt.

Her nephew Tommy Wildcat said his aunt was "really connected spiritually" to the ceremonial grounds and was a medicine keeper.

Neal said her mother also liked to grow things and had a natural knack for it. She always had large gardens and grew tomatoes and cucumbers that she would sell in the summer.

—Corinna Drum Neal, daughter
Interviewed by Will Chavez

1971: From Left to Right: Mattie, Tom, Helen, Nellie, Rosella, Luman, Ella; Seated is Squirrel Wildcat.

From top: Mattie Drum family photo, courtesy of family; Corrina Neal Drum of Gore with finger-woven belts made by her mother, Corinna Drum Nea!, daughter of Mattie Drum, photo by Will Chavez; Finger-Woven Belt by Mattie Drum, photo by David Fitzgerald

william foster

August 13, 1920
Rocky Mountain, Oklahoma

William M. Foster was born at home at Rocky Mountain, near Stilwell, Oklahoma, to original enrollees John and Jennie Batt Foster. He had three brothers and two sisters and attended Rocky Mountain School. Grandpa John, his dad, was a stomp-dance leader at Sugar Mountain. He passed away when my dad was eleven years old, and Dad was left with the responsibility of raising the family and taking care of the animals. He lived through the Great Depression. When he was a young man, he would get into his covered wagon and go to Stilwell to see Susie Locust. He married her in 1942. They were married for about 63 years. When Mom and Dad first married, they lived in a two-room log house, and I remember him telling us about the outlaws that used to go through that area on a trail. Sometimes, gunshots would hit the side of the log house.

Dad was a veteran of World War II— a Navy Seaman, First Class. He served in the Phillipines, but never really talked much about that. Except for a brief time in 1957, when the family moved to Gary, Indiana, he spent most of his life in Adair County. He was a steel worker in Indiana, but when lay offs came, he and Mom returned to Rocky Mountain, and he started working at the Rocky Mountain school system. He was employed there for over thirty years. Dad was also a deputy sheriff and did some night watchman work. He was a deacon at Echota Baptist Church for years. We all grew up going to Echota Baptist Church; it was the Foster family church.

From top: William Foster bow and arrow; William Foster family; William Foster

Our family lived on Grandpa John's allotment land. Dad was a hard-working man. He and Mom had five children—Bill, Charles, Kenneth, Rose and Sue. He cut a lot of wood and worked at the school, but he still found time to do a lot of family things—family visits, spending time on the creek with family members. With my mom's family, we would go fishing (or) pick strawberries. I remember that he used his pickup to haul strawberries and beans. We were always taught that family was important.

He used to plow the garden with our horse, Bill. After he plowed the garden, Dad would sometimes put me on Bill's back. One day, he plowed the garden, unhooked the plow, and Bill just walked off and kept on walking. He never came back.

Dad also raised pigs. We'd have an annual hog butchering for family every October and share the meat. Basically, it was a fresh hog fry. He also loved dogs; we always had four or five old dogs around the house. He didn't like to kill bigger animals—deer—but he would hunt squirrel and rabbit for food, and he would fish. I remember that we used to go fishing at night; all night long we'd fish for catfish (and) have coffee and a bonfire.

As kids, he would have us watch him do stuff to learn. We would make fence posts, cut wood, (and) work with cars. He was pretty much a self-taught carpenter and craftsman. He and Mom also taught Cherokee classes. They taught Cherokee to missionaries for several years at Cedar Tree Assembly grounds, Indian Baptist, over at Briggs.

He taught us how to recognize plants and trees—what was good medicine to use for coughs and colds. Mom taught us food things—finding mushrooms (and) which greens were good to eat. Dad told us stories in the evenings—ghost stories, everyday stories, and family stories. I remember him telling us the story about how Grandpa got shot. I think Grandpa was a deputy.

I passed on some of the ghost stories to my kids. Dad really loved to do magic tricks every now and then; he liked trying to fool us. He was pretty good, too. He even played ball with us and the grandkids until he was about seventy years old. He ran the bases and everything.

Dad taught us how to be self-reliant; we did our own mechanic work like rebuilding and tuning up cars (and) fixing flats. We learned how to do repairs and stuff around the house. He made sure that we went to school.

Continued on page 263

david neugin

August 26, 1920
Fourteen Mile Creek, Oklahoma

When visiting the Neugin household I was greeted by Maxine Neugin, wife of Cherokee National Treasure David Neugin. Neugin had passed on from this earth, but it was evident that not only his memory but also his stories were still being carried on by the family. As one family member after another entered, I quickly took down their names. Katherine Neugin White, his daughter, had pictures in hand to share memories of her father and his unique skills in Cherokee traditions and art. Katherine's daughter, Rebecca White Keys, David's granddaughter, also arrived soon after. Maxine pointed out that Rebecca is named for the historical Rebecca Neugin who died at the age of 115 on July 15, 1932, in the state of Oklahoma, and was considered to be the oldest survivor of the Trail of Tears.

Bryan Shade, David's nephew, had shown the way to the Neugin home, located along Fourteen Mile Creek, and was also present when David's son, Bobby, entered the room. As everyone got settled around the living room of the Neugin home, conversation sparked, and stories were told together by family. Pictures were passed around the room showing this National Treasure at work, from skinning groundhogs for bowstrings to heirloom pictures of Cornstalk Shoots from days gone by.

Above: David Neugin's father, Buck Neugin, shooting at Cornstalk Shoot, photo courtesy of family; Bows and Arrows made by David Neugin displayed on family quilt, photo courtesy of family; Below: Bow knotches, left with groundhog skin bow string made by David Neugin, photo courtesy of family

As the family told the history of David Neugin, the audio recorder caught priceless conversation documenting memories and little known information about the beginnings of the Tsa-la-gi Heritage Center and Ancient Village, as well as stories of a husband, father, and grandfather who still evokes pride and honor among family and friends.

Maxine Neugin, wife: Marty Hagerstrand hired me, I worked with Betty Smith at the Ancient Village. I was the first one hired there when it started.

Katherine Neugin White, daughter: We all went when Mom worked out there. I don't remember if we got paid or not, but we played a lot. They had ponds, and we swam in them. We learned to stomp out there, and we learned from William Cabbagehead. We also had to wear those wigs! They were hot!

Katherine: William came from a long line of medicine people. That was always interesting. His family (members) were always medicine makers, and he was from Tailholt.

Continued on page 264

Photo courtesy of family

sally lacy

September 11, 1920
Bull Hollow, Oklahoma

Sally Lacy was born to Sam Lacy and Susie Redbird on September 11, 1920. She was raised by her grandmother, Nancy Big Acorn, and grew up east of Kenwood in the Bull Hollow community. She was full-blood Cherokee and had one son, Henry James Buck. They remained close throughout her life. Sally also had five grandchildren—Lisa, Choogie, Melissa, Theresa, and George.

Granddaughter Theresa Buck recalls that, "She took good care of us and of our uncle, Eli Big Acorn, wo was blind. She and my dad both spoke Cherokee, but he had so much trouble in school that he didn't teach us Cherokee." Because of this, Sally spoke English to her grandchildren. "She was a good cook, too. Where we lived, there was an apple tree and she would go out with us, and we would pick those apples so that she could cook them for us. I remember one day I saw her eating spinach. I'd never eaten it before. I tasted it and I've liked it ever since. She only drank Pepsi and black coffee."

"She would get us all up early and we would go to the museum and to Oaks when they had their arts and crafts going and where she would sell her baskets."

Theresa said that it was likely that the biggest collection that anyone had of Sally's baskets would be Kelly's Store in Jay, Oklahoma. The store would eagerly purchase Sally's baskets and would display them on the window ledge of the store. People could see Sally's baskets as they walked by or shopped.

Sally taught basket making at the recreation center in Claremore, Oklahoma. Anytime that she was invited to show her baskets or to teach, she always said yes. In fact, she would share her basketry skills if anyone ever asked her to do so. Kenwood community had a grandparent program, and Sally and her brother would spend time with the children. She participated regularly in that program.

Sally learned basket making from her Grandmother, Nancy. While Sally was learning to make baskets, her brother learned how to make turtle-shell shakers.

Just as Sally's grandmother raised her, Sally also raised her grandchildren. Theresa said, "She never wanted us to get in trouble. She was really good to us. I think I got her artistic nature because I enjoy making things. My older brother, James, can draw so he and my other brother got the drawing skills."

Theresa recalled that Sally often brought her own Mother over sometimes. When Theresa and her siblings were young, Sally kept them in touch with the Lacy side of the family. "I remember every Wednesday morning, at Steely Baptist Church, the older ladies of the church would get

Continued on page 265

Clockwise from top; Sally Lacy Weaving, photo by Pamela Jumper Thurman; Large doublewall lidded buckbrush storage basket by Sally Lacy; Sally Lacy with son Henry

basketry 1990

"I am a traditional basket weaver. To be able to call yourself a traditional basket weaver, you need to gather your own material—go out and get your own reed, and process it the way it needs to be processed. Even if you know how to get it, there's a difference in knowing how to get it and then doing it yourself. That's the way I feel about it. I feel like I can totally say I am a traditional basket maker if I go out and get my own reed and dye. I would say that you have to go out and get the honeysuckle, and you do all the necessary steps to make a basket, and dig your own blood root or whatever color you wanted or you are going to use. To me, that is a traditional basket, knowing what to gather—the best. You know you can gather anything, but it should be the best kind you can find."

—Bessie Russell

"I've always looked at baskets and wanted to learn how to make baskets. My grandparents would make baskets. But they didn't teach me. I just watched. Somehow or another, as I grew up, they didn't make baskets anymore. They didn't show anybody else how to make them. As I got older, I kept wanting to learn to make baskets. I love making baskets. I love the flat reed. It is relaxing to forget about everything else outside the door and just make baskets. A lot of people—when I teach them, they don't have the patience for it. Usually I tell them, I hope they have patience—because that's what it takes to make a basket. And a lot of people want to learn how to make a basket so they can make money. And that's to O.K., but I think you have to have the love for what you're doing before you can make a good basket. I'm not saying people make ugly baskets or anything like that. I'm just saying you have to love what you do. It's like cooking. If you love cooking, people's going to love your food."

—Betty Frogg

"A basket that I make is a living thing. People ask me, 'How do you 'keep' a basket?' as in how do you keep one from getting old and falling apart. It just depends. Like people, baskets that are living will get old. They will age over time. But, that basket has lived and has a lot of stories to tell. A lot of hands have touched it. For this reason, I use most of my baskets. All have different purposes to me. I always think of our traditional basketry as an art form that has prevailed all the trials and tribulations of the Cherokee people. Basketry and other traditional arts represent to me tradition and pride in those who came before us. It is amazing, and somehow comforting to me, to know that we continue that tradition today over a thousand years later."

—Shawna Morton Cain

"One of my favorite things to do is go and dig blood root. I never take too much. That is a no-no. But, I really enjoy going out with other basket weavers—and now, with my grandkids—to dig blood root. Blood root is one of our oldest dyes that we used way back and we still use today. There is a certain way to gather it and a certain time to get it that is best, but that is knowledge that we pass to each other after we know that someone is a serious basket maker and someone who won't take too much. If we take too much, there won't be any left. It is already getting harder and harder to find."

—Thelma Forrest

Pictured left: Ella Mae Blackbear Buckbrush Baby Cradle Basket, photo courtesy of Cherokee Heritage Center; This page, left to right: Thelma Forrest with her baskets; Kathryn Kelly baskets; Bessie Russell and Lena Blackbird holding baskets together

minnie handle jumper

July 25, 1922
Barber, Oklahoma

Minnie Handle Jumper's corncob dolls are unique in that no one makes the dolls she once made using corncobs that were served during lunches and dinners to her family.

Her daughter, Carolyn Dunn, said her mother learned how to make her dolls from her grandmother, Cartayah Chunestudy. She said that early on, Minnie gave the dolls to friends and family, but later she began to sell her dolls. Her sets of dolls that included a woman with a baby on her back and two little girls were popular among buyers. "People were buying those sets for $500," Carolyn said. She said it's likely not many of her mother's dolls exist. She keeps a set of them in her work office. She also doesn't know of anyone else who made corncob dolls like the ones her mother made.

"They were just the cutest little dolls. She would make clothes for them like bonnets like they wore a long time ago," said another daughter, Sandra Whitecrow. "It was always just girl dolls that she made. She would even sew on their faces like their little eyes and their nose. And they would have the cutest (prairie) dresses on that my mom would sew. She did it all by hand."

Sandra also said her mother would make long sleeves for her dolls' dresses and gathered the sleeves at the wrist. She also used cardboard pieces to make a bill for her bonnets so that they extended over the dolls' faces. "I used to watch her make them. I think it would relax her. And I think she did it because it reminded her of her mother," Sandra said.

For her dolls, Minnie would dry out corncobs left from family dinners. She grew

the corn in her own garden. Carolyn said she and her sisters would dry out the corncobs for their mother if they wanted dolls. "I just dried out corncobs for her, and that's how she would make them. I would go over to her house and watch her make them," she said. Carolyn said it would take about two weeks for her to make a full set of dolls.

Minnie would put her dolls in the Cherokee Master Craftsman Shows in the 1990s. Cherokee National Treasures were called "Master Craftsmen" back then, and the shows were only for Master Craftsmen. Carolyn said that when her mother received the award in 1992, she likely just smiled because she was a quiet person. "You know how those older elder ladies are; they just kind of grin and go on, but you could tell she had that pride in her smile, too," Sandra said.

—by Will Chavez

Clockwise from top left: Minnie Jumper holding daughter Alice; Cloth doll made by Minnie Jumper; Doll made by Minnie Jumper. Photos courtesy of Alice Jumper Wilder

john a. ketcher

June 5, 1922
Yonkers, Oklahoma

"I lost my mother, and because of that bad luck I had, it really helped me."

I started school at Yonkers, Oklahoma, and it was a one-room school. I started when I was six years old like most kids. When I went to school, we had to walk half a mile and had a difficult time learning the English language 'cause I came from a Cherokee-speaking family, though my mom spoke some English 'cause she went to Chilocco Indian School. Both my father and mother were the same amount of Cherokee. My father never spoke Cherokee. My father's side was Frank Ketcher, and they did not speak Cherokee. I was orphaned when I was about ten years old when my mother passed away due to pneumonia. At the time, we were living just outside of Wagoner.

My mother was a Downing. And after she died, my mother's sister, Annie Batt, became my mother. When my mother passed away, no one was interested in coming to take care of us. I tried to go back to school at Yonkers and stayed with my Grandpa Downing and Katie Fisher, and they found out we had a hard time getting to school 'cause it was three miles one way. I often missed school 'cause of weather. But family found out there was an orphanage/boarding school for Cherokees in Tahlequah that would take us in—my half-sister and cousin—because we were half-orphaned. We were eligible for the school in Tahlequah, Oklahoma, which is now Cherokee Nation Sequoyah Indian High School. So I have a long history with Sequoyah. In fact, it is so close to me I thought of it as my second home.

"If my mother had lived, I would not have been sent to a boarding school."

When I first came to Sequoyah, I was still in third grade and was three years behind. They told me I could go to the next grade if I liked, but I told them I wasn't ready. After I started

Photo by David Fitzgerald

getting toward ninth grade in Sequoyah, you could become eligible to learn a vocation. Sequoyah was named Sequoyah Vocational School at the time. And what they did, was after becoming a ninth grader, we could take a vocation and take classes and get hands-on experience. They wanted you to try out all the vocational things. We had shop class, which comes into play later on when we get to the weaving part, because that is where our looms were built, and that is the first thing Mr. Ames had to do when he came to Sequoyah.

So, when I became a ninth grader, they would change every semester, I think, for the vocational part; each day would be half a day academic, and the other half would be vocational. So after they changed it again, they put me there—loom weaving as one of the first classes, 'cause by then, Mr. Ames had started a classroom which was located in the basement of the girls' dormitory at the time. They had made these looms up at the shop, using shop boys learning how to use saws and planes and even a lathe for those round things that go on a loom. He had enough to start a class, and they only consisted of six people because that is all the looms they had, but they kept making them in shop class.

Continued on page 265

Clockwise from top left: Loom weaving by John Ketcher, photo by David Fitzgerald; John and wife Colleen Ketcher by John Ketcher's weaving and historic loom at Cherokee Heritage Center's Adam's Corner, photo by Roger Cain; John Ketcher Deputy Chief of Cherokee Nation, photo by David Fitzgerald

mildred justice ketcher

November 26. 1922
Tahlequah, Oklahoma

Mildred Justice Ketcher, is a Cherokee National Treasure who could often be found, on any nice day, enjoying her flower gardens and her basket making. She is shown in one photo on her backyard patio on Keetoowah Street in Tahlequah, Oklahoma.

Growing up, I remember that it was not uncommon to find an array of friends, visitors and, sometimes, tourists who were visiting the area, gathering at her home. Eager to share her knowledge with those interested, she would pull up another chair and patiently encourage and demonstrate her basket-making techniques. She was always especially excited when capturing and incorporating the enthusiastic interests of youngsters. No matter what phase of production, her guests would be encouraged in their efforts, and it wasn't long before they would be well-initiated into the process. What a sight it was—an assortment of guests and the frequent visiting strangers, sitting in the shade—talking, enjoying a cool drink, and enjoying their own handiwork.

The backyard fence on Keetoowah Street was lined with fragrant honeysuckle which provided a lot of the material for Mildred's traditional Cherokee baskets.

From top filmstrip: Walt Justice Family (back: Arthur, Walt, Freddie (Walt's wife), Jim; front: Jean, Lillian, Mildred); Mildred Ketcher's homestead; Mildred Ketcher teaching a class; Mildred Ketcher buckbrush basket with natural blood root and black walnut dyes, photo by David Fitzgerald; Mildred Ketcher buckbrush double wall basket with black walnut dye, photo by David Fitzgerald

Periodic ventures into the familiar countryside yielded many natural ingredients for the dying processes.

In the confines of her fragrant yard, one could find the typical impromptu "backyard day"—gathering and stripping and the preparing and mixing of natural dyes for the weaving and shaping of baskets under Mildred's helpful guidance. At the end of the day, crafters could leave with their project, regardless of the stage of completion, and sometimes, wearing the dyes as their newly found badges of honor. This occurrence was repeated for as long as I can remember.

For three to four years that I know of, Mildred and her husband, John, traveled to Ocmulgee National Monument near Macon, Georgia, where she demonstrated/taught basketry as an artist-in-residence during the summer months. Each year that she returned, she would share pictures, memories and friendships. She continued to correspond with others who shared that common interest long after the tenure. She always enjoyed her creations, and she especially enjoyed viewing and holding the creations of others. While much of her concentration focused on the use of honeysuckle, she also experimented with pine needles, split oak and willow.

Continued on page 266

Photo courtesy of family

jennie jean sapp

February 21, 1923
Taggs Flat, Oklahoma

Jennie Proctor was born at home to Thomas and Katie Proctor in Delaware County. The family lived at Taggs Flat near Bull Hollow. She grew up near Steely Church. Jennie had five brothers and four sisters. Her younger sister, Marie Proctor, is also a Cherokee National Treasure. Of the ten children, only Rosie, Jenny, and Marie made baskets.

Steely Baptist Church used to be a school, and that is where Jennie attended school. She achieved a third-grade education, which was an accomplishment in those days. She could speak, read, and write Cherokee. She also spoke English pretty well.

Jennie's mother, Katie, made the regular, round Cherokee baskets, but she was not able to make them as often as she might have wanted. Jennie was very resourceful, and when she discovered dynamite wire at a landfill, she collected it, stripped the plastic covers, and started weaving. She was looking through a magazine and saw a photo of a crocheted swan. She knew that she could weave that wire into a swan, just like the magazine photo, and she did. That photo started her weaving, and it was also what started her weaving unusual baskets in the shape of animals and birds. She wove some ducks but needed beaks, so she used pinewood and carved beaks for the ducks.

In the fall, Jennie would go out to harvest buck brush. It would take a couple of

Above (filmstrip): Jennie Sapp and Jennie Buckskin making buck brush baskets at Bull Hollow, Cherokee Nation of Oklahoma, circa 1970; Basket by Jennie Sapp; Jennie Sapp; Left: Duck Basket made from coated wire by Jennie Sapp from the collection of Kathryn Kelley, photo by Roger Cain; Below: Basketry by Jenny Sapp, photos courtesy of family

weeks to cook it and clean it before she could start on her crafts. She would collect a lot of buck brush vines and honeysuckle vines so that she had plenty to work with. She would sometimes work with commercial reed because she couldn't always make enough of her art to supply the buyers. She worked very hard to fulfill the orders. She would go to the arts and crafts events to sell her baskets and would often go on weekends to display and sell. She had her own loom and made saddle blankets and place mats. Around Christmas time, Jennie would make Christmas bells and decorate them. She made frogs with their mouths wide open, turkeys, swans, ducks, eagles, dogs, owls, and rabbits. Few weavers had this skill.

Her daughter, Annie Loy, recalled a time when a lady called from Colorado and requested a purse. She wanted Jennie to make her a purse that looked like a fish. Jennie made it. Where the fins of the fish are located became the handles.

Continued on page 266

carving

1990

 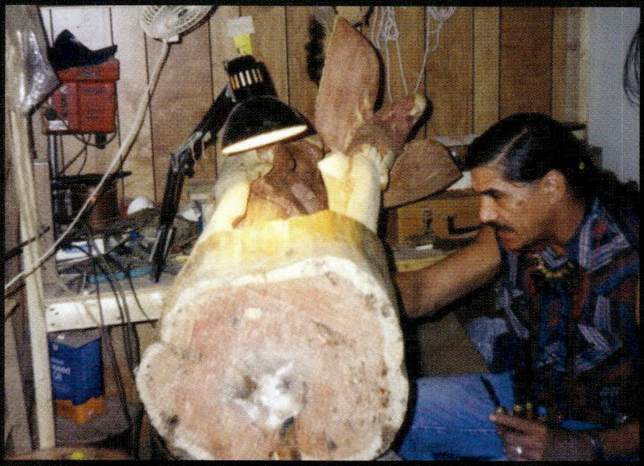 

"I want to represent American Indian people with pride and dignity.... My ideas and themes come from the philosophies of Native Americans about spirituality, family, respect for life, animals, and all that is around us, and the Great Creator."

—Eddie Morrison

"Clarence Downing, first artist to be recognized as a Cherokee Treasure for carving, was world-renowned for his many fine carvings made of sandstone and wood. His carvings are on display throughout the world, including Japan, China, Rome and the Vatican.

"I was taught if something good exists, it never dies. It's always there and just needs to be stumbled upon again. Maybe this was one way the old Indian people thought they could communicate with us here in the future. Even though the designs are very, very old, they haven't lost their vitality or freshness. They have so much strength and so much power in them that sometimes, in the art world, we want to incorporate that into our work somehow to give (the art) strength, to capture that. So that's what I've been trying to do, capture that strength and vitality. If other people can see this, then they can feel it, too."

—Knokovtee Scott

"By cutting away and releasing the images in each piece of wood, my carving helps me to express my traditions and beliefs in the old ways of the Cherokee."

—Luther "Toby" Hughes

"Richard Rowe was a knife maker, carver, and a gig maker. He used springs out of older cars—no older than 1949 though—to make gigs and knives. His knives are owned by some very famous people. One is in the possession of President Bill Clinton, another with Governor Frank Keating, and another with Senator Kelly Haney."

—Joe Byrd, Speaker of the Tribal Council

"I remember Dad bringing home some wood cutouts of bears, ducks, and other animals—even a tall cutout of a giraffe. He brought home this one particular small wooden cutout that was very intriguing to me. The cutout looked like the shape of a small drag-racing car. It was out of walnut wood with a big body and a long piece of flat wood attached to it. I would play with it, pretending it was a racing car.

"Later my dad came looking for that piece of wood and found out I had been playing with it. He took the small cutout and began carving on it. It turned out to be a little mouse with a long tail. That was so fantastic, I didn't know that piece of wood was a cutout of a mouse."

— Sammy Still on his father, Sam Lee Still

"When I think about our dad's art, I think about the times when he would seem not to be doing anything special that required time or a need to be by himself to express creativity, but a few minutes later, he would hold up a painting of a deer or maybe a woodcarving of the Cherokee clans or a horse and wagon set or even a tiny pair of wooden cowboy boots. You wouldn't know that he was creating art right there just a few feet away in the house or outside on the porch, but when he showed it to you, all you could do was be amazed."

—Gerald Wofford

"I just play around right here. This is where I carve around, just make stuff. Either here (or) on one of these hills, I'll go up there to a little sitting spot, and I'll just sit there all day and carve."

—Thomas Muskrat

Pictured left: Sequoyah carved wooden bust by Clarence Downing, photo by David Fitzgerald; This page, left to right: Peach pit carving by Hastings Shade, photo by Jeremy Charles; Toby Hughes working in his shop, courtesy of Cherokee National Archives; Deer antler carving by Thomas Muskrat, photo by Jeremy Charles

scott rackliff

May 29, 1923
Rocky Ford, Oklahoma

Cherokee artist Scott Rackliff was named a Cherokee National Treasure in 1991 for flint knapping and carving, but his friends said he could make just about anything from wood or stone. He spent many years working at the Cherokee Heritage Center, giving visitors a good glimpse of Cherokee craftsmanship. "Scott was what we called the 'Village Chief.' He helped people when they needed something in the Ancient Village at the Cherokee Heritage Center. He knew quite a bit about blowguns, bows, and flint knapping," said current Diligwa Villager Danny McCarter. "He was an all-around artist, and that's what we all teased him about and called him 'Great Scott.' He was always coming up with something. He was real crafty. He could pick up things off the ground and make something out of it."

McCarter recalled a time when Rackliff learned that Osage people used cedar wood for their bows, while the Cherokee used Bois D'arc and locust trees for theirs. Rackliff found a cedar tree that had been cut down near the Ancient Village, took a piece of the wood, used his hatchet, and in three days fashioned a bow. "What he did was take his hatchet and kind of roughed it out. He also carved his arrow out of cedar. He carved the arrowhead and everything out of the limb itself," McCarter recalled. "He could take something and just look at it and make something. One time he made a Bois D'arc knife. He was carving around on a piece of Bois D'arc, and the next thing we know, he had butcher knife-looking thing, and he's over there cutting watermelons with it."

Cherokee Heritage Center employee Ken Foster recalls Rackliff was "a good guy and a real craftsman" who liked to talk about his bows or his other interests. Foster also said, "He was stout." He said one of the last times he saw him, Rackliff was finishing a small bow with a thirty-pound pull. When Foster asked why he was making such a small bow, Rackliff said he wanted to make sure to kill his next deer without his arrow penetrating all the way through the deer.

"I can save my arrows that way," Rackliff told Foster.

Anna Sixkiller worked with Rackliff in the Ancient Village in the 1970s and 1980s. She said he worked on arrowheads, bows and arrows, lances, blowguns and darts, and stone pipes, among other things. She said he also could make utensils, like spoons, out of natural materials. "I think he just learned by watching or by looking at art pieces," she said. She also said he once made a canoe by slowly burning out the center of a large tree like Cherokee men did in ancient times.

She said when he wasn't showing his skills to visitors in the Ancient Village, he and the other villagers maintained the buildings in the village and the wooden fence surrounding it. One of the requirements for being named a Cherokee National Treasure is that an artist teaches others what they know. "All of the boys—like Danny (McCarter)—would come to him,. All of the young guys in the village, he probably taught all of them to do many different things and not just one thing," she said..

McCarter said many of the people who work in the village pick up skills like bow and arrow making, flint knapping, blowgun making, making stickball sticks and other traditional skills, but he added Rackliff must have grown up learning all of the skills he brought to the village.

"I think his family was just that way. They probably used their blowguns. They probably used their bows at that time," he said.

McCarter said he is always glad to see people like Rackliff, who died in 1994, receive the Cherokee National Treasure award. "The thing about Scott is he liked to talk to people. People would stop and talk to him because he had all of his bows with him. He also made stickball sticks. He was always trying to teach us how to make them. There wasn't anything he couldn't do."

—by Will Chavez

Top: Scott Rackliff Spear Point, photo by David Fitzgerald; From left: Scott Rackliff demonstrating flintknapping at the Tsa La Gi Ancient Village, photo courtesy of the Cherokee National Historical Society; Scott Rackliff in Adam's Corner General Store, photo courtesy of Cherokee National Historical Society

tom webber wildcat

August 11, 1922
Greenleaf Lake State Park, Oklahoma

Tom Wildcat was known to many as *Su-we-gi*, and he was the son of Squirrel Webber Wildcat and Polly Tehee Wildcat. Both his parents were original enrollees on the Cherokee Nation Dawes Final Roll, and both enrolled as full-blood citizens of the Cherokee Nation.

Tom grew up on his mother's allotment land in the southern region of the Cherokee Nation near Greenleaf Lake State Park. Tom was trilingual, as he was a fluent speaker in Cherokee, Creek, and English. At that time, many traditional stomp-dance people resided all over the area. He became a stomp-dance leader at the age of nine, and as a boy, Tom learned the traditional Cherokee art of making turtle-shell shakers from his mother, Polly, who learned the custom from her parents and siblings.

Tom was the second oldest in his family, and he helped his parents with chores. He would plow the garden with a couple of mules in the early days of their large gardens. The family would grow acres of vegetables, including corn, beans, potatoes, watermelons, cucumbers, and cantaloupe melons.

Tom and his siblings walked to the local school and rode their horses everywhere—even to the stomp grounds—until automobiles took over their lives.

Living the heritage and surviving in the modern world was all around, but

Right: Tom Webber Wildcat Turtle Shackles and claybeads, photo courtesy of family; Below: Tom Webber Wildcat receiving National Living Treasure at Cherokee Holiday with then Deputy Chief Garland Eagle, photo courtesy of family; Tom Webber Wildcat family, photo courtesy of family

nothing stopped Tom and the Wildcat family from going to the stomp dance. They would dress up in their best clothes, shine their boots, and load up for the evening stomp dance.

The Wildcats were a strong stomp dance family. Tom was featured in a 1995 *National Geographic Magazine*, "Rekindling the Fire," and a 1995 American Express commercial, called "Charge Against Hunger." He is also on the cover of a beautiful coffee table book called *Cherokee*.

Mr. Tom Webber Wildcat raised his family in the traditional Cherokee customs of the stomp-dance heritage, teaching them by living the heritage daily, as he lived it. Through his efforts, the heritage of the stomp dance and Cherokee customs is preserved and perpetuated. His family proudly carries on that heritage today.

Tom Wildcat was honored with the title of Cherokee National Treasure in 1995 for (making) turtle-shell shakers. He left a legacy that can be heard through his family, friends and all who knew him.

—Tommy Wildcat, son

NOTE: *Stomp dance is the terminology used to describe the old structural heritage of the Cherokee tribal towns, where the language is spoken, tobacco used, prayers, medicine, Seven Clans kinship families, and the chief, council, and medicine man are followed like Christian ministers and retain the protocol of the ceremonies.*

betty scraper garner

February 23, 1924
Tahlequah, Oklahoma

Betty Scraper Garner was born and lived in the Old Green community west of Westville, Oklahoma, in Adair County. She attended high school at Haskell in Lawrence, Kansas. Betty enlisted in the Navy WAVES (Women Accepted for Voluntary Emergency Service) and was stationed at various naval bases in the country during World War II. After she was honorably discharged, she began her career in the Bureau of Indian Affairs. She worked at Jones Academy in Hartshorne, Oklahoma, as a dormitory matron. She retired in 1973, a year after her husband, Wallace C. Garner, retired from the Bureau of Indian Affairs. During her first years of retirement, Betty and her sister, Lenora Hamilton, took basket-weaving classes taught by basket-weaver Thelma Forrest.

After the classes ended, Betty continued to weave baskets from commercial reeds and dyes. She taught her children and grandchildren to weave. Her family represented three generations of basket weavers. Over several years, Betty and her daughters would weave together in the evenings and weekends and sell their baskets to local gift shops in Cherokee, Adair and Sequoyah counties. Betty enjoyed working and weaving

with white-oak splints, honeysuckle and buck-brush runners. With the assistance of her family and close friends to split the white oak, Betty would use natural dye materials and weave the white-oak splints to make "large waste baskets" and "egg baskets" as she called them.

In the summer time, she hosted several tourists in her home. The garage was converted to a den where she displayed her baskets and other craft items, as well as those of her children and grandchildren. Several gift shop owners/managers would call her to see if she would open her home to those wanting to see and purchase her baskets. Betty enjoyed having her guests wander through the den, admiring the baskets (made by) her and her family. She made a few sales, too.

During the early 1990s, Betty was asked to teach at area community centers in Tahlequah, Muskogee, Bell, Watts, and Porter. She loved teaching others and especially the elderly. Betty would say that basket weaving was therapeutic for our hands and fingers. Most could weave the wider flat reed better, and some of her students entered their baskets in fairs and won ribbons. They would display their winning baskets in class.

Continued on page 267

From top: Tribute pot from grandson Bryan Waytula, photo by Jeremy Charles; Betty weaving with granddaughter; Honeysuckle double-wall lidded basket, photo by David Fitzgerald;

clesta manley

November 23, 1924
Pryor, Oklahoma

"My greatest honor was to be recognized as a Cherokee Artist."
--Clesta Martin Manley

Photo by Will Chavez

Stepping inside the Manley home is like entering another world. On her walls are framed paintings and prints of her art work—pictures of flowers, animals, Cherokee women, the *Nanyehi,* abstract art, and so much more. "Amazing Grace" is the name she gave to one painting of the Saline Court House and women in Cherokee dresses holding hands in a circle with a man playing a flute standing by. The women are members of the Indian Women's Pocahontas Club who were gathered at the Saline Court house one June day. Clesta has been an active member of the Pocahontas Club for forty years. The women were singing and offering prayers of blessing and thankfulness, as the Court House was lost to the Cherokee during the time of the Dawes Act but has now been returned.

Clesta is the daughter of Mack and Edna Martin. She grew up in Boatman, Mayes County, on her father's allotment close to the Grand River. Her grandfather built a three-story house on her father's land because he liked it better than his own allotment. Clesta loved sitting in a third-story window at her grandfather's because she could see the Grand River and the birds that landed there. She was a country girl and loved riding her father's quarter horses and looking for places to paint. The family lived on the allotments until the land was taken from her father and grandfather because of the construction of the Pensacola Dam.

Clesta had five brothers who were "always out fishing and hunting" and did not want her tagging along with them. So her dad, who was good at drawing, introduced her to drawing before she started school. She was so excited when she started school and got her first crayons and could add color to her drawings. One day, when she was in third grade and looking out the classroom window, she saw a squirrel in a tree, and she started drawing. Her teacher saw it and praised her, then showed the drawing to other teachers. They told her she was so good she would be a great artist one day. After that, she started drawing and coloring every chance she got. When her mother painted the walls, she would take any leftover paint and paint on rocks and anything else she could find.

In high school, Clesta was good at math and thought it would be a good idea to become a CPA. She decided to

Continued on page 267

Clockwise from top; Clesta Manley at work on her painting Amazing Grace, photo by Will Chavez; Clesta Manley at home, photo by January Hoskin; Clesta Manley with Saline Courthouse paintings, photo by January Hoskin

traditional clothing
1990

"Although widely recognized as the only maker of buffalo grass dolls, Lorene Drywater was designated as a Cherokee National Living Treasure in 1990 for her traditional clothing such as tear dresses and ribbon shirts.

"Lorene also made little dresses for her buffalo grass dolls. Each doll received a cotton calico "tear" dress with detailed trim and petticoats.

"I learned to sew by watching my mama. I started sewing as soon as I knew how to hold a needle."

—Lorene Drywater

"When I put my first tear dress on, that sweet Ruth England made for me, I turned cartwheels in it, just because I could."

—Tonia Hogner Weavel on Ruth England

"The tear dress was practical for two reasons: The fullness of the gathered bodice and skirt gave the wearer freedom of movement to do the labor of daily work chores, and the one-piece construction allowed women to bend and stretch without fretting with the problem of keeping a waist tucked in or hooked to a skirt."

—Wendell Cochran

"Mama made most of our clothes. We'd get flour in the twenty-five-pound sack, and those sacks would have a design, and she'd save enough of those—maybe she'd get enough of one kind—to make a dress. Well, when I was in high school, I learned how to sew. And that's where I get my love for sewing, I guess."

—Edith Catcher Knight

Pictured left: Traditional clothing, photo courtesy of the Cherokee Heritage Center; This page, left to right: Traditional Clothing provided by family; Ruth England's Granddaughter in tear dress, photo provided by family; Traditional clothing

sam lee still

January 28, 1925
Tahlequah, Oklahoma

Sam Lee Still began carving on wood in the early '70s. I remember living in Cherokee, North Carolina, where my dad would attend a wood-carving class taught by Amanda Crowe, an Eastern Band Cherokee woman who was very famous for her wood carvings and also taught carving at the Cherokee High School.

My dad would work all day as a road foreman for the Bureau of Indian Affairs, come home in the evening, eat supper, and then leave to attend wood-carving classes two nights a week.

I remember Dad bringing home some wood cutouts of bears, ducks, and other animals—even a tall cutout of a giraffe. He brought home this one particular small wooden cutout that was very intriguing to me. The cutout looked like the shape of a small, drag-racing car. It was out of walnut wood, with a big body and a long piece of flat wood attached to it. I would play with it, pretending it was a racing car.

Later, my dad came looking for that piece of wood and found out I had been playing with it. He took the small cutout and began carving on it. It turned out to be a little mouse with a long tail. That was so fantastic; I didn't know that piece of wood was a cutout of a mouse.

My dad was very talented and became a good wood carver, carving wooden bears, ducks, and even a nice looking giraffe which stood three feet tall.

I began taking interest in wood carving, and so did my sister. My dad would bring home some wooden cutouts for me and my sister to carve on. We began carving small wooden animals. Of course, after a while, I began cutting my fingers on my pocket knife, and my sister lost interest, so we both decided to stop carving. But my dad became well known locally for his wood carvings.

We would go back home to Oklahoma to visit family and friends, and on one such occasion, my father met a person who told my dad that he should set up a table to display and sell his wood carvings. He informed my dad about the annual Cherokee National Holiday event where he could show and sell his artwork. So my dad took this gentleman's advice, and we returned during the Cherokee National Holiday weekend, displaying and selling his carvings. My mother helped him, and my sister and I even had some small wooden animal carvings we displayed and sold.

When we moved back to Oklahoma, my dad continued carving. My mom and dad would travel on weekends to arts and crafts shows to display and sell his carvings. They would travel throughout Oklahoma, into Arkansas, Kansas, and to many other different craft shows. This is where he met other famous wood carvers. One was the world-famous Willard Stone; they became very close friends, along with fellow carvers Calvin Berry and a man named Darling. They all became very close friends.

Clockwise from top: Cherokee Nation Seal earned by Sam Still; Sam Still's Duck Carving; Sam Still with son, Sam Jr., displaying wood carvings

What I remember the most about my father was his artistic talent. He never graduated high school, but to me he was a very intelligent man who was a very creative and loving person.

— Sammy Still Jr.

linda lou mouse hansen

March 25, 1925
Bull Hollow, Oklahoma

Linda Lou Mouse Hansen: In her passing, her last name was Ryder. She had been married to my father, Jess Mouse Hansen, for many years, and at that time she lived with us at Dry Creek. She knew how to cook, prepare wild game, *tsistanv* (crawdads), *atsadi* (fish), and how to can food. Linda canned all the vegetables my father raised—green beans, corn, and potatoes. She knew a lot about plants and herbs that grew out in the wild; she knew what kind of plants and herbs to pick.

Linda's artistic side: she could do beadwork; she beaded all through her life to the day of her passing. She also did basket weaving. (She was) a very gifted woman. She had a hearing disability and learned sign language. Later on in her life, she received several surgeries to correct her hearing and overcame her disability, learning how to speak.

Linda was a very talented woman who overcame many adversities along with her hearing disability. She didn't learn to drive a vehicle until in her mid-forties. Once she learned how to drive, she expanded her horizons, traveling to Tahlequah to buy beads and selling her beadwork. She was a very remarkable lady. Linda would even drive to Cookson to sell her beadwork. Bull Hollow to Cookson is quite some distance to drive, but she traveled there and traded.

My mother grew up during the '50s and witnessed the Depression and World War

Clockwise from top: Turtle Basket by Linda Mouse Hansen, photo by David Fitzgerald; Linda Mouse Hansen buckbrush basket, photo by Sam Still; Reed baskets by Linda Mouse Hansen, photo by David Fitzgerald

11. She lived through two sons going to Vietnam during the war in the '60s and '70s, and she witnessed both of the sons returning home. She was a mother of five boys and two girls.

She was bilingual and could play the piano and loved to sing. Linda was a woman of her time who did the best she could under a lot of hardships and circumstances.

In the 1960s, there was an initiative program—provided by federal grant money—at the community center in Bull Hollow, five miles from our house. There a group of ladies started weaving classes. They would weave baskets, and I think they even weaved rugs. The same program was introduced at the community center in Oak Hill, near Jay, Oklahoma.

Recruiters would come by individuals' houses and recruit women to attend these initiative programs where the ladies would socialize as they weaved. This is where many of the community ladies learned how to weave, do beadwork, and even to can food. I know at our church, the women would gather on Wednesdays and sew quilts and socialize.

I remember my mom as being artistic, because I have some of her traits. I did stage and drama in school, and she had that dramatic flair in her personal life by just being herself. She was from the Peavine area; how she ended up in the Bull Hollow, Kenwood area, I'll never know.

Linda Lou Mouse Hansen enjoyed life. In spite of the challenges and hardships she faced, she still had a song in her heart and a smile on her face.

Even to this day, even though my father and mother were divorced for many years, they lay side by side in the Dry Creek cemetery in the Bull Hollow area. I can't wait to see her again.

I am the youngest of the seven children she had.

— Woody Hansen, Linda's son
Interviewed by Sammy Still Jr.

mary foreman

September 24, 1926
Oaks, Oklahoma

Mary Downing was born to Joseph and Hattie (Leach) Downing from Snake Creek in Adair County. She was the oldest of the Downing children. Mary attended what used to be called Buffalo School near Leach, then Smith Chapel. She was designated as a master craftsman during the 1990 Cherokee National Holiday.

Basket making was a family tradition. Mary's mom, Hattie, made baskets. Mary made them. Her sister, Louisa (Soap), made them, and now her younger sister, Joann, makes them, too. Mary's daughter, Hattie, and son, Billy, also learned how to make baskets, and Mary's granddaughter, Marcella, makes baskets. The three other grandchildren carry on the family tradition as well. Their brother, Clarence, was a wood and stone carver, who was also named as a Cherokee National Treasure.

Mary's mother and a sister were quilters, and they made beautiful crepe paper flowers—a vanishing art—for Memorial Day. Mary started doing beadwork when she was in her early thirties. Her sister, Louisa Downing Soap, bought a little loom and brought it home so that she could make a bracelet. When she showed the bracelet to Mary, Mary said, "We can do that."

"Mary went right out and bought a bunch of beads, all in different colors. Mary just started making things from her head—medallions, bracelets. I asked her how to make those things, and she said I would have to learn it for myself. She couldn't tell me how it was done; she said it was always different. She told me to draw it and then start right in the middle. So I learned from her how to bead," Louisa said.

After they had learned to bead, Mary started making baskets, and then Louisa started making baskets. Louisa said that their mom used to make baskets out of honeysuckle. Honeysuckle grew right outside of their house, and it was just going everywhere. So they started gathering that honeysuckle, and Mary started peeling the vines. She tried hard to remember how their mom fixed that honeysuckle to make her baskets. She worked with it and worked with it and, finally, she remembered how it was done. The next time Louisa went over to see Mary, Mary said "Now we can go get them sticks, because I know how to do it." She showed Louisa how to do it. Honeysuckle runners were her favorite material to use. Louisa said that that she would often go with Mary to gather the honeysuckle. The best parts of the bush

Continued on page 268

Clockwise from top: Doublewall Buckbrush lidded basket with blood root and blackwalnut dyes by Mary Foreman; Buckbrush Pitcher and Saucer basket with black walnut dye by Mary Foreman; Oblong doublewall Buckbrush storage or gathering basket by Mary Foreman. Photos by David Fitzgerald

anna mitchell

October 26, 1926
Jay, Oklahoma

My husband always wanted a clay pipe, like Sequoyah. And one day, I said to Bob, "I'll make you one." Little did I know there was more to it than making mud pies. So, I went down to make these pipes. It was dry summer. My kids rode their bikes up and down the dip—a ten-foot hole. I went down there and there was this clay. So, I started playing with it and trying to make pots. And that day, I put them in the sun and went back to the house and left them. I was working. The next day I came home—the pots, the pipes, they were all cracked. I thought, "My ancestors used to make pottery. I wonder what it looked like. And that started the whole thing."

For me, it was seeking out designs of anything from the Southeast—what we were about, what our ancestors' legacy would have been to us as a people because you wonder about the design. You get into this thing of, "Is it really Cherokee or is it this tribe or is it that tribe?"

What I found out (about) being a potter was I couldn't find anybody to ask to show me how to make pottery like the Cherokees or even what the designs were. Once I got into clay, well, then, I started wondering how our ancestors used to make pottery, wondered what it looked like. I never intended to get into pottery. Then, when I did, I didn't have any designs or anything to look to.

So, later on, I found this book at Gilcrease (Museum). It was a little golden book of different tribal arts. And they had a little section on the Southeast. That was the first inkling that I thought about anything Southeast. That led me to know where to look. You know, anything Southeast, anything of that culture. I mainly wanted to know what the signs were. It didn't matter to me, at that time, if it came off of a shell or a pot or a petroglyph or whatever. As long as one is Southeast, you know, I wanted people to see that's the kind of designs we had. It didn't matter if it was on a pot or not because nobody was doing it!

And I remember the first time I entered a show and an anthropologist or an archaeologist from somewhere asked me, "Are you just copying these designs off something?"

I said, "No, this is my pot. I made it. It's Cherokee. I didn't copy it. I just designed it from something I saw that's Southeast." That's all I can tell you."

And so, he said, "I just wondered if you just copied this."

I said, "No, I'm not. I'm just making my pots."

I got all kinds of questions like that. Nobody had seen a Cherokee pot, especially in the Southwest. You had to almost bully your way to let them know that. Where I've been and the questions and the fences I've had to climb over is something else when you're trying to do something that nobody else was ever stupid enough to try and do. But it got interesting, the more I got into it. You can say, to me, it wasn't lost. And I didn't, necessarily, go out to find it. But I wanted to see where it was. So, eventually, I became a potter—and to the best of my ability.

Southwest was totally different. At that time, they thought—the world (thought)—that they were the only potters. And they started (Santa Fe) Indian Market

Continued on page 268

From top: Young Anna Belle, photo courtesy of family; Anna and Bob Mitchell, photo courtesy of family; Effigy pipe by Anna Mitchell

Photo by David Fitzgerald

lee foreman

October 19, 1928
Cloud Creek, Oklahoma

Lee Foreman is a full-blood Cherokee living in the Clouds Creek community. For many years, Lee has maintained the Cloud Creek Marble Field which is located north of Little Kansas and west of Colcord on Foreman family land. The Cloud Creek field is a popular gathering place for nightly games of Indian marbles. Players from all the surrounding communities play throughout the year. Lee believes the Cherokee tradition of playing marbles is a good, positive tradition to keep for people of all ages and abilities.

In 1996, at the age of 67, Lee was a player on the championship marble team at the Cherokee National Holiday Tournament. The following year, his team won second place. Since 1988, when he helped plan the first tournament, Lee has been actively involved in the management of the tournament and the daily maintenance of the marble ground. His only regret is that the tournament is held on the same weekend as the quarter meeting at Cloud Creek Baptist Church where he is a deacon. Since his priority is his church, he rarely comes to Tahlequah for the tournament finals unless his team is competing for the title. Even then, he takes no time for celebration but hurries back home to get ready for the Saturday evening service.

In 1987, Lee participated in the Lost Arts Project, a joint effort of the Cherokee Nation, the

Cherokee Heritage Center, and the Northeastern State University Bilingual Education Center. Throughout this project, the description and history of the game of Indian Marbles was recorded, and the first of the annual Cherokee National Holiday Tournaments was planned.

For several years, Lee along with his wife, Minnie, daughter, Jewell, and his brother, Andy, have traveled to Tahlequah to teach the game of Indian Marbles to the Cherokee Heritage classes at Northeastern State University. Lee is always eager to share his knowledge and skills with any student who wants to learn. In addition to the rules and strategies of the game, he also teaches about the skills of stone-marble making and the fine craftsmanship involved in preparing the marble field.

One marble story told by Lee and his brothers is about their father, Richard Foreman, who worked at a sawmill near their home. When they were children, their father would play marbles just about every weekend. At the time, the marble game was played with handmade stone marbles. And since the competition was fierce and there were many good "hitters," the stone marbles would sometimes break apart from a solid hit. Therefore, it was always necessary to have an extra marble on hand to continue the game if your marble was broken. So marble players were always on the lookout for good, rounded rocks to make into marbles. The process for making a marble involved chipping the stone to make it as round and smooth as possible. One clear memory Lee has of his father is the pecking sound that could be heard in the distance as his father walked home from the sawmill through the woods after a day of work. Richard Foreman would be shaping a new marble as he walked.

Continued on page 269

Clockwise from top: Lee Foreman throwing marbles picture from Lost Arts Project brochure, 1987; Lee Foreman and Dennis Snell at Cloud Creek marble field; Lee Foreman (at right) at marble tournament

oom weaving

1990

"My favorite is just loom weaving, and that's all I do. In 1951, I had my sixteenth birthday down at Sequoyah Weavers. At the beginning, I just went over to see what was going on at the weaving shop. And there were a lot of women there. I really didn't pay attention to who was doing what. They asked me if I wanted to learn. They didn't say weaving or what. They said, 'Would you like to learn?' And I said, 'Yeah.' And then Bill Ames gave me two boxes of yarn—red and black.

"They told me, 'Go string it.' So, I made the warp and then, when I roll the warp and brought it in the weaving shop, then I had help threading it. And it took a whole day. And then the next day I would weave, and it took a whole day weaving. I was pretty young. I was the youngest student there. I can't remember how many people were there. They were doing just different things—learning different things. They taught baskets. They taught beadwork. They taught tailoring clothes.

"See, that's why I was really pushing loom weaving! I wanted someone to learn and then turn around and teach somebody. And I want to hear them say, 'I taught so 'n' so,' while I'm still living! I want to see it while I am still able to move, and do something, and pass it on to somebody. And, in turn, I want to hear them say, 'I taught 'n' so.' Yeah, that's what I wanted to do. That's what I asked for, anyway. John Ketcher and I talked about that between us."

—Dorothy Ice

"One of the churches, the private church. Not the big Assembly Ground Church, the one that sits on back on the other side of the grave yard. Well, that's where they started. They had room for about two looms, and that's where they were when I took them over. So, meanwhile, we begin to look around; if we were going to teach quite a few people, we needed a bigger place. And, I guess the director, Mr. Ames, had read in the paper (that) this army camp over by Braggs would begin to close down when they got all their soldiers out of there. They begin to say they were going to sell all the barracks and all the things there because they were closing down. I guess he got in touch with them. Being a government facility, anyway, we were able to get one. They cut it in half—two sections. And we had some government trucks that hauled it back in two pieces. They just went right on and took it out to Briggs, and this lady, Ms. Hair, she's still living, and her family owned all that strip in there. And, they said that you could put it there if you're going to start the loom weaving there. They allowed Mr. Ames to build that on their land. So we used again our carpentry-shop people. Our electrician boys learned how to wire it up, and we had electricity in there. Only thing we didn't have was water, 'cause there were no rural lines in those days."

—John Ketcher

"Wynona learned her weaving techniques from her mother, Winnie, also a Cherokee National Treasure. Winnie was part of the Sequoyah Weavers group and later, Wynona started going to the weavers building to learn as well. Wynona recalled that she and her mama spent a lot of time at the Sequoyah Indian Weavers Building. Wynona's mother began weaving in 1948. After Wynona started going to the weavers building with her mom, they would weave and talk for hours.

"Wynona started out making rag rugs and wall hangings and then finally moved on to weaving afghans. She said that she was about eighteen to twenty years old when her mama finally talked her into weaving. Wynona holds valuable history of the Sequoyah Weaver's Building. She said that when she was small, she would go over to the building with her mother. John Ketcher was often there and she remembered William 'Bill' Ames as being the driving force behind the formation of the Sequoyah Weavers. She believed that the group was formed as a result of a Bureau of Indian Affairs funding project. Although the funding was discontinued sometime in the 1950s, the building and Wynona, the weaver, remain."

—Wynona Dreadfulwater

Pictured left: John and Dorothy with historic loom and spinning wheel at CHC, photo by Roger Cain; This page, left to right: Briggs weaving hall where Sequoyah Weavers were housed, photo by Pamela Jumper; Sequoyah Weavers at Briggs, OK; Early Loom weaving, courtesy of John Ketcher

albert charles wofford

July 2, 1929
Rose, Oklahoma

Photo by David Fitzgerald

Our dad, Albert Charles Wofford, is a full-blood Cherokee Indian who makes his home in Pryor, Oklahoma. He was born in Rose, Oklahoma. His mother and father, Nancy and James Wofford, raised seven children, living near the towns of Locust Grove, Salina, and Kenwood.

Our dad still possesses part of his family's allotted land near Locust Grove. It is called Bryant Hollow and is the part of the region called the "Goingsnake" district.

It was through the temperament of our dad's father, a World War I veteran, and his mother that our dad learned that being Cherokee could be expressed in service to people through hard work and becoming creative, not only to share his art but also (to share) a piece of his heart and soul as well.

Our dad's introduction to art is a unique one. Having started at a young age, he always had the desire to discover things on his own. Spending an afternoon while hunting, playing baseball, or gigging crawdads near Snake Creek, he would pick up or cut a piece of wood off a tree and begin to carve something from it with his pocket knife. Later, it would be drawing or painting that would also allow our dad to express his creativity as a Cherokee artist, one whom I was honored to nominate as a Cherokee National Treasure in 1999.

When I think about our dad's art, I think about the times when he would seem not to be doing anything special that required time or a need to be by himself to express creativity, but a few minutes later, he would hold up a painting of a deer or maybe a woodcarving of the Cherokee clans or a horse and wagon set or even a tiny pair of wooden cowboy boots. You wouldn't know that he was creating art right there just a few feet away in the house or outside on the porch, but when he showed it to you, all you could do was be amazed.

Our dad's art makes me think of the times he grew up in a World War, through a depression in the 1930s, and being called to military service. The art of our dad grew even more with a desire to create, whether it was the format of woodcarving, painting, or making replicas of churches or courthouses from a century ago.

Clockwise from top: James and Nancy Wofford, parents of Albert Wofford, stand in front of the First United Methodist Church in Salina; Albert and Lena Wofford; Albert Wofford studies the woodwork he has created to honor the Seven Clans of the Cherokee Nation. Photo by Gerald Wofford

When I think about our dad and the art that he has created, many thoughts come to my mind—thoughts about how he expressed his art through his life.

His artwork makes me think about a man who worked hard his entire life, the example that showed in days of his youth picking cotton near Salina and Locust Grove, and proved valuable as he got older and hauled hay along with his brothers, Joe and Robert. The work ethic they possessed made them the fastest hay haulers in Mayes County, often being tested by competitors who thought they could do it quicker. They soon found out who was the best when the competitors had only half of their task completed while the Wofford boys were putting the last bale of hay in the barn and calling it a day.

Continued on page 269

ella mae blackbear

August 23, 1930
Kenwood, Oklahoma

Sometimes when I start a basket, I don't know even how I'm going to end up or how big it is going to be. It's a lot more work either way dying and buckbrush,gathering them and processing them, and striping and trimming. Best time to get it is after it's frost. And that way, there are no snakes and spiders and stuff like that. Well, Mom did more of the gathering. I did the carrying. When she'd get a handful, then I'd have to pack it. Well, I guess I did gather a few. I was just mostly her extra hand.

You have to put them in a big pot and put some water in there and let them boil. You boil them. You have to test them every now and then, to strip them off. It takes at least fifteen to twenty hours of rapid boiling. It seems like the harder they boil, the quicker they get done. And then after that, you can test it—take a little bit off the tail end—and then they are ready to be stripped.

What I think about? That's a thousand miles away. Oh, just whatever comes, I get to thinking. Seems like the more I think, the faster I work. And sometimes I sing. And then when I'm singing, I mean, I'm going full speed. I don't know; seems like singing really helps. Keeps my mind on. I've learned a lot of songs by heart. I just sing. Like if I'm driving. When I sing, the faster I go. And I have to watch that. That's right. I have to be careful. I catch myself going too fast sometimes!

This is how it starts. You crisscross six on this side and six on the other side. There was one lady; she was looking at a basket, and she said, "Where do you start?" When you look at something, you wouldn't know where they start. The bigger the basket, the more you have to put in extra; I call them extra spokes. I don't know why I keep putting this in my mouth. I'm always doing that! If I see one that is real good or long for weaving, here it goes...like this (*between her teeth.*) You just have to kind of mold it in place.

From top: Ella Mae Blackbear Buckbrush Baby Cradle Basket, photo courtesy of Cherokee Heritage Center; Ella Mae Blackbear buckbrush baskets, photo by David Fitzgerald; Ella Mae Blackbear lidded buckbrush basket, photo by David Fitzgerald

Far as I can remember was when I was in the second grade. And I don't ever remember Mom teaching me how to do this. As far as I remember, I already knew how it was done. But about ten (years old), I imagine. I remember one time I was making a basket. I was always running strings on the same direction, over and over. She'd make me rip it out and say, "If you're going to sell this basket, you better do it right." (That) is what she told me. Once you got it all pushed in, you wouldn't know where you started.

When I first went back to baskets— over the last five or six years — I didn't know where I was going to start selling them. I didn't know who to contact. And the first I knew, I went to that Cherokee Tsa-la-gi (gift shop) over at Tahlequah. I didn't even know if I was going to sell them or not. And then seemed like it just started from there. Then they took them to shows like Dallas and some of the (other) places they went, and here I am now.

Continued on page 270

kathryn kelley

December 6, 1930
Rocky Mountain, Oklahoma

Photo by Jeremy Charles

I was born in 1930. Mother said the midwife who delivered me was named Ms. Thirsty. Daddy's name was Johnson Key, and Mother's name was Bertha Allen. The only grandparent who I know was Dad's mother, Kate. I started school, 1-8, at Rocky Mountain. When I went to school, there were two rooms. Of course, I walked to school. That's what it was like. We carried our lunch most of the time. In the winter—I don't know why, (maybe) when it started to turn cold—they had someone cook the lunch. We'd go out and sit on the place out on the rocks at the edges of the school ground and eat.

There's always some real big-mouth person, and there was this one girl; she was always blabbing. My sister stayed in the Cherokee Tuberculosis Center for years. I'll never forget, we were out there eating our lunch one day. This same girl was standing up there blabbing about how she didn't like Indians and talking about how bad they were and everything. And pretty soon, she turned around to me and said, "How's your sister getting along?"

That made me so mad. I just wanted to hit her. It just went through my mind right away, "You don't like Indians! Why are you asking about my sister?"

Kathryn at 16 years of age with father, Johnson Keith, at home in Rocky Mountain

I was born on my daddy's allotted land at Rocky Mountain. He built a house on his land. I was born in that house and lived there until I graduated high school. He was getting pretty old then. He said, "I can't work this farm anymore. I'm going to sell this place and move." Just like that, it was put up for sale one day, and it was gone the next. We moved to Tahlequah. I must have been about eighteen or nineteen years old. I graduated from Cave Springs down there close to Bunch. I had to walk about a mile to catch the bus. It was a pretty small school. We didn't have more than something like nine or ten in the graduating class. Then, about the time I graduated from high school, that's when Daddy sold the farm and we moved to Tahlequah. Right away, I enrolled in Northeastern State Teacher's College (now Northeastern State University).

My husband, Bob, and I were about seniors in college when we met. And I was just really lucky, I guess, that Daddy moved there after he sold the house. Otherwise, I might not have gone to college. But I would work in the summer and save my money, and I'd make enough money to pay for two semesters—fall semester and spring semester. First semester was $33; I'll never forget that. At the time, it was a lot. My mom and dad lived there by the old high school in Tahlequah. I went through college living there. Then after I graduated, Bob and I were married, and we moved to Tulsa. I started teaching the second grade and stayed there for thirty years in two different schools.

Daddy had these old Indian ways, you know. And I don't know why he did it. You know, they believed in these spooks and conjuring and everything. Every so often, we'd have to get up before sun up—well, barely coming daylight—and go down to the spring and wash our faces. Daddy would throw that water

Continued on page270

Kathryn Kelley holding her miniature baskets, photo by Roger Cain

"Fancy Baskets" by Kathryn Kelley
Photo by Jeremy Charles

betty bean smith

March 26, 1931
Lost City, Oklahoma

I was born out in the country, in a home, a log cabin (in) Shady Grove Community, because Shady Grove School was just about two or three miles from there. My father was from that community. He was raised around there. And my mother was raised around this other side of the creek. James Bean, my dad, always told me to go for what I believed in. Don't let anybody run me down. And my mother was Cora Mae Bean. She was full-blood Cherokee. Dad was, too. She was a fluent speaker. He wasn't because he got punished (for speaking Cherokee) at school. He graduated at Chilloco Indian School. He was a basketball player and a baseball player.

I got Living Treasure for traditional cooking (of) foods. Well, see, Wilma Mankiller came to my house, and I cooked a traditional dinner for her. I invited her to my house and promised to cook a traditional Cherokee cooking. She brought Charlie and two little boys, and I cooked crawdads, catfish, I think it was wild onions and cornbread, beans. We cooked quite a bit. We had already eaten so we just sat in the living room while they ate so we wouldn't bother them. Charlie ate so much (that) he said, "I am just sick."

Wilma said, "It's been a long time since I ate a meal like that. And you can cook like that!"

I said, "Yeah, that's the way I've always cooked. Raised the kids like that."

She said, "It is delicious." She really enjoyed herself on that. We visited for a while and

Clockwise from top: Betty promoting the Tsa-la-gi Village Courtesy of the Cherokee Historical Society; Betty training for ancient village, courtesy of artist; Betty Jo Smith with son Rex Smith and granddaughter Feather Trevino at Cherokee Ancient Village, photo by Jeremy Charles

they left. That was a year or two before I got National Treasure. I was surprised whenever I got that award.

I started working in the Tsa-La-Gi Village in 1967. They started the village, I believe, in '66, and it was completed in '67 in June. Chief Bill Keeler was the director of it (the Cherokee Heritage Center) more or less. Bill Keeler had a lot to do with all of that. Well, he would go out to the community. When I was a child, Earl Boyd Pearce (and) Virgil Herrington—they came out to the community and had meetings with Cherokees out there. I bet not very many people know it. I remember that because I was a child, about 10 or 11 years old. And my father, oh, they came back there for the Keetoowah meeting. I don't know how much they talked about or anything, being a kid. My dad signed us up as Keetoowah members. But the building (that the documents) were in burned up and all the history is gone. And I always tell some of our kids, we really were Keetoowah members years back. But, there's no proof of it. It was kept in private homes. And Chief Bill Keeler used to go to the stomp dances and participate. See, he did things like that.

Back then, at the ancient village, we were on our training mission, getting acquainted with making pottery and anything that would be traditional to Cherokees. We even had training classes.

Continued on page 271

traditional foods

1991

"I got Living Treasure for traditional cooking—foods. Well, see, Wilma Mankiller came to my house and I cooked a traditional dinner for her. I invited her to my house and promised to cook a traditional Cherokee cooking. She brought Charlie and two little boys and I cooked crawdads, catfish, I think it was, wild onions and cornbread, beans. We cooked quite a bit. We had already eaten so we just sat in the living room while they ate so we wouldn't bother them.

Charlie ate so much (that) he said, "I am just sick."

Wilma said, "It's been a long time since I ate a meal like that. And you can cook like that!"

I said, "Yeah, that's the way I've always cooked. Raised the kids like that."

She said, "It is delicious." She really enjoyed herself on that. We visited for a while and they left. That was a year or two before I got National Treasure. I was surprised whenever I got that award."

—Betty Smith

"My daddy used to make a log, cut the log, cut a hole in it, and grind the hominy and ***kvnvchi****. That's what he used to do. He do it and pound it up and that was interesting like what they do now. Well, you get a rock and you pound on the hickory nuts first as much as you can. And you have a colander and you sift all the goodies out of there. We used to take all the goodies out of the hull; we put it in there. The kids done that. When we got through with that and then he pound it, there were little hulls in there yet. They just roll it up and make that* ***kvnvchi****. You put that* ***kvnvchi*** *in hot water and check on it and get all the hulls out of it and use that liquid and usually hominy grits; now they put it in rice. I like hominy grits better. They used to have a store in Tahlequah. They have hominy all the time. My daddy and her daddy. We didn't care much for rice. We used hominy."*

—Lizzie Whitekiller

Pictured left: Roger Cain This page, left to right: Edith Catcher Knight using her traditional Kanon to crush hickory nuts. Mocker Hickory and Shag Bark Hickory nuts are Edith's Choice for making the ancient traditional soup ***Kvnvchi****: Traditional foods Betty Jo Smith art; Crawdad in water*

vyrl keeter

October 28, 1931
Stilwell, Oklahoma

Photo by Linda Martin

Vyrl was born near Stilwell, Oklahoma, on October 28, 1931—in the Stoney Point community—to his parents, Tom and Margaret Keeter. There were eight children in the Keeter family, and Vryl's mentor was his oldest brother, Ray, who could both read and write Cherokee fluently. His brother, once retired, became a minister to Cherokee churches.

Vyrl first went to school at Mulberry Rural Elementary and later to Horn Elementary, but he graduated from Stilwell High School. "We grew up as a working family. Growing green beans and cattle ranching on the open range. A major goal for all was a formal education beyond high school," he said. "Six of us have college degrees and two have vocational degrees."

Vyrl currently lives in Muskogee (where he has lived) since returning from Europe while in the military, but he said he would always consider Stilwell his home. He stressed that he and his family were churchgoers and believed in a higher power. "Personally, I firmly believe in life after life with two forces—good versus evil in present life with good always prevailing through a supreme being," he said.

Vyrl shared stories about the property where he was raised, fondly pointing out that three creeks—Horn, Mulberry and Caney Creeks—all of which flowed into the Illinois River ran through it,. "Two mountains—the Tome White

From left: Vyrl Keeter Flintknapping, photo by Linda Martin; Vyrl Keeter touching up a knapped point, photo by Linda Martin; 2016 Cherokee National Treasure Vyrl Keeter, photo by Linda Martin

Mountain and Coon Mountain—also ran through our property,. I became interested in the many artifacts that I found in this area; (they) made me wonder how they were made and by whom."

Recently awarded what he considers his greatest honor, (that) of being named a Cherokee National Treasure in the ancient art of flint knapping, Vyrl said he's been perfecting his craft for near fifty years. "I have developed most of my skills by trial and error. Also learning from others at knapping and watching films along with my long-past grandfather, John Dale," he added.

After finishing his military career during the Korean War, Vyrl returned to Oklahoma and married his high school sweetheart. Bobbi Rae Garrett. He completed his bachelor's degree and later his master's degree at Northeastern State University. He also completed some post-graduate work at the University of Tulsa. "During this time I was employed by the Muskogee School district as a classroom teacher, then football coach, and later (as) a secondary principal," he said.

Vyrl retired as the director of athletics and continues today to practice his craft. All through the years, he said he continued to work at flint knapping. As the years went by, Vyrl became more serious, he said, in both the physical aspect and the history and culture of different tribes and how they exchanged materials, methods, and styles of knapping. "My primary goal is to continue the art of flint knapping as passed down through my ancestors, who used to make tools for their way of living," he said. He said that it's very memorable to watch the look and expression on children's faces while he demonstrates the art.

Continued on page 271

Maxine Stick weaving buckbrush in her weaving chair, photo courtesy of family

maxine stick

December 15, 1951
Kenwood, Oklahoma

My mom, Maxine Stick, was a second-generation buckbrush basket weaver. Her mom was also a weaver. I am a third-generation weaver. My mom always sat in the kitchen, in a certain spot and on a certain chair. To this day, we have that chair. It still sits in the kitchen. She even had to have a certain-size box for her material. I suppose that is where we, her children, get our meticulous way of doing things. For that, I am very thankful. She taught us that no matter what we were doing, we were to give it the best we had.

I am the youngest of seven. She had six girls and one boy. My sister and I are twelve years apart. So growing up, I had lots of time with my mom. I remember driving her to church. On Wednesdays, we would go to the church. She would cook for the women that were there sewing quilts. We would spend all day there. She was a woman of faith and had a deep love for God. And she loved to cook. I can still recall seeing her in the kitchen, steam on the windows from the heat of the stove. She cooked for every holiday. I suppose it was just a means to have some family time. I can still hear her singing in Cherokee as she cooked.

My mom was my greatest teacher. She could not go any place without sparking up a conversation with a total stranger. By the end of the conversation, she had a new friend. She was always welcoming anyone into her home. Like every

From top: Photo by Forrest Blackbear; Maxine Stick's buckbrush basketry at home, photo courtesy of family; Buckbrush weaving with natural dyes by Maxine Stick

other elder, she felt the need to feed everyone who came through. I could not tell you how many people have come and gone through her kitchen. She taught us that no matter how a person chose to live their life, they were still a person. Because of her generosity and love of family and friends, we have carried on that tradition.

I have had countless, from the heart, conversations with her in that kitchen. I sat at the table, eating whatever was on the table, while she sat on her chair weaving a basket. I remember she would tell me what kind of basket she was going to weave before she even started. If we weren't in the kitchen, we were outside. She taught me to weave in bits and pieces. Somewhere, in those moments, I picked up what she was teaching me. Now that I look back at those moments, they weren't just about learning to weave a basket. They were life lessons as well. These are lessons that I carry with me every day.

She always seemed to be doing something with buck brush.

My brother always gathered the buckbrush for her. She would clean the leaves and things off, and my brother would do the boiling process. Once all that was done and the buckbrush was ready to be stripped, it became a family affair. She, my brother, and my sisters would all sit outside and strip the material clean. I would sit outside with them but rarely helped. I just enjoyed the conversations and the laughs. A ll these conversations were in Cherokee. Things always seem funnier when they are in Cherokee. She and I had many dirt-road memories looking for plants to use as a dye.

Continued on page 272

wanna lou barton

April 22, 1932
Vian, Oklahoma

Wanna Lou Barton, of Catoosa, was born on April 24, 1932, in Vian, Oklahoma. Her parents were Eli Hendricks Sr. and Peachie Smith Hendricks. Barton's mother, Peachie, was who taught her how to make traditional Cherokee turtle shackles. Her mother taught her how to clean the turtle shells, fill the shells with river pebbles, and add the leather. Wanna began making shell shakers in 1986. Women wear turtle shell shackles/shakers during Cherokee stomp dances.

Barton married and had two daughters. One also continued in the tradition of making turtle shell shackles, and the other does beadwork. She retired from the Indian Health Service in 1994 to take care of her mother in Claremore until her mother's passing.

"I first met Wanna Lou a few years before her passing. When she walked into the room, it just lit up! We were working with a nonprofit organization that worked with Cherokee National Treasures, especially Elders. Wanna Lou joined this organization and began actively participating in projects related to plants that Cherokees were known to have used, plants she had grown up using for medicinal and food purposes. I remember the first plant she taught us was the Maypop. I had always heard this plant called Passion Flower but had no idea it was an indigenous plant to the Americas. Wanna Lou taught us about this plant and others by telling stories. She told us that to say the name of the fruit some call Maypop in English, we should say *Uwaga*

or *Uwaka* in Cherokee. Her stories would intertwine her life experiences with how the plant was used and the Cherokee ways to say them. She talked about busting open the Maypops or fruit of this vine plant to "suck on the seeds" as she put it. My husband now grows Passion Flowers in our yard, and I always think of Wanna Lou! I can just see her mouth pucker up talking about how the seeds were sweet but sour and made a nice treat at the end of summer and early spring.

"I remember walking to school, and we would stop to pick those wild apricots or Maypops. They were a real treat!" Wanna Lou would explain that many of the plants around us are not only to eat but can also be used for medicinal purposes. She talked about the roots of the Passion Flower being a good medicine.

While Wanna Lou was distinguished as a Cherokee National Treasure for her skill in making turtle-shell shakers for ceremonial Stomp Grounds, she was also a very talented artist in beadwork. I remember she was working at the Hard Rock Casino when I met her, and she was showing and entering beautiful beadwork pieces into the Cherokee Art Market competitions. She just had an eye for nature! That is what I enjoyed most about her—the way she always seemed to incorporate nature into all of her art work. I will always regret that I did not get to meet Wanna Lou earlier in my lifetime. She was a teacher by heart and had a lot of Cherokee knowledge that she was always happy to share."

—By Jami Murphy
Interview with Shawna Morton Cain

Clockwise from top left: Wanna Lou Barton's beaded bracelet, "Butterfly on Moss"; turtle-shell shackles made by Wanna Lou Burton; Wanna Lou Barton, Cherokee Heritage Center Homecoming Show 2002

Photo by Jeremy Charles

lorene drywater

June, 19, 1932
Steely Hollow, Oklahoma

You learn a lot more when you get out in the woods. In the classroom, all you hear is the words. When I was a little bitty thing—I guess I must have been around three, four—that's where Mama started teaching me.'Cause I was the only one always crying for a doll, and, I kept saying, "Mom, I want a doll. Can you buy me a doll?"

"Oh, we don't have money to buy a doll," she said. When Mama made it for me—she helped me make one for my playhouse—she'd hand it to me, and she said, "Now go find me another grass."

I work wherever the grass catches me.

As she handed me the doll, I thought, "Oh, my, that is the most beautiful doll I have ever earned." I mean, oh, my, it was like every time we'd go off somewhere to visit, to Grandma up on the mountain, we enjoyed it so much. And the reason I like this here is because that's how I climbed the mountain to see my grandmother. On the foot trail through there, there'd be a lot of this grass. I'd ask, "Mama, next time, can we bring a hoe?"

"O.K., we'll bring hoe."

Next time we walk up that way, no hoe. That grass made my feet itch!

My grandmother used to say, "We landed in a place they called Red Land." I was a baby when I got old enough to know what that was. That's where we were, this place. Red Land is between Sallisaw and Muldrow, Oklahoma, south off 64 Highway. That's where she was taught to make her Buffalo Grass Dolls. Grandmother grew up and raised her own family—three girls, three boys. She taught the girls to make Buffalo Grass dolls and weave baskets of canes and young tender hickory tree skins. Boys were taught other things. As they all grew older, they were taught to farm, mend fences, and build log houses.

One of the three girls is my mother. When my grandmother passed away, some friends wondered how old she was. Mama didn't know. Only thing Grandma knew was she was told her birthday was the week before Christmas. These friends went to the county court house and welfare department and they came up with it. Grandma was 108 or 112 years old when she went to rest.

My mother grew up, married my dad, and they raised seven of us—five girls and two boys. We would have been 12 of us if not for three miscarriages. One was two years old. Another lived a day-and-a-half after birth; I remember her crying from the moment she was born. She never stopped crying till she went to sleep. Next day, they took her away in a horse-pulled wagon. If I remember right, there were three wagons with people in them.

Continued on page 272

Lorene Drywater, photo by Linda Martin

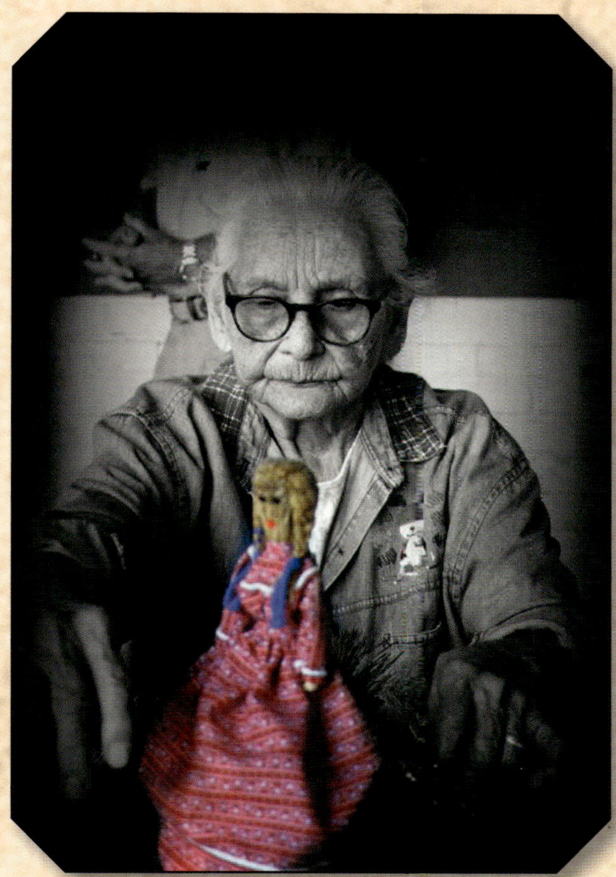

Buffalo Grass Dolls on the hill, photo by Jeremy Charles

Lorene Drywater's mother

turtle shell shakers

1991

"It might take all day to clean them if we have thirty or forty. We clean them all. We drill holes in them. We have all of the rocks ready, and the wiring to keep them tight so they won't open up when they dry. If the weather is hot, they dry really fast, and that way, you can put them together really fast."

—Nancy Smith

"Eva Mae learned to make shackles from her mother, Easter, who learned how to make them from her parents. Eva Mae made shackles for so many people, it would be hard to count how many she made in her lifetime but likely hundreds. She made shells for all of her daughters and most of her granddaughters and taught her six daughters and several granddaughters how to shake shackles. - *Daughters Sadie Ringgold and Ellen Murdoch on Eva Mae Smith*

"As far as I can say, they are called "shackles". You can call them ***Daksi.*** *I started making them because my aunt wouldn't make them for me anymore. She told me, 'OK, just sit. You're on your own.' I'd say I was about seventeen. That's when she quit making them; it was up to me to make my own. "*

—Vivian Leaf Bush

""Women do not sing. Only the men sing. The Cherokee stomp dance is not a powwow."

"It is distinct, the way of the Cherokees. It is a way that was almost lost. Men, women, and children dance around the ceremonial fire. A man leads a group as the shakers—only women—set the rhythm to his step and song."

—Tammy Wildcat speaking of her father, Tom Webber Wildcat

"Wanna Lou Barton's mother, Peachie, taught her who how to make traditional Cherokee turtle shackles. Her mother taught her how to clean the turtle shells, fill the shells with river pebbles, and add the leather. She began making shell shakers in 1986. "

—Shawna Morton Cain on Wanna Lou Barton

"Lisa Smith attaches the shells to the boot tops, which allows women to fold the leather around their shins and tie the shells to their legs. She said it is getting tougher to find used boots made of real leather and not manmade or synthetic leather. She also searches for leather for leather strips that she uses to tie the shells together and wire (that) she uses to fasten the shells to the boot tops. During stomp dances, women and girls wear her shackles under traditional Cherokee skirts."

- Lisa Smith

Pictured left: Shackles made by Eva Pigeon Smith; This page, left to right: Small shackles made for a child; Turtle shell shackles; Jimi Dawn Hornbuckle wearing shackles made for her by her Grandmother Eva Mae, photo provided by daughters Sadie Ringgold and Ellen Murdoch

Photo by David Fitzgerald

marie proctor

October 21, 1932
Taggs Flat, Delaware County, Oklahoma

Four miles east of Kenwood, nestled away from the road, is a small house with an eighty-four-year-old lady who holds onto a hospital bracelet with her birthdate. She says this is for those who question her age. Her name is Marie Proctor—a full-blood Cherokee whose English is minimal (and) a lady who knows no strangers and welcomes anyone into her home. Her home is like any other elder Native American home. Inviting. Comfortable. Very calming, and the only thing you hear is the faint sound of a radio. Her Cherokee hymn book and Bible lie on a table next to a recliner. Although this is not her childhood home, she has been a part of the Kenwood community all her life. Marie Proctor was born to Thomas and Katie Proctor in Delaware County, the youngest of ten children. The family lived at Taggs Flat near Bull Hollow. Her older sister is a basket weaver and a Cherokee National Treasure. Of the ten children, only Rosie, Jennie, and Marie made baskets.

Marie attended school in the building that is now Steely Baptist Church. Her mother, Katie made baskets in the double-wall Cherokee style. It is likely that the girls learned some basket-making skills from Katie.

Marie spent countless Sundays walking to church. She would spend Wednesdays with the elder ladies of the church sewing quilts. She also sewed quilts at home. She has a picture on her wall that shows her presenting former Chief Chad Smith with a quilt that she had sewn. She talked of the many people who had bought her quilts.

Marie was a recipient of the Cherokee National Living Treasure award in 2000 for her art of Buck Brush Basket Weaving. She weaved with buck brush, honeysuckle, and commercial reed. She passed the trade on to her daughter, Rosie Chewie. Rosie and her husband did most of the gathering of material and preparation. Marie has also taught the art of basket weaving to others; using nature's materials, she adds color to her baskets with dyes made from wild berries, walnuts, and blood root that she has gathered along with buck brush, which grows abundantly around her home.

Aside from weaving her beautiful baskets, she also does quilting. Marie's daughter, Rosie, who is deceased, was a recipient of the 2003 Cherokee National Living Treasure award for her basketry weaving in buck brush and honeysuckle. Marie is the

Continued on page 273

Photos: from top: Marie holds a basket weaving that uses naturel dyes.. Photo by Stephanie Stick. Middle and lower: Marie with her sewing machine. Photos by David Fitzgerald.

eva mae pigeon smith

March 19, 1933
Pinhook Corner, Oklahoma

Photo courtesy of family

Eva Mae Pigeon was born March 19, 1933, near Marble City, Oklahoma, to Sam and Easter Bush Pigeon. Sam and Easter had seven children—Watie, Sie, Eva Mae, Dewey, Autry "Jay", Willie, and Robert. Eva Mae was the only daughter among six sons. Her family later settled near Bunch, Oklahoma, where she grew up. She was only able to attend school through the sixth grade because she was needed at home to work and help the family.

Eva Mae married William Lee Smith on September 9, 1949. William and Eva made their home near Pinhook Corner, near Vian, Oklahoma. They attended Stokes Smith Stomp Grounds where William served as Chief of the *Kee-too-wah Society*, the old Cherokee religion. Though they had seven children, the same number as Eva's parents, William and Eva Mae had six daughters—Doris, Lila, Dorothiea, Geneva, Sadie,and Ellen and one son—William David.

Eva Mae worked hard all of her life, first at her parents' home, keeping up with six brothers, working in the fields, cooking and cleaning, and later, keeping up with her own children and household. Eva took care of the family's cattle, horses, dogs, and sometimes kittens. Family gatherings were common at the Smith home. There was always way too much food and lots of laughter. She would say it was a sin to let people go hungry. No one went hungry around her house.

Eva Mae was recognized with the title of Cherokee National Treasure, or master artist, for her skill in making turtle-shell shackles. Shackles are worn on

the legs of the women at traditional stomp dances, and the making of them is special. Eva grew up shaking turtle-shell shackles in ceremonial dances and became a skilled turtle-shell shackle maker. Eva was particular about how she made her shackles and who she made shackles for. She wanted them used for ceremonial purposes only and not for resale.

In Eva's words "Shackles are made out of turtles. You get a turtle, and you kill it, and clean it. Then you drill holes in it after you get through cleaning it real good. You find a certain kind of rocks, and you put maybe a handful in each shell. Then you tie a string around them and hang them up in a dry place and wait for them to get real dry. Then you take thirteen shells for one shackle. It takes twenty-six to make a whole pair. You get an old boot top or some kind of leather, and you put your turtle shells on there. You run a wire through there to hold them on there. Then after you get thirteen on there, you put strips of leather on them so that they don't rattle all the time."

Eva Mae learned to make shackles from her mother, Easter, who learned how to make them from her parents, "a long time ago". Eva Mae made shackles for so many people, it would be hard to count how many she made in her lifetime, but (it was) likely hundreds. She made shells for all her daughters and most of her granddaughters and taught her six daughters and several granddaughters how to shake shackles.

Continued on page 273

Photo from top: Eva Mae and five of her brothers (front - Waite, Sie, Willie; back - Robert, Eva Mae, Jay); Eva and her sister-in-law, Nancy Smith; William Smith with Eva Mae and William's brother, Junior Smith with his wife Nancy; Eva Mae and William Lee Smith; One of Eva Mae's special turtle shells, photo by Sadie Ringgold; Turtle Shell Shackles made by Eva Smith

lena blackbird

August 24, 1933
Rocky Ford, Oklahoma

Lena Blackbird: I grew up around here at Rocky Ford and went to school here in Rocky Ford.

Lisa Forrest, Lena's daughter: She went to Sequoyah Vocational Training School for two weeks! My grandpa, her dad, and his friend, Bob Belt, they went through all the paperwork to get her in there. And what did they say? "We dropped her off there, and she got back before we did." They took Lena and got everything ready and took her to Sequoyah School and we drove back and Lena was already home before they got back. (She laughed.)

Lena: Yeah, I didn't stay very long.

Lisa: My grandpa, her dad, they went through all the paperwork to get you in Sequoyah, and they dropped you off and you made it home before they did. (She laughed.)

Lena: After I learned how to make baskets, I just loved doing it. Some of them would just work with them and just finished them real fast so they could have a lot of baskets so they could make the money. I didn't think that way. I just loved doing it, took my time and everything. My favorite is honeysuckle. I like that honeysuckle, but it's getting scarce. You can hardly get any anymore. That's what I like to use to make my baskets. I've made a lot of commercial reed baskets. The first basket I entered was made with honeysuckle. Somebody told me to enter it at Muskogee, and I took it up there and that was my first basket to enter in that show.

Photo by Jeremy Charles

Clockwise from left; Lena Blackbird in Tsa-ia-gi Ancient Villiage, Tahlequah, Ok, photo courtesy of Cherokee National Historical Society; Honeysuckle Vase basket by Lena Blackbird, photo by Jeremy Charles; 2003 Cherokee Heritage Center Trail of Tears Art Show, large double-wall, lidded honeysuckle basket.

And I won Best of Show on it.

Lisa: I remember you telling me about that. They called all the names—first, second, whatever they had in there. Everybody was saying, "They didn't call Lena's name!" You know everybody wanted her to win. Finally when they said "Best of Show," they called her name for that.

Lena: No, I had no idea. I thought the first place was the last one that they was gonna call.

Lisa: Yeah we have entered shows together. The first year I entered anything, you entered. That was your last time. It was the basket with the corn cascading off.

Lena: I remember. That was where I had the corn from big to little and had them tied onto the knob on the lid.

Lisa: She's taught me everything I do and know. She still critiques me. I say, "Mom what's this look like?" And she'll tell me. I remember when we first started, she was grading me A, B, or C. (She laughed.)

Lena: She's been weaving for about six years, and she's already won awards.

Lisa: I quit work in 2008 but it was like 2007 when she taught me. I thought, "Well, I'm sitting here, She could teach me how to weave." It was a lot of fun! I don't think I can shape as well as she did. She's just a natural at learning. She's a natural at getting those nice shapes.

Lena: Making baskets is shaping them even and just right. Just like for me, it was hard for me at first.

Lisa: She's taught three generations now.

Lena: They know how. Just like Lisa, she's the one that has really turned on to it.

Lena: I used to work at the village. I haven't been to the

Continued on page 273

Photo by David Fitzgerald

eunice o'field

December 11, 1934
Kenwood, Oklahoma

Eunice Raper O'Field was born in the family home at Kenwood—during the cold month of December—to George and Jennie Wickliffe Raper. She had a brother, John, and three sisters—Marie, Ruth, and Flossie.

Eunice was a lifetime resident of Kenwood, Salina, and Mayes County. As a young girl, she attended school in Kenwood and then attended Jay High School. At an early age, she became a Christian and was baptized in the Euwasha Baptist Church. Eunice taught Sunday school classes and was a Girl's Auxiliary leader in her church for several years. She enjoyed reading her Bible, gospel music, raising indoor and outdoor flowers, and sewing.

For her skill in weaving and quilting, Eunice O'Field was designated as a master craftsman during the 1991 Cherokee National Holiday by then Chief Wilma Mankiller. Eunice was widely known as a skilled basket maker using natural materials such as buck brush and honeysuckle and was also very talented in beadwork. Eunice was an award-winning quilter and was honored in 2000 for her Lone Star Quilt at the Heritage Homecoming Show. At the time of her death, her photograph, in poster size, and a list of her accomplishments were on display at the Smithsonian Museum in Washington, D.C. Her works in weaving, Native bead work, and basket weaving were in high demand by collectors.

Clockwise from top left: Eunice O'Field with her baskets; Eunice O'Field weaving on loom, photo provided by family; Basket by Eunice O'Field

Eunice married Edward O'Field on July 2, 1954, in Stilwell, Oklahoma. Family was important to Eunice. When her children were young, the family enjoyed cookouts, swimming, and camping on Saline Creek.

Eunice O'Field passed away on January 19, 2002, in Pryor, Oklahoma. She was survived by her children—Rosetta, Loretta, Debbie, Jeff, Phillip, and Mary. She had eighteen grandchildren and eight great-grandchildren.

—Mary Bendabout, daughter

Interviewed by Pamela Jumper Thurman

flint knapping

1991

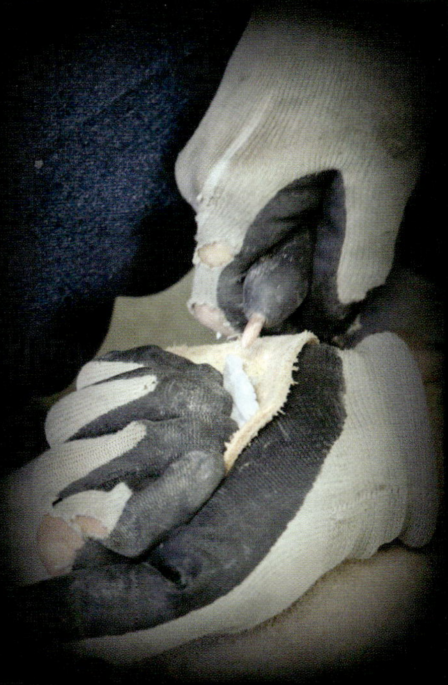  

About Scott Rackliffe as a traditional artist and flint knapper: McCarter said many of the people who work in the village pick up skills like bow-and-arrow making, flint knapping, blowgun making, making stickball sticks, and other traditional skills, but he also said Rackliff must have grown up learning all of the skills he brought to the village. "I think his family was just that way. They probably used their blowguns. They probably used their bows at that time," he said.

—Danny McCarter

"Actually, just playing with this stuff as a child just never quit. Before I started public schools—and I can tell you almost the exact spot; I can get you in the general area—where I started flint knapping. Out past the lake, Highway 100. You know the Juicy Pig Store? You used to be able to drive down to the lakes down there. But, they've blocked it off and you can't do that now anywhere. But, we drove down there and we were fishing. And my mom and dad, you know, maybe no fish were biting or something. I was just small. But, my dad picked up an arrowhead and he said, "We used to hunt with these." And you know if you go down there, you find arrowheads. I don't know about nowadays. But we used to. He said, "We used to hunt with these."

And being a kid I asked, "How did they make them?" Just question after question.

He looked around, took a couple of rocks, and just started hitting it. You know, looking at it and knocking flakes off it. He made a big bi-face or hatchet head—whatever you call it. And he just said, "Like that."

I sat there and watched him do it. And I can do the same thing now. Just takes minutes to actually rough them out.

He said, "Like that." Then he just threw it down. Put it back down and we kept going. But, I went home and tried it.

—Noel Grayson

"When I pop a large stone and it splits open showing the beautiful color...and make a nice arrow point it causes the youngsters to want to know more and study the Indian culture and history," Vryl said. "I suppose I shall never stop teaching the art of knapping."

—Vyrl Keeter

Pictured left: Flintknapped points by Noel Grayson, photo by Roger Cain; This page, left to right: Vyrl Keeter Flintknapping, photo by Linda Martin; Noel Grayson flintknapping by Lake Tenkiller, photo by Jeremy Charles; Scott Rackliff at the Tsa La Gi Ancient Village

clarence downing

May 31, 1935
Oaks, Oklahoma

Clarence Lee "Jim" Downing, a full-blood Cherokee, was born at Snake Creek in Mayes County. His parents were Joseph Downing and Hattie Leach. He married Annas L. Cummings in September 1976, and they lived in the Oaks area all their lives. The two had four children — Jimmie, Timmie, Vickie Christie, and Janelle Settlemyre. Clarence worked in construction before becoming a Cherokee Nation master craftsman. He was known widely for his carvings of sandstone and wood. He was featured in an article by Jim Etter with *The Oklahoman* in 1990. The article featuring Clarence talked about his sculptures and where he gets his ideas. Below is a portion of that article.

Carved Images Keep Indian Artist Company

by Jim Etter

Downing, a full-blood Cherokee Indian sculptor, produces images of other people, most of them members of his tribe. Some, like Sequoyah, are famous. Others resemble persons, living or dead, (that) he's known throughout his native eastern Oklahoma.

"This one here, that's the 'Trail of Tears,'" said Downing, sitting at a mound of wood shavings behind his home in this small Delaware County community and pointing his chisel toward a large bust of an aging man with sad eyes and drops of moisture streaking his dark face. Nearby was the bust of the famed creator of the Cherokee alphabet, complete with turban and

Clockwise from top: Clarence Downing Sandstone Turtle Sculpture photo by D. Fitzgerald; Sequoyah carved wooden bust by Clarence Downing, photo by D. Fitzgerald; Clarence Downing mask, photo by Jeremy Charles

pipe, and other pieces, some with leather headbands and with turquoise stones for eyes. "And that one, that's a Cherokee medicine man," he said, indicating the representation of a contemporary man with a large, flat-brimmed hat and with the look of an Indian healer. Downing, 55, said he began making people from wood about 20 years ago. A disabling accident he had at a Tulsa metal plant provided him with the time to practice, he said.

Since then, he estimates he's made hundreds of pieces, mostly busts and some life-size figures, by sawing, sanding, chiseling and carving from walnut and catalpa woods.

He sells most of them, usually through gift shops at places such as nearby Miami, Oklahoma, Locust Grove, Tahlequah, Jay, Henryetta and Siloam Springs, Arkansas. He said one of his sculptures has been purchased by Oklahoma Governor Henry Bellmon and another by a Catholic nun who said she was taking it to Rome. One of his few artworks not of a Cherokee subject is a Kawliga-type cigar store

Continued on page 274

Photo by Roger Cain

dorothy dreadfulwater ice

December 26, 1935
Briggs, Oklahoma

We'll start out with Dorothy Dreadfulwater and when we go into '57, the year I married, then we'll go into "Ice." I was born December 26, 1935. My father was Mike Dreadfulwater. My mother was Emma Bark, from around Vian, Marble City, just all around. Dreadfulwaters were from around Chewey and Briggs. I was born in Cherokee County, out in the country, at home.

What do you call those women? Midwives! I wish I knew her English name. I remember hers was just Old Lady Grasshopper. That's all I remember. I have seen her after I grew up a little bit. I don't know where she came from. They had to cross a river to get her. So, I don't know where she lived. Wish I knew.

I have one sister and three brothers. The boys were born at Hastings. My sister was born in Adair County. I was raised in Briggs community. I still live there. I'm a fluent speaker! And I teach the language. And, I love it! Yes, I am (certified) through both Nations. That was the only language that was spoken around home—Cherokee. I like to teach. That's why I do it, 'cause I want to, and I want to share it. If I didn't, I wouldn't even try to teach it. I'm pushing it, too!

My favorite is just loom weaving, and that's all I do. I don't do baskets anymore. I don't do beadwork anymore. In 1951, I had my sixteenth birthday down at Sequoyah Weavers. At the beginning, I just went over to see what was going on at the weaving shop. There were a lot of women there; I really didn't pay attention to who was doing what. They asked me if I wanted to learn. They didn't say weaving or what. They said, "Would you like to learn?"

And I said, "Yeah."

And then Bill Ames gave me two boxes of yarn—red and black. They told me, "Go string it."

So, I made the warp and then, when I rolled the warp and brought it in the weaving shop, I had help threading it. It took a whole day. The next day I would weave, and it took a whole day weaving. I was pretty young. I was the youngest student there. I can't remember how many people were there. They were doing just different things—learning different things. They taught baskets. They taught beadwork. They taught tailoring clothes.

See that's why I was really pushing loom weaving! I wanted someone to learn and then turn around and teach somebody. And I want to hear them say, "I taught so 'n' so," while I'm still living! I want to see it while I am still able to move. Yeah, that's what I wanted to do. That's what I asked for, anyway. John Ketcher and I talked about that between us.

I drove a bus for 25 years, and I worked in the school system for 27 years at Briggs School. I always wanted to learn to drive when I was real young. When we went to Grandma's house around Jay, we would go up No. 10 highway, and it was all dirt road. When the wheels got dry, they would rattle. Dad would pull on the side of the road there or in the road. Mom had a coffee can in the car, and then I'd get out and pour water on the spokes until they got tight, and we'd leave again. And when they started rattling again, we'd stop somewhere.

Continued on page 274

From top: Dorothy Dreadfulwater Ice dancing; Dorothy in white buckskin dress she made at the Briggs Weaving Center, "I had that buckskin dress hanging on the ceiling. I'm holding that doll 'cause Bill Ames said it looked like me."; Dorothy at 16 years of age at loom in Sequoyah Weavers Building, Briggs, Oklahoma.

al herrin

March 13, 1936
Tahlequah, Oklahoma

Photo by Jeremy Charles

I was born March 13, 1936, in the hospital in Muskogee. We lived in Okay at the time. My parents had a farm there. I guess I lived there for the first five years of my life, and I don't remember much about it. Then we started moving around. It was my dad was trying to get work in different places. About the middle of third grade, that's when we moved here, to Tahlequah. I had gone to eight different schools in that length of time.

Anyway, we moved back to Muskogee, in the Cherokee Nation around Tahlequah, and I was fascinated by the bows and arrows I'd see being used mainly at cornstalk shoots that we have around this country. I just became fascinated with them.

A Cherokee full blood by the name of Richard McLemore made a little bow. It was about 3 feet long and had a string on it made of squirrel hide. The arrows were made of dogwood, and the feathers were hawk feathers or duck feathers—whatever he could find. They were tied onto the arrows with sinew. Richard had a forge out behind his house where he lived; he would make cornstalk spikes or gigs, all different kinds of things out of metal. He made these points for his arrows; he called them barrel hoop points. I guess in the old days, they made them out of barrel hoops.

I shot it for a little while, and a kid strung it backwards and broke it. So when I was eight years old, I decided I'd make myself one. It's made out of Bois d' arc wood, and I made the string out of fox-squirrel hide. I shot for several years with that. When the compound bow came out, why, I just had the feeling that it was getting too away from where archery should be, and so I went back to making these old bows. I've been making them since about the 1980s.

I started by going out, gathering wood and really getting serious about making them. These are the only ones I shoot—not these all-wood bows. This is what I hunt with and everything.

To even go out into the woods with equipment that you've made yourself—the bow and the arrows, literally everything you've made yourself—is a great feeling. To go out and harvest a deer or something with a bow like this is really a great, great feeling. I hunted a lot, which put food on our table. We ate deer meat a lot.

From top: Al Herrin teaching bowry at Cherokee Heritage Center; Al Herrin, photo by Jami Murphy; Tools for bow and arrow making, photo by Jeremy Charles

The Cornstalk Shoot is old; it had been going on a long, long time—centuries, probably. I've seen conflicting stories about the beginning of Cornstalk shooting. One is that it was a children's game with bows and arrows. But I believe that it goes back to the ancient Cherokees and it was practiced for warfare. Cherokee towns were built with a wall around them. They cleared the area around the wall on the outside, just like the English (did) castles, and the archers would stand upon the walls on the walkways to shoot these guys coming across the open area. English archers practiced shooting at long distances; they shot very heavy bows and the bows actually were very similar to Cherokee bows. There was one time, especially, in the 1500s, when English archers were the terrors of the world. They wiped out French armies. They would shoot these huge volleys of arrows in there and just kill those guys like mice. Well, I believe that the Cherokees did basically the same thing. The cornstalk shooting was, say you shoot cornstalks at 100 yards. So it was a method of shooting and practicing in long distance, and it was a defensive mechanism. I think that's the beginnings of Cornstalk Shooting. And it comes down today. It is competitive.

The Cherokees were one of the tribes that maintained the making of bows and arrows. In a lot of the tribes, it became completely lost, but the Cherokees continued to make them and this is the design that's basically been handed down. I think, personally, it's very similar to what the Cherokees were making before the time of Columbus.

Colonel Martin Hagerstrand, at the Cherokee Heritage Center, started this project—"The Lost Arts Project"—to try to rescue some traditional Cherokee things that were about to be lost." It was bows and arrows, blowguns, marbles, gigs and maybe one other. These

Continued on page 235

nadine wilbourn

April 24, 1936
Rocky Ford and Locust Grove, Oklahoma

Photo courtesy of Cherokee National Historical Society

Nadine Mankiller was born in Cherokee County to Charlie Mankiller and Fannie Nofire on April 20, 1936. She grew up in the Rocky Mountain/Barber area, though she moved to Locust Grove in her later years. Nadine was a Cherokee speaker who attended elementary school at Indian Day School in Barber community.

Her son, Darrell Chuculate recalled that she once talked about walking a lot—walking to school, to church, and to community events. She met Mose Chuculate in Barber, and they married in 1954 when Nadine was eighteen years old. They had five boys and one girl: John, now deceased, Darrell, William, Felix, Clifford, and Lorene. Darrell recalled, "When we were younger, my dad and his brothers used to be in a little band, a kind of Saturday night band, and she loved music. She especially loved gospel music."

Both Lorene Chuculate and Darrell Chuculate agreed that their mother liked to be outdoors; she liked gardening and enjoyed playing sports. Lorene said one of her favorite memories of her mother was that, "She used to play sports with us, even at an older age; she played softball and badminton, and I used to laugh at her because when she would score a point or catch a ball, she would just scream."

Clockwise from top: Nadie Wilbourn baskets, photo by David Fitzgerald; Nadine Wilbourn The Daily Times, April 14; Nadine Wilbourn with grandchild Patricia Thomas, who carries on her grandmother's basket-making art.

Family outings often included camping trips, fishing, and catching crawdads. Darrell said that his mother could make frybread and beans taste so good and that she was a great cook—"one of the best."

Nadine once worked at a tree nursery, proving again that she enjoyed being outside and even working at jobs that allowed her to be in the outside environment that she loved so much.

Lorene said that Nadine really liked to travel. "We'd go to Arkansas almost every Sunday just to drive. She went to Cherokee, North Carolina, Niagara Falls, Florida, and Wisconsin."

Both her children said that Nadine was very craftsy. "She did a lot of crocheting; she could do beadwork. When her eyesight started to fail, she just used bigger beads. She made those plastic craft holders for Kleenex boxes, and she crocheted a lot. She crocheted a lot of blankets," said Lorene.

Nadine retired from Oklahoma Children's Center in 1984 and began working in the historical village at the Cherokee Heritage Center, demonstrating the art of basket weaving. At that time, she

Continued on page 275

doll making

1992

Photo by Jeremy Charles

bessie russell

June 22, 1938
Rocky Ford, Oklahoma

I was born in the Rocky Ford community in a little old cabin house where I had seven siblings. That's how many was in that little log house. I was born in June in the hottest time of the year, you might say. My mama—Nancy Tail was her maiden name—always told me that she had gone up to the fields to pick blackberries around that time. She said that she went up to where a big bunch of neighbors or people would go up on the hill and pick for half a day or until they got what they wanted. She said that's what she did on that morning. That evening or that night was when I was born. It's a wonder I wasn't born out there in the blackberry patch.

I was probably about three or four when we moved up there on the other side of Rocky Ford in a small wood house that was a government home. I had four brothers and three sisters, and we all lived in that, except my oldest brother who went to the Army. We never thought nothing about it, because it's what we were used to. So, my dad, John Rackleff, and my brother would plant corn and beans and make a garden in the springtime. For winter, they sold the corn to pay the bills. But for winter, I don't really remember what they did to survive on—to make money to buy the things we needed. Mom canned, they jellied, and stuff like that. We knew every kind of berry or anything that was edible. Sometimes we wonder why we didn't get poisoned, because we ate everything.

When I got older, I was a tomboy, I guess you would say. I was the only girl on the softball team, the school team. I got to play with the boys. I was good! I don't even know what position I played. I just played everywhere.

If you really want to jump ahead, when we lived in Hennessey, I played ball out there, and we spent half of the summer, or most of the summer, at the ball fields. We'd either be practicing or we would have a game. My kids kind of grew up on the ball field. The team that I joined was the worst team out there. I tell you we would have games, and we'd get beat like crazy. Our main problem was nobody knew how to pitch. If you don't have a pitcher, you're going to get slaughtered.

It was the early '60s when the oil boom came in, and that's when Chief's old boss called us back to Hennessey because they were having so much work. That's who we became friends with was the oil people; oil field trash is what they were called. We just fit right in. But I stayed with the same team, only we just got a coach this time. That's when Chief and my nephew started coaching us. And, that's when we started getting better. The first year they coached us, we came in fourth place. The second year, we came in third place. Third, second, and then we were Number One! We still couldn't find a good pitcher.

So, I started practicing. We had a concrete garage, and I'd pick out one concrete block, like a target. I practiced and I practiced. I started getting better and better. So, I think it was two years, maybe three, I was the pitcher. But what stands out for me during that time was the high school girls. They

Continued on page 276

From top: Bessie Russell as a youngster; Bessie and Chief, ball team; "Turtle Pond and Lilypads" honeysuckle basketry, from the collection of Jim Cosby. Photo by Jami Murphy

richard rowe

March 28, 1939
Moodys, Oklahoma

Photo courtesy of family

Richard Rowe was born at home near Moodys, Oklahoma, to Dick Rowe and Maggie Raper. His grandparents were Jack and Jennie Jumper Rowe, on his father's side, and George Raper and Lydia Buck on his mother's side. Family recalled that he spent a great deal of his time with his paternal grandparents. He spent his younger life in Moodys, and he loved to run to school each day. He attended Ballou School for his elementary years and, later, paid his own way through college to obtain a degree—likely in criminal justice—from Northeastern State University in Tahlequah, Oklahoma.

In his younger years, he was an athletic person; he enjoyed running and won medals for that skill. He was also an adventurer. His nephew, Thurman Ritchie, said, "He would gas up the truck and come and get me, and we would just go on the spur of the moment. We would just take off. He was something else, Richard was."

Thurman also laughed at the memory of Richard's riding his roller suitcase down the hill. The family spoke of an Olympic medal—one that he kept with him throughout his adult life—that meant a lot to Richard. They also recalled that he always wore necklaces with eagle claws.

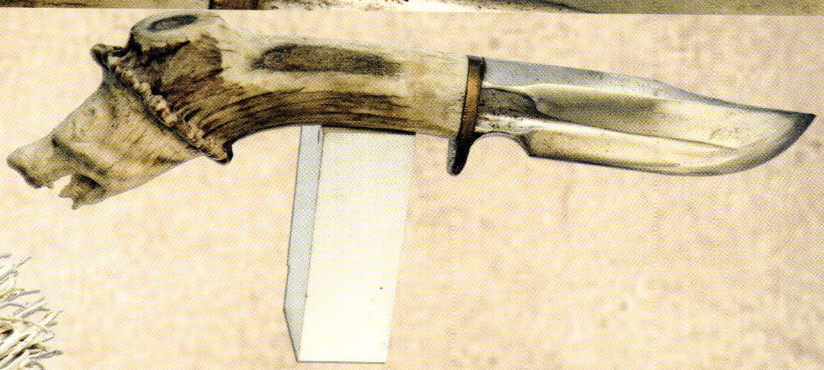

Clockwise from left: Eagle-carved-handled knife with sheath, bear-claw necklace by Richard Rowe, photo by David Fitzgerald; Knife with carved handle by Richard Rowe, photo by David Fitzgerald; Unfinished White Buffalo, Richard's last project, photo by Pamela Jumper Thurman

Grandniece Jamie Ritchie said that Richard loved cornbread and that he would trade her items for her cornbread or call her and pay her two dollars to make him a pan of cornbread. He would instruct her on just how he liked it. In fact, the family said that even when it came to his art, he loved trading and would often trade his carvings and handmade knives for other things. Jamie also shared a memory of his generosity: "He always remembered us and brought us stuff when he traveled." He would return to Moodys and stay with the Ritchie family at times, then take off on another adventure.

He traveled to Alaska, Oregon, and Canada, and while in Canada, worked for a mining company where he refined and mixed gold. He knew exactly how much copper and other ingredients were needed to refine the gold. For years after he left, the company that employed him continued to send him gold for his retirement pay.

Niece Madonna Rowe Ritchie said, "He was generous in teaching others how to carve. Some of the carvers that he instructed or helped were Perry Vanbuskirk, Hastings Shade, and Thomas Muskrat." She said there were many others as

Continued on page 276

Photo by Jeremy Charles

ruth england

April 23, 1939
Tyler Springs, Oklahoma

Brendalee Lassiter, Ruth's granddaughter: When were you born? Where did you all live?

Ruth England: I remember we were living in Lyon's Switch when I was born over here in Tyler Springs on top of the hill. Up the hill, where the old house used to be? That's why we moved. But I don't remember when we moved down there. I was about five or six (when) we moved to Lyon's Switch. As far as I know, then we moved back. I think I was about nine when I started school. It was at Peavine. England Hollow land was my Grandpa Soap. I don't know why they call it England, because we lived there I guess.

Brendalee: And you were just raised up with everybody talking Cherokee?

Ruth: Uh, huh. Most of them. I was raised by my grandma. I was born around here in Adair County. I was born at home. My mother's name was Eliza, and my dad was John. Eliza Wall was my mom. They were both from around here—Stilwell. I used to live in England Hollow; some people call it Peavine. My grandma was Nanny Scraper. My grandpa was Mose Soap. That was on my mom's side. I don't know too much on my dad's side. Well, my dad, his name was Soap. Satuski Soap. I don't even know if that is a Cherokee name or not.

Ruth: When I was almost eighteen, I had my first child. I have six kids—five girls and a boy. Johnny's the oldest. I think I got nineteen grandkids, and I don't know how many great-grandkids.

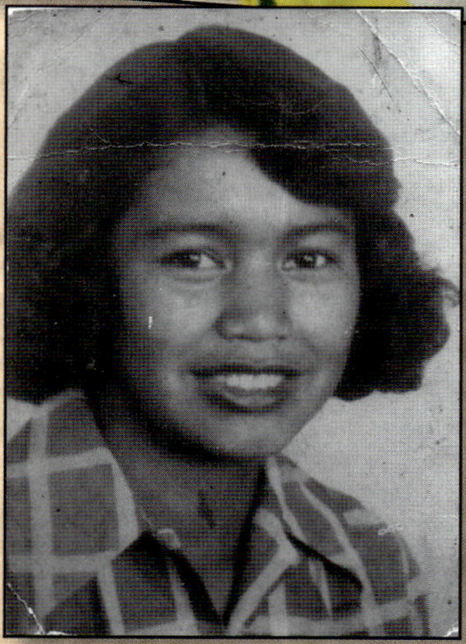

From top; Wearing Grandma's Sewing, Ruth England and family, Stilwell, Oklahoma, photo by Jeremy Charles; Ruth working on tear dress while grandkids are watching, photo by Roger Cain; Ruth England, photo courtesy of family

Brendalee: You have twenty-three great-grandkids?

Ruth: I don't know.

Brendalee: Well, something like that. (She laughed.) But you didn't learn English until you got with Grandpa England?

Ruth: Well, I did learn it in school a little bit. I do speak Cherokee. I grew up speaking Cherokee from my parents. Well, everybody was talking Cherokee when I grew up. When I met (my husband) Bob, I was about seventeen. In school, they taught in English. There weren't any teachers that spoke Cherokee. Our teacher was Oak Ketcher. I don't know what the other one was.

Brendalee: Was it all Indian kids that went to Peavine?

Ruth: Uh, huh. Maybe there would be one White one. I went to seventh grade at that school. Then in eighth, I went to Maryetta School. I went to East Peavine to school when I was nine. We had to walk to school, about five miles. We had two teachers at the school. That was first to fourth and fifth to the eighth, I think it was.

Continued on page 277

Photo by Jeremy Charles

edith catcher knight

December 6, 1939
England Hollow, Oklahoma

There were a lot of things that I just go by hearsay. The first thing I remember is the day we moved. We rode on the back of a big old truck. I guess I must have been about three and had lived there on Orchard Road all through grade school and high school. I remember how we played with some of the other kids who lived around there. We'd roll an old tire for miles—just rolled it. Everybody would have an old tire. And I remember the way I learned to drive a car. There was an old sycamore tree out in our yard, and I found a stand and a lid off a lard bucket. I nailed that lid to the tree. I would just sit there and really drive that car.

We didn't have a car at home. To go to town, we'd have to catch a ride—even on a wagon. Our neighbor would always go to town on Saturday. We'd catch a ride with him and his wagon. If it was strawberry-picking time, maybe we'd get a taxi back—that is, whenever it was 25 cents a mile. But, we walked most of the time. From where we lived, we'd walk across a field and Davis Mountain to come out in town. That's when everybody would spend all day in town, sitting in front of the stores and visiting.

Then the ice wagon would come by. They had these little pieces of cardboard, and if you wanted (the driver) to leave five pounds of ice, you'd leave that cardboard where "5" would show. If you wanted 10 pounds, you'd turn the cardboard upside down where "10" would show. Drivers delivered it out in the country. You know where the ice house was there in Stilwell? Well, that's where it came from. They'd load up big old blocks, and the driver would break those blocks up. We had an ice box; you put the ice in the top and the stuff on the bottom stayed cool until the ice melted.

My mama's name was Lula, and Dad was William. They called him Bill Catcher. They taught us to like to fish. That's something that has stayed with me all these years. From where we lived on the old homeplace on Orchard Road, it was, maybe, three miles to get to the place where Dad liked to fish. We'd walk down to Evansville Creek, and then there was backwater he called the "Old Slew." Well, we had to wade the creek to get to where he wanted to fish. Boy, that water was cold! Caught some big fish out of there, he did, with an old cane pole. I don't know how they fished with it—just a cane pole—after using my rod and reel.

We had to carry water from the branch (creek) down there. I'd leave my buckets in the morning, and then, when I came back, I'd take fresh water to the house—(as I was going) back and forth to school. To do the laundry, we had a well, but we had rusty water at home. So we would load up the clothes in a galvanized tub on an old wheel barrow. I've still got that wheel barrow outside. We'd load it up with soap and clothes, and we'd go back down there to that branch on the backside of the property. And somebody had a big old black washtub. There were some other people—from the other side of the hill—who used that same area. So, we'd use that big old iron pot to boil our white clothes. That was my job—to keep the fire burning under that pot. Mama would wash on the wash board, and we had plenty of water for rinsing and everything, but we'd use that pot to boil our clothes. We used homemade soap. Mom knew how to make lye soap. When we got them all washed, we'd wring them out, take them back up to the house and hang them out. That was all the time.

I'd be thirsty by the time I got to the spring where we got the water because I'd been running. I'd just lay down and get me a drink out of that spring. Well, I did that one day, and low and behold, the spring was full of snakes—a big old ball of them. Anyway, I didn't get a drink that day! I just backed off, got my buckets and kept going. No water that day. I told Mama. She may not have believed me. She may have thought I just didn't want to carry that water up that hill. We did that all through high school and grade school.

Continued on page 277

clockwise from left: Edith's grade school portrait; Edith Catcher Knight photo by David Fitzgerald; Edith dresses photo by Jeremy Charles

cherokee marbles

1999

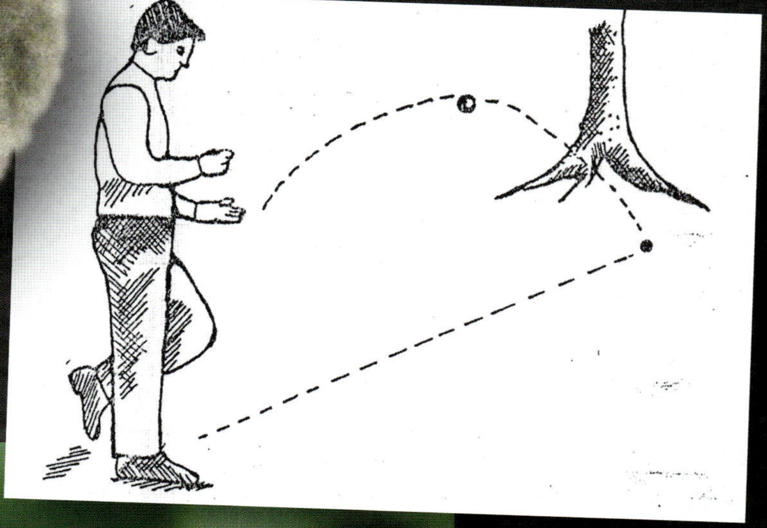

from Lee Foreman

page 1

Clouds Creek Marble Tourn.

Rules 1984

Both teams will throw from the second hole.
Whichever team that moves their marble closer to the first hole will move first.

Each player shall stand behind the hole. when throwing towards the first hole.

you will lose one turn if your foot goes past the position of the hole when throwing.

you will lose one turn.

If you throw or move the wrong marble.

If you carry your marble around while setting up the other marble.

page 2

you will lose one turn.

If you touch or move your opponent's marble while your marble is still in the hole. after making it.

If your opponent's knock your marble out of the hole after losing a turn. you do not need to remake it again.

If you step past the position of your marble when hitting and hit your opponent you will lose your turn right there.
But if you miss then you will lose your next turn to move.

For sidearm or overhand throw when hitting.

Nothing more than the fingers may go past the position of the marble when making the hole.

page 3

your hand or arm may go past the position of your marble.

When hitting.

Or when making the hole outside the six foot circle or mark.

When inside the six foot circle nothing more then the fingers may go past the position of the marble when making the hole.

Unless your marble is inside the six inch [illegible] circle. then you may pick up your marble and put it in the hole.

A hit will not count if the marble bounces than two times. Or if it rolls more then six inches after one bounce.

If the marble should slipped out of your hand, you may move again if the marble does not roll forward over 6 inches

page 4

you may move the marble not more then 2 inches forward or back But not sideways when setting up.

If your marble fall into a hole you do not need while hitting or moving. you must move on to the next hole that you need.

And if you [illegible] have already won you must go back to the first hole you do not need to renew it not needed.

If you make the hole you need by accident after missing your opponent's you may move again next turn.

no steel marble

you must not sidearm to hit at an angle to get to your opponent marble.

page 5

Hitting your opponent a third time after using up your two. shots you will lose two turns

After winning you will rest your marble 6 inches from the hole. After resting one turn you may move again.

you will not lose any one of your two shots for hitting the wrong marble.

you will lose two turns for running over your opponent's marble on purpose to keep him from making a hole.

you will forfeit the game for running over your opponent's marble on purpose when his marble is inside the 6 in circle when the distance is too far for you to hit. when he's trying to win.

“The Clouds Creek Field is a popular gathering place for nightly games of Indian marbles. Players from all the surrounding communities play throughout the year. Lee believes the Cherokee tradition of playing marbles is a good, positive tradition to keep for people of all ages and abilities.”

—Linda Vann on Lee Foreman

Pictured left: Traditional stone marbles made by Sam Lee Still, photo by David Fitzgerald; Cherokee marble diagram; Stone marble, photo by Roger Cain. This page: Hand written rules by Lee Foreman

Photo by David Fitzgerald

thelma forrest

February 9, 1940
Tahlequah, Oklahoma

Linda Vann was taking care of the Living Treasures when I started. I worked at the Heritage Center and she would come and get me on the days that she would like to visit the candidates for the upcoming Treasures. We would go out to their hometowns and we would visit. If it was a small town, we might go to the grocery store or elsewhere to talk to the people. We would go to their homes, and you could tell by going to someone's home that they really are working on their art and see what they have. And they'll bring out their stuff. We would see if it was commercial or traditional and just visit with them—mostly to see their community. Community people would know what they're doing or have been doing and how long they have been doing it. That is what being a Living Treasure is all about—being traditional and carrying on the traditional art ways.

I worked with John Ketcher way back in the '70s. He was my boss when we were going out and working with communities, helping start up teaching traditional arts like basketry and loom-weaving and lots of other stuff. We would work to help them market their art work and to encourage them to continue to make Cherokee art. We went to rural areas, way out. John was good at what he did and the program was a success.

It wasn't until the '80s that I went to Cherokee, North Carolina, to learn from their master basket weavers. They were using a lot of river cane and white oak when I was there. We went there; that was Mrs. Mildred Ketcher and Ms. Vivian McCullough. Ms. McCullough had grown up there, and she knew everybody. So we went and we spent almost a week. We got to meet way out in the country. Later on, I went another year and they wouldn't even talk to you if they didn't know you. So, Ms. Vivian McCullough would go up, and we would stand outside and she would get out. You could see the curtains move, and then they would come out the door and say, "Oh, Vivian!" If it weren't for that, they weren't going to see us. There was a lady who even took us out just past her yard. She cut down an oak tree and showed us how she split it and everything. So they just showed us everything. Wherever Vivian took us, we were always welcome and they would tell us whatever we had a question about.

Thelma Forrest with grandchildren Laney Sinali Tinaci Cully, Forrest Kurt Cully, and Kendall Lynn McCoy. Photo by Jeremy Charles.

Then we went to this lady who worked in the village or ran the village basket-making part there. Vivian went in and we talked to her. She asked me, "What are you going to do with the patterns?" We were wanting patterns. I said that we were going to be teaching it here. We were teaching it out in the community. So she went to her bedroom and got a little brown box, and she got a big bunch of patterns and gave them to me. I should have kept them because they were all on the old paper that she had done. So when I moved from working in the Cherokee Nation Education Department, I left them because I thought that's where they should be. I should have kept them because they probably finally got thrown away. We came back here and, sad to say, they wanted to keep doing the double-wall honeysuckle and buck-brush baskets. No one was too interested. I don't know if the reason was that it was kind of hard with all the counting and that stuff. I introduced it everywhere that I taught—Kenwood, Oaks, Westville. Wherever we had classes, I would show it. But, now, you see more of the patterns. I came by to talk to Katherine at the Heritage Center and they were weaving that

Continued on page 278

Thelma Forrest river cane basket with blood root and black walnut dyes. Photo by David Fitzgerald.

nancy smith

April 15, 1940
Vian, Oklahoma

At a Cherokee stomp dance, rhythm is kept by the sound of pebbles encased in turtle shells which are tied to the legs of women participating in the dance. The making of turtle-shell shackles is a summertime activity for Cherokee National Treasure Nancy Smith. During that time, small box turtles are gathered to use for the shackles, and the hot weather is beneficial for drying the shells before they are tied to leather pieces to enable them to be worn on a woman's legs during a stomp dance. Men sing traditional songs to lead a stomp dance counterclockwise around a fire while women and girls dance, joining them, keeping the rhythm with the sound of the pebbles in the shells. The shackles are wrapped around the shins and tied around the calves. Pebbles in the shells, when shaken by the women during a stomp dance, give the dance a rhythm as the sound is paired with a male singer leading the dance.

Smith, 76, can't recall how many turtle-shell shackles she has made over the years. By word of mouth, people find out she makes the shackles, she said, and she makes an average of ten shackles a year. Along with selling shackles to numerous local women, she said she has sold many to Cherokee people in the old Cherokee homelands in North Carolina. Smith has also made them for people of the Muscogee (Creek) Nation, a neighboring tribe west of the Cherokee Nation, who also have stomp dances.

Her sister-in-law, Eva Smith, (also a Cherokee National Treasure), started her making turtle-shell shackles thirty-five to forty years ago, she said. Importantly, she showed her what kinds of rocks or pebbles were best to use inside the shells. "Mostly," she said, "we go to the creek, to pick up the pebbles. Later, it got to where we couldn't get to a creek, so we just went

Above: ***Daksi*** *or Turtle Shell Shackles made by Nancy Smith. Right: Nancy Smith. Photos by David Fitzgerald*

out on the (gravel) road because that's where the gravel comes from anyway, and we picked up the pebbles there."

Traditionally, box turtles are caught and put in a cage until they are ready to be "cleaned" or hollowed out. Once hollowed out, pebbles are placed inside the shell, and it is resealed so that when the shell is shaken, the pebbles inside will rattle. "It might take all day to clean them if we have thirty or forty. We clean them all; we drill holes in them (shells). We have all of the rocks ready, and the (steel) wiring to keep them tight so they won't open up when they dry. If the weather is hot, they dry really fast, and that way, you can put them together really fast," she said. "We just can't keep extra turtles because someone is always wanting a pair (of shackles)."

Turtle shells are attached to leather boot tops from old cowboy boots Smith finds at garage sales and at thrift stores. It usually takes about two weeks to finish a pair of shackles from cleaning them, drilling holes in them, waiting on them to dry, putting pebbles inside, tying the shells together with leather straps, and then attaching them to the leather boot tops by placing wires through the drilled holes. Then they are tied using leather through metal grommets so the leather won't tear from the weight of the shells. She also shellacs the shells to make them last longer and to make them "prettier" by giving them a shine.

"Some younger women can't handle the weight of too many shells," Smith said. Normally, thirteen turtle shells are attached to each shackle. For young women who need lighter shackles, Smith will use nine to eleven turtle shells for each set of shackles that are worn under a traditional, colorful Cherokee skirt.

Thirteen shells weigh about twelve pounds, and nine shells weigh about seven pounds. She also accommodates young children so that they can participate in the dances, and usually places only four shells on each shackle to lessen the weight. "If they're heavy, they're not enjoyable for anyone to be struggling with them," Smith explained. She said she wore thirteen shells on each leg during the time she participated in stomp dances, from a young age until she was about sixty years old.

Smith has shown two of her daughters, Diane and Lisa, how to make turtle shell shackles, and over the years

Continued on page 279

Photo courtesy of Cherokee National Historical Society

wendell cochran

July 19, 1940
Tahlequah, Oklahoma

Attempting to encapsulate the contributions of Cherokee National Living Treasure Wendell Cochran as an innovator, artist, and articulate historian is a feat not possible within the pages of this text. Wendell's participation in conceptualizing, cultivating, and recording the history of Cherokee dress stands the test of time as contemporary Cherokees continue to honor and proudly wear the Cherokee tear dress into the Twenty-First Century.

The Cherokee Tear Dress Eyewitness Accounts
Information compiled and written
by Wendell Cochran
Excerpts Copyright 2001

This is the account of the Cherokee tear dress according to the recollections of Marion Hagerstrand, the wife of Colonel Martin Hagerstrand who was the founder and Executive Director of the Cherokee National Historical Society at Tsa-la-gi. Mrs. Hagerstrand is an enrolled member of the Cherokee Nation and lives in Tahlequah, Oklahoma. Although Marion was not involved in the day-to-day operations of the facility, she was a constant companion to the colonel and was privy to all of the planning and development of the grounds, the buildings, and the outdoor theater from its earliest conception through development and construction. She is a knowledgeable source of tribal history in the formative years of the modern Cherokee Government during the 1960s and 1970s.

Mrs. Hagerstrand was actively involved in the outdoor drama, The Trail of Tears. *The drama opened in 1969 as a brand new production with a script by Kermit Hunter. Marion, who is an accomplished seamstress, volunteered to work in the costume shop as a stitcher during the rehearsal and construction period leading up to the opening.*

Because the Trail of Tears *drama is a semi-fictional historical accounting of the Cherokee at the end of the trail in 1839 through the trouble and turmoil as they established a government and settled into their new homeland in the west, costumes for the drama had to be created from scratch. The costumier for the first year was a New York-trained designer who knew little about Indians or what they wore historically. Her costumes for the white people were copies (of styles) of the 1830 to 1860. Dresses for the women were a problem because there were not any documents or photographs she could copy. It was decided that she would dress all of the Cherokee woman characters in replicas of the tear dress that had been made for Virginia Stroud. It was the only existing example of what "might" have been worn. Of course, the original tear dress had only been authenticated back one hundred years, which would have been after the Civil War. The trail had taken place thirty years earlier.*

Continued on page 279

From top: Feather Smith Treveno wedding dress made by Wendell Cochran, photo by Jeremy Charles; Wendell Cochran; Three Boogers in a Row sketch by Wendell Cochran

thomas muskrat

April 6, 1941
Bell, Oklahoma

I was born in Huntmill Holler, south of Oak Ridge. I grew up, didn't have a birth certificate. Sue (wife) just wrote to Oklahoma City and they had one. My dad was a "tie hacker" on that certificate—laid them railroad ties. After, he went into the Navy. He was in the Navy, and I guess my mom left me and my brother. That's when our grandparents found us. So they went through court and got us. They raised us around here (Bell Community).

When I started school, I couldn't even talk English. All I knew was Cherokee. That set me back three or four years. I didn't complete high school. Then I joined the service. My dad (and) my uncles went, too. Frank (brother) was in the Marines. I chose to go to the Army in 1958 or '59. When I was in there, every once in a while someone would mention Vietnam: "One of these years, we're gonna be in a war with Vietnam." After I got out, it wasn't too long (before) we was in a war with Vietnam. I didn't get to go, but I heard a little bit about what was happening.

See, when I finished grade school, they shipped me to a boarding school—Chilocco Indian School. I got up there and got to making friends, and there was guys there could play the drum. Weekends we didn't have nothing to do. We'd get out in the yard and play the drums, the ones that could sing. Most of them was from out West. We got to dancing and they got to showing me. I learned everything right there at Chilocco Indian School. 'Cause, when you go to a Pow Wow, you can get in (and) start dancing with them. But there's more than dancing. You gotta know the rules that's inside the circle. Respect is (the) number one thing. What you learn is respect. It's just I've done it so much in there, it's just kindly got in me.

Well, when I came home, I'd hear the Native Americans living right here in this community talk about the other tribes. They'd never seen them, and they'd just kept filling my brain up, talking about these other tribes. Tthey'd wonder how they lived, what they'd done, what their traditional ways was, and just stuff like that. Right there is when I decided, bring the Pow Wow to Bell, Oklahoma. It was tough. We started having meetings on it. I started explaining the Pow Wow. It wasn't religious. Get together, different tribes got together and had a good time. You joked. You laughed. Kindly exchange the culture with another tribe, and it just went on and on about other tribes' ways and your way.

Sometimes at Chilocco, they'd ask me if I wanted to join them. I respected their ways, so I would do their ways, and then, sometimes, they'd ask if we could do my ways. That's when I started talking about the Pow Wow around here at home. We had a few meetings (at Cherokee Nation). They asked me, "Have you brought in people from your community to be involved in this?"

I said, "Very few."

They said, "What's the church people say?"

I said, "I don't know. The Pow Wow is not religious. It's not a Stomp Dance. Stomp Dance is religious; it's like going to church every Sunday. It ain't that. It's a get together, an exchange of culture and have a good time. What I've learned from that, you make friends that becomes a family. People will adopt each other. People will start treating each other like families, helping each other. This is something that this community needs, if this community would come out. All I want to do is show the other tribe to the East (and) the Cherokee tribe in Bell, Oklahoma."

Well, here come another meeting. First thing, they jumped in and said, "Beer money! You're using beer money!" I said, "OK, I know about every one of you church members go to convenient store, buy something. That change you get: is that beer money? Have you thought about it?"

Well, nobody couldn't answer me. I said, "OK, this is a tax write off from that beer company. I don't call it beer money. It's just money that

Continued on page 280

Clockwise from top: Thomas Muskrat; Thomas Muskrat's barn, photo by Roger Cain; Thomas Muskrat, photo by Jeremy Charles

stickball (A ne jo di) 2001

Stickball resembles the modern European game of lacrosse, using ball sticks which are made by hand from hickory. A small ball, made of deer hair and hide, is tossed into the air by the medicine man. The male players use a pair of the sticks, and female players use their bare hands.

In earlier times, only the men with the greatest athletic ability played the game. The game was oftentimes played to settle disputes, and the conjurer for each team often became as important to the team as (were) the players themselves. Seven points are scored when the ball strikes a wooden fish or ball on the top of a pole approximately twenty-eight feet in height, and two points are awarded when the ball strikes the pole.

In earlier days, there would be a dance before the ballgame. The ballplayers were the participants of the dance, along with seven women dancers. Each woman represented one of the clans. Throughout the dance, the women would step on black beads, which represented the players of the opposing team. The conjurer had placed these black beads on a large flat rock. Today, stickball is an important part of the day's activities at ceremonial Stomp Grounds, being necessary to play before the Stomp Dance can ever begin.

It is also a recreational sport at other times between community teams. There are also intertribal teams made up of players from Cherokee, Muscogee (Creek), Yuchi, Natchez, and other area communities.

Information provided by the Cherokee Nation Cultural Resource Center.

Pictured left: Ball sticks hanging from the rafters by David Comingdeer; This page, left to right: Making stickball sticks by David Comingdeer; Betty Smith playing stickball at the Tsa-La-Gi Ancient Village; Willie Jumper photo

hastings shade

May 20, 1941
Evening Shade, Oklahoma

Photo by David Fitzgerald

In the spring of 1997, a creature was seen on the Illinois River. Two young men who were fishing saw it. It is known as the *uktena*. It is said to be an enormous snake with horns and it has a crystal embedded in its forehead. According to myths and legends, the *uktena* is the deadliest creature in the world. It is also a huge part of the traditional Cherokee and Keetoowah world. Elders have said that whenever this entity is seen, some great event in the Giduwa society is going to happen.

In 1999, Hastings Shade was elected to the office of Deputy Chief of the Cherokee Nation of Oklahoma. He was the last full-blood, traditional Cherokee to hold an office in the tribe. Many programs at Cherokee Nation—concerning history, culture, and language—were created and or inspired by Hastings Shade. You won't see his name on any building or material distributed by those programs because his heart was concerned with the continuation of the Giduwa people rather than trying to carve his name into the history books. Hastings didn't really care who claimed credit for his ideas as long as they got done. That was his heart; that was his spirit. He cared more about the people rather than notoriety.

I knew and loved Hastings Shade for half my life. I wish I had known him longer because he taught me so much about our culture. After my great-aunt, Maggie Turtle, died in 1981 at the age of 98, Hastings became my "Immediate Elder" to whom I would go if I had any questions concerning history, traditions, or language. Many was the time when we

Pictured right: Hastings Shade gigging Buffalo Fish with hand forged gig, photo courtesy of National Public Radio; (below) Hand-forged hatchet made by Hastings Shade; Carvings, forged gigs and marble making set by Hastings Shade

would sit at his kitchen table eating whatever his wife, Loretta, had cooked for us or sat in the living room of his small, unassuming house or in the work shed where he forged and made his crafts. We would talk for hours about different things concerning our people, and of course, sharing stories and laughing. Hastings loved to laugh. His gruff countenance softened with a huge smile, a mischievous twinkle in his eyes, and his belly laugh was contagious. He often told jokes and amusing little stories of his childhood that kept me in stitches.

He could have retired, but Hastings jumped at the chance to work for the Cherokee Nation dealing with language and culture where I had the good luck to work with him on several projects, some of which were so progressive that they were not followed up on back then but are today part of the programs and curriculum. Hastings, Durbin Feeling—a world-renowned linguist— and I had the first computers that were programmed with the Cherokee syllabary as part of the word processor's font. Thanks to this innovation, Hastings began writing books about our culture, history, and language. One such book, "Myths, Legends and Old Sayings" is a tome of remarkable information about our people. He also developed a word-find game book using the syllabary. There is a "World Info" book that he was working on over the years depicting the world according to *Giduwa* teachings. This volume, even though he wasn't able to complete it, is a large book reminding one of an encyclopedia. I was lucky enough to help him recreate the old, small Cherokee Hymnal into a large, easy-to-read book for use by the elders; this project was dumped by a

Continued on page 281

luther "toby" hughes

June 12. 1941
Old Green, Oklahoma

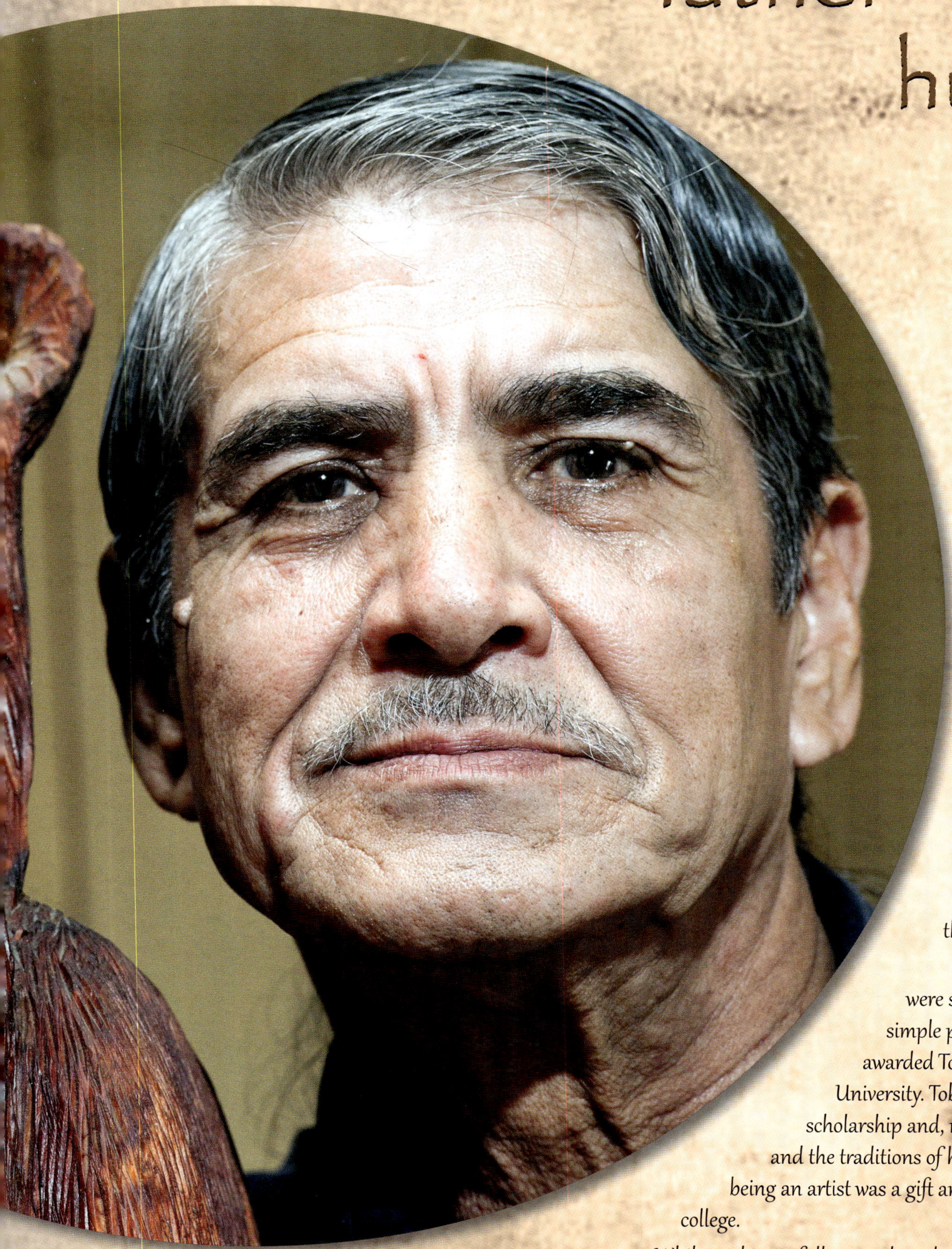

Luther "Toby" Hughes was born in 1941 in Westville, Oklahoma. He was raised by his grandparents, Ely and Nannie Sam Hammer, who were of both Cherokee and Creek descent.

As a young boy, Toby would sit quietly and listen to elders speak of things from long ago. He was taught traditional Cherokee ways by his grandfather. At an early age, he learned the Cherokee language. He did not learn English until he started to school.

He excelled in school and amazed teachers with brilliant art projects he carved—using crude knives—from pieces of wood. Toby is proud to say that he was the first male of the Hammer family to finish high school.

The Westville School District personnel were so impressed with his ability to turn a simple piece of wood into a work of art that they awarded Toby a scholarship to New Mexico State University. Toby, however, decided to forego the NMSU scholarship and, rather, to remain near his homeland and the traditions of his people. In his heart, he believed that being an artist was a gift and not something a person could learn in college.

While working a full-time job and raising a family, he always found time to

Clockwise: Toby Hughes with National Living Treasure proclamation, photo by Cherokee National Archives; Toby Hughes' Crooked Face Mask, photo by Jeremy Charles; Toby Hughes working in his shop, photo by Cherokee National Archives

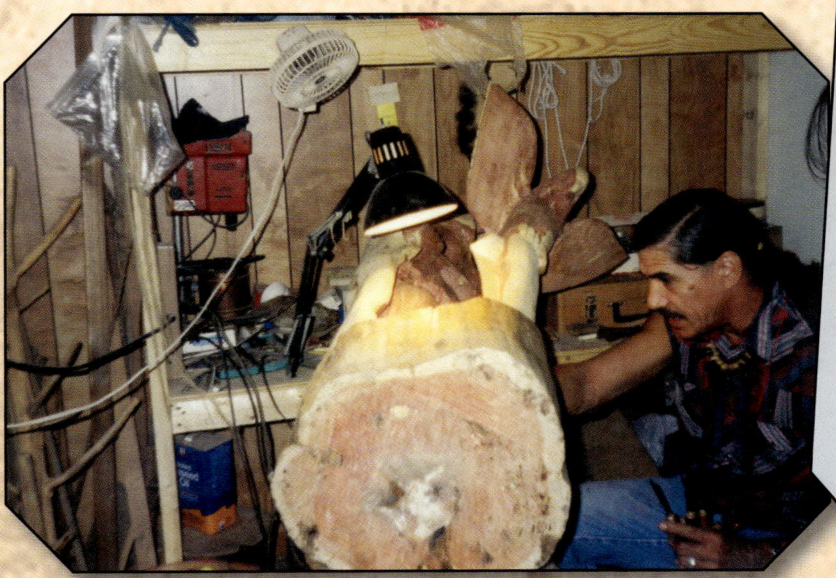

slip back into the world of nature. There, he would find perfect pieces of wood or bone on which to carve. He sold his carvings out of his home for a small price, keeping in mind that the working man also enjoyed Indian art.

In all his years of working as an artist, Toby has entered only two competitive art shows. He found that some shows were biased and political, and there was no place for that in his world. He continued to sell his art to individuals and galleries in Oklahoma, and he's proud to say his art is scattered throughout the nation and abroad. Whether it be a miniature carving less than two inches tall carved from a deer antler or a three-foot wood sculpture, each piece reflects his Indian heritage. Love for Indian art keeps Toby carving from wood he has found in the hollow, as do the words of wisdom his grandfather spoke so long ago: be proud of who you are and never forget you are an Indian."

— Luther "Toby" Hughes
From his Cherokee Nation National Treasure Nomination Form

sue girty thompson

June 13, 1942
Woodall, Oklahoma

I was born Edna Sue Girty at Hastings Hospital, in Tahlequah, Oklahoma. My parents were Tobacco Girty (*Tsoli*) and Jennie Whitewater Girty. Our family is from what is now the Camp Gruber area. When I was just a kid, the government took over the dam and Camp Gruber, but our family is from that Gore and Braggs area. My family sold that land and moved to Hulbert for a while, but then my grandma found land near Woodall, and that's where we wound up moving. All of us lived right there. A couple of brothers did eventually move away—one to Lawrence, Kansas, and one to to Dallas.

We are full-blood Cherokee, so I am a lifelong Cherokee language speaker. In fact, everyone in my family—four brothers, one sister and three cousins—spoke Cherokee. Mom and Grandma spoke only Cherokee. After speaking English all day at school, we would keep talking to each other in English until we got to the supper table. Grandma (*Elisi*) would say *"Jalagi ijiwoniha,"* ("You all speak Cherokee"). I taught my mom and grandma to speak some English. My mom could then do her own business, like at the bank.

When I was growing up, everyone spoke Cherokee; our neighbors who visited spoke the language, and the Cherokee people who shopped at the store in Tahlequah, also spoke Cherokee. I only knew those people by their Cherokee names. When you went to the grocery store, Willis Store, everyone spoke Cherokee. When we would see each other at Christmas time, you had to say "*Da nis da yo hi hv ado neth* (Christmas gift)" before the other person said it, or you had to

give them something—maybe snuff or a hanky, but you had to give them something. It was fun!

At church, the elders read the Cherokee New Testament for their Sunday School class. The minister, Reverend Jim Pickup, preached the whole sermon in Cherokee at the New Greenleaf Church. That's where I first I heard my grandma, Betsy Phillips Whitewater, reading a verse. I spoke Cherokee, but I really wanted to learn how to read it. I knew that my grandma and dad could read Cherokee, so I wanted to learn, too. No one else was really learning it. In Sunday School, Grandma would read Cherokee out of the New Testament that was written in the language. I was young and I would sit next to my grandma, and I wondered how they understood it. Then one day, I asked Mrs. Bowlin, at church, how to read Cherokee. She said to start with John 1:1: "In the beginning was the word, and the word was with God, and the word was God."

ᏗᏓᎴᏂᏍᎬ ᎧᏃᎮᏛ ᎡᎮᎢ, ᎠᎴ ᎾᏍᎩ ᎧᏃᎮᏛ ᎤᏁᎳᏅᎯ ᎢᏧᎳᎭ ᎠᏁᎮᎢ, ᎠᎴ ᎾᏍᎩ ᎧᏃᎮᏛ ᎤᏁᎳᏅᎯ ᎨᏎᎢ.

She suggested that I read from this particular paragraph because the verse was repetitious. I didn't learn the Cherokee syllabary first. I just kept flipping back and forth between the Cherokee New Testament to the syllabary. I was in my twenties when I began to read; the more I began to understand, the more I would read. That's how I learned to read Cherokee.

Benny Smith, at Haskell, asked my brother, Andy Girty, if he would come and work for a while in Native American studies. Andy wrote his own curriculum and taught Cherokee. He loved it because he learned even more as he went along. He was at Haskell for sixty years. He retired from Haskell. I also

Continued on page 272

Clockwise from top: Sue Thompson teaching Cherokee language to students in Adam's Corner one-room school house; Sue Thompson teaching Cherokee language to Kelsey Galilo Morgan *and Jolie* Qualayuga *Morgan. Both are graduates of Cherokee Nation Immersion Charter School. Photo by Jeremy Charles*

Photo by David Fitzgerald

jess oosahwee

July 28, 1942
Shady Grove, Oklahoma

I guess blowgun making was passed down from elders in my family. I can remember when we were just boys. We would use sumac and make blowguns to use as we spent our time in the woods and along the creeks in the Shady Grove Community of Cherokee County. About the only time in my life when I wasn't active in cultural activities was while I was in the U.S. Navy. Later, I worked at the Cherokee Village and "perfected" making blowguns and darts (learning) from William Cabbagehead. We use the native cane for making blowguns and the thistle for making darts. The shaft of the dart is made from different materials. Skewers are popular nowadays, but you can use river cane, rose bush, Bois d'arc or just about any hard wood.

Making and shooting blowguns has always been

a "family thing" for us. Cousins, aunts, nieces, nephews—everyone participated when a competition was scheduled, and many times, family members would be the winners. It was pretty tough competition, too. There used to be a "Thistle Society." To be recognized as a member, you had to win the Cherokee National Holiday Tournament and outshoot a previous Thistle Society member. I can think of nine (Thistle Society members), and four of them are close family members.

I spent some time in Lawrence, Kansas. I went to Haskell and made a lot of friends who were from other tribes and other states. I learned more about the Cherokee cultural arts from friends from the Eastern Band in North Carolina. These ways are important, and I have tried to keep them alive for my children and grandchildren. I am proud that my son was a champion blowgun shooter, and his two sons have gotten into the competition at Cherokee Holiday.

Continued on page 281

From top: Jess demonstrating the blow gun shoot at Tsa-la-gi Cherokee Heritage Center; Jess as Tsa-la-gi villager, photos courtesy of Cherokee National Historical Society. Wilma Mankiller and Jess Oosahwee at Cherokee National Holiday, photo courtesy of Cherokee Phoenix

Photo by Jeremy Charles

jim buckhorn

September 13, 1943
Pumpkin Hollow, Oklahoma

Robert McLemore was my grandpa. He was from Pumpkin Hollow. Yeah, that's where I learned my bow making. When I started watching him, I was about twelve years old. Fourteen years old is when he gave me that little stick to make a bow. I got pretty good, but he'd say, "No, No, No, you don't do that. You do this!"

I said, "OK."

And then finally he said, "Let's try it again." He helped me, kindly, to find the growth ring in that wood. I did that. "Now you're gettin' close." That's all he told me. "Now you're on your own."

And I made that bow. I had it 3 1/2 years. Boy, I killed a lot of birds and bunnies with that. It turned out good. Then it was time to make another one. And just right after that, when I finished up on the third bow that we made—that he helped me make—he passed away. I kept that bow for a long time. It was a great one; I do know that. He'd be sitting on the porch in that rocking chair and he'd say, "Set me up this snuff can on the corner post." He hit it every shot and never missed. I couldn't do that.

I got older and got to where I could do pretty good after that. Then I went on ahead and started making them on my own. And he said, "Yeah, you done that all right. You done OK."

Jim Buckhorn and daughter, Regina Foreman, photo by Jeremy Charles

Then finally, when I turned 16, I had one spare. This other guy, he said, "Want to sell that bow?"

I said, "Yeah, I'll sell it. For how much?"

"Fifty cents."

And that's what I sold it for! My grandpa, his bows were the ones that were only a dollar-and-a-half. But he made beautiful bows! But you know, that was just something that my grandpa would do and make a wood carving, making bows and arrows. And that's what I did, what he left off. I'm still doing it even right now.

In 1975 shooting with the Green Country Bow Hunter Association, I was the first person ever to "Robin Hood," splitting a bull's-eye arrow with a second arrow.

People use them. Some of them, they hang them on a wall. Some of them, they shoot in the tournaments. All my bows, mostly, have been shot in a tournament. The Cornstalk Shoot, something like that. See, just like my daughter, the bow she's shooting now. It comes from where a limb was just there; it was really a crooked limb. I told her to wait three times. One day, I looked at it again and said, "That's going to make a good bow." And it did! So far, she's won two tournaments with it. She shoots good. Now I've got my daughter started on making bows and arrows. There's some arrows that she made that turned out beautiful. I make my own cornstalk points, and I just do all my work in the back.

I've got two bows in the truck that I brought today in case I need them to look at. Both are made in the traditional Indian way. The bow string is the only thing that is modern. But the wood and the way I carved it—everything is done the traditional way. No

Continued on page 281

Jim Buckhorn's senior picture

quilting

2001

"My grandmother has been hand quilting since she was twelve years old. She has told me stories of how they used to sew quilts with my aunt and the other ladies at the church. She said that when you first began quilting, the younger girls worked on baby quilts for women who had a baby in their community. The older ladies worked on quilts for sick or elderly."

—From Polly Jane Whitekiller's nomination form for Cherokee National Treasure

"Margaret Wilson of Tahlequah was recognized as a Cherokee Master Craftsman in Hand Sewn Quilting in 2001. At that time, she had hand quilted for over thirty-two years. She told of her mother taking her on Wednesdays to Johnson Prairie Church to sew with the ladies. Margaret also does the old-fashioned type of quilting known as tacked quilting, where the quilt is held together by twine instead of the quilting thread."

—Cherokee Nation News Release, October 19, 2001 on Margaret Wilson

"How do you get young people interested in making quilts? You invite them to your home—that's sewing, anymore. I don't know if they be interested, but you put something up somewhere and invite little kids.Boys can do it too. I saw a man at Hastings. He made a quilt. He entered it in the show down there at the Cherokee Nation. He made a good quilt. That was a man."

—Lizzie Jane Whitekiller

*Pictured left: Margaret Wilson hand sewing a quilt, photo by Sammy Still;
This page, left to right: Quilt by Lizzy Jane Whitekiller, heirloom photo;
Hand-sewn quilts by Polly Whitekiller; Syllabary quilt by Polly Whitekiller,
photo by David Fitzgerald*

wynona "chicken" dreadfulwater

May 4, 1944
Briggs, Oklahoma

Photo by Pamela Jumper Thurman

Wynona Hair was born to Lucille "Winnie" Chair and Zeke Hair at Hastings Hospital in Tahlequah, Oklahoma. Paternal grandparents were Mose Hair and Sallie McCarter and maternal grandparents were Rev. Jim Chair and Lizzie Wilson. Wynona is called "Chicken" to those who know and love her. Her grandmother told her that her nickname came about because, when she was very young, the family lived in a very old log cabin. When it would rain, the rain would blow in through the small cracks between the logs. People would say that Lucille was home with her chicken—Wynona—under her wing. From that point, everyone started calling Wynona "Chicken." Wynona laughed and said that everyone in her family had nicknames. Her brothers are the late Benny Dreadfulwater, Franklin "Jody" Dreadfulwater, the late James "Chooch" Dreadfulwater, and the late Raymond "Babe" Dreadfulwater. Her sisters are Athena "Squirty" and Clara "Puddin'". (Clara). She said that there really wasn't much to do growing up. "I've lived in Briggs all my life. Mama took care of our grandfather and that's where we lived, right there in Briggs"

Wynona learned her weaving techniques from her mother, Winnie, also a Cherokee National Treasure—1990 for weaving. Winnie was part of

From top: Wynona at the loom; Carrying on the family tradition.
All pictures by Pamela Jumper Thurman

the Sequoyah Weavers group and later, Wynona started going to the Weavers building to learn as well. Wynona recalled that she and her mama spent a lot of time at the Sequoyah Indian Weavers building. Wynona's mother began weaving in 1948. After Wynona started going to the Weavers building with her mom, they would weave and talk for hours. Wynona started out making rag rugs and wall hangings and then finally moved on to weaving afghans. She said that she was about eighteen to twenty years old when her mama finally talked her into weaving.

Wynona holds valuable history of the Sequoyah Weaver's Building. She said that when she was small, she would go over to the building with her mother. John Ketcher was often there and she remembered William "Bill" Ames as being the driving force behind the formation of the Sequoyah Weavers. She believed that the group was formed as a result of a Bureau of Indian Affairs funding project. Although the funding was discontinued sometime in the 1950s, the building and Wynona, the weaver, remain.

The building is in disrepair, but Wynona said, "...It's still sturdy. Someone broke in and stole our wood stove so we can't weave in the winter now; it gets too cold. My boys would cut wood for us so that we could keep warm."

She said that she wished that the Cherokee Nation would come out and fix the building because it is historic. She said that some years back, a group came from Colorado and sheetrocked and painted the interior of the building. They added carpet and really fixed it up. Others came and wanted to fix the building, but they wanted a deed.

Wynona said that Mr. Ames had once said that when the last weaver finished there, the place would be theirs. Wynona is that last weaver. Despite health challenges, she still teaches anyone who wants to come out. One of her cousins comes in occasionally to weave. Winnie taught the cousin to weave as well. So sometimes, Wynona has

Continued on page 282

anna sixkiller

March 25, 1945
Tahlequah, Oklahoma

Photo by David Fitzgerald

I grew up on a small farm in a little community called Leach, Oklahoma. Mom and Dad grew everything we ate. It was a different time. I had chores every day. With different seasons, we did different things. In the springtime, we got everything in the ground that we needed for the winter. This was our survival for winter. During the summer, we picked fruit or even greens in the wild. Mama would pick fruit—apples, strawberries, things like that. We would can as much as we could and make jelly, and dry all the summer stuff like roots and vegetables. I was the helper. Mom had a little baby, and I took care of the baby. But when Mama needed me, I was there. In the fall, we harvested some of the berries that come out, and then the nuts—hickory nuts and things like that for winter food like *kvnvchi* and things like that.

Two crops are to be harvested at this time, corn and potatoes and all the things that you have planted. We harvested and stored it for the winter. We didn't buy much. We had corn, and my daddy would take it to the mill (so) we had cornmeal and flour, too. We bought coffee, salt, and a little sugar; we also had honey stored. In wintertime, we did like sewing. Momma made all our clothes. Maybe we bought coats sometimes if she didn't have time to make us a coat. But, nevertheless, that was my life growing up, as far back as I can remember. I cannot ever remember going to bed hungry.

The first school I started was in Kansas, Oklahoma. When I was in the second grade, there were several of us in the class. Sometimes, we didn't fully understand what the teacher was telling us to do. So one of us would talk in our language and (we would) try to help each other and we would get in trouble. Sometimes, we would have to stay in recess, for maybe a week because we spoke our language. But that didn't discourage me from talking the language. I always will. Furthermore, I read and write; that is my job as of today. That was my first school, and then the district boundaries changed, so I could go to a little school called Leach. I finished there and went on to Oaks Mission School.

I've had a happy life—learning about how to think differently. I didn't finish high school. I dropped out. I went back later to adult education classes and got my diploma. I got married. I have three kids who are grown up, married and have kids. I have grandkids, and have taught them to do what was taught to me. Both my girls can do baskets. My son liked to draw. He was an artist but when he got all grown up and married, he put that aside, so he worked and supported his family.

When we were growing up, we would go visit my grandma, who was really my grandma's sister. Her name was Maggie Spade. Sometimes we'd find her sitting by a little stream and she was

Continued on page 282

Clockwise from top: Anna Sixkiller weaving at Flat Rocks, Goat's Bluff, in Cherokee County, photo by Sammy Still Jr.; Anna Sixkiller Cherokee National Treasure 1991; Anna Sixkiller demonstrating basketry at the Tsa-la-gi Ancient Village in Tahlequah. Photos courtesy of Sammy Still Jr. and the Cherokee National Historical Society

jane osti

July 30, 1945
Tahlequah, Oklahoma

I was born at Hastings Hospital in Tahlequah, Oklahoma. My parents are Dolly Smith Hitchcock and Jesse Hitchcock (deceased). My grandparents on my Indian side of the family were Nellie Rackleff Smith and Lemick Smith. My great-grandmothers were Lizzy Sunday and Sarah Bluebird. I grew up in the Teresita and Rocky Ford area. My relatives had allotted land from Teresita and Rocky Ford all the way to Oaks. I went to grade school mostly at Teresita and high school at Oaks Mission.

The only art that I can remember in my youth were pictures in the Bible and on calendars. The aunt that I lived with for a lot of years didn't have much, but she took great care of her house and made wonderful gardens that supplied a lot of our food. In many ways, her life was an art because she made everything that she had to work with beautiful. I may have gotten my love of interior design and gardening from her example.

I moved to Southern California with my brother, who was in the navy, when I was in my early twenties. I later moved to San Francisco. I took my first art class in community college at the age of 33. From the first class, I knew that art was what I wanted to do. The smell of oil paint still calls to me. I took every art class available for about seven years, 15-18 hours each semester. I moved back to Oklahoma in 1985 and enrolled at Northeastern State University. I was only a few hours away from getting my bachelor's degree. I had to take the required pottery and sculpture class for the Bachelor of Arts degree. I fell in love with

the clay and have continued on that path for almost thirty years now.

I was fortunate to meet Anna Sixkiller Mitchell during that first year of working with clay. My admiration for Anna, her cultural knowledge, her passion for clay, and her beautiful pottery was my inspiration to learn about, and to make, Southeastern/Cherokee pottery. Anna lived in Vinita. I moved there in the mid-nineties and worked closely with her for about a year. Her wonderful husband, Bob, and I would sit on the porch after a day of firing or pottery making and drink some of his homemade "stuff" that he got from a friend. Those are great memories. He was so supportive and so very proud of Anna. Anna was a lot of things to me—my friend, my teacher, and my inspiration. I will always miss her. She walked on a few years ago.

Red Earth was my first big show in 1990. I took a sculpture that I had done of Anna to enter in competition. It received an Honorable Mention. I have continued to do Indian markets and museum shows for the past twenty-five years. We now have our very own Cherokee Art Market held annually in Oklahoma. In the early years, I did at least ten out- of-state shows every year. That has changed with the purchase of our work for the Cherokee casinos, Cherokee clinics, and the Cherokee Art Market. Keeping some of our art in Cherokee country has many benefits. Our art is being displayed, preserved, and used for educational purposes throughout the Cherokee Nation.

Dr. Noble at NSU suggested that I teach my first class about 1989 or 1990. Since then, I have taught at my studio, JOM programs, and Cherokee Nation and as adjunct teacher at NSU. My love of teaching has a lot to do with keeping the tradition of pottery making alive. I have learned that you have

Continued on page 283

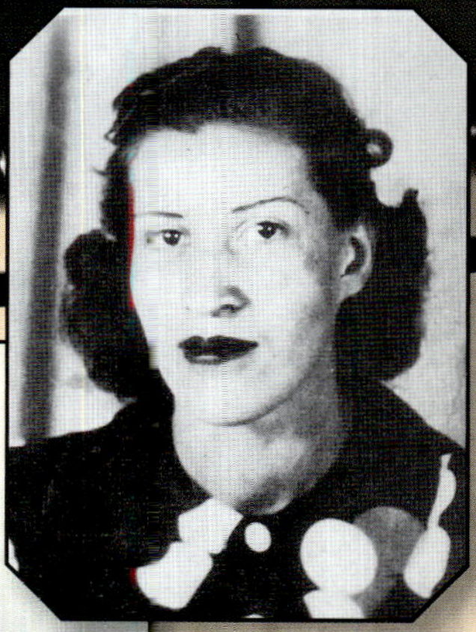

From top: Jane Osti's art; Jane Osti's mother; Lillie Brooke Vann, Jane Osti's granddaughter receives First Place in pottery, Youth Division, Santa Fe Indian Market.

durbin feeling

April 2, 1946
Little Rock, Oklahoma

I was about twelve years old. Of course, this would be back in the early or mid-'50s. My dad didn't have a steady job. He just had a few things he did—building fences and things like that. Whenever he was idle, he would read the *New Testament* every day. So, he's sitting around outside, and me and my brother and my sister really never played together. I was kind of a loner. They played together more than all of us. But once in a while, we would all get together and play. But mostly it was just me. I noticed my dad reading while he was sitting there. And I'd come running by there, and I took notice. So I stopped one day, and I stood by his lap, and he was holding his *Bible*, reading along. When he noticed that I was interested, he took his pen out of his pocket, and he would guide me where he was reading. As long as I stood there. Sometimes I'd just dart off. But another time I'd come and stand a little longer.

After a while, I spent a lot of time listening to him and watching him read, and every time he would do that, guide along. I got to memorizing words that were short. The word like this—two letters *te a*. Or Jesus—*Jesa*. So those little sight words like that. I just kind of got used to it. Later on, Mom had a *New Testament,* and when she wasn't using it, I would use hers. I'd pick it up and begin to look at it. Sometimes, it would start with a letter I knew, and I would start reading as far as I could. Inevitably there would be some word that I wouldn't be able to pronounce. I'd go back to the back of the book where it had a pronunciation guide and find the letter to find out how to say it and then come back and start reading again. (I) kept on reading until I came to another one I didn't know and (I would) do the same thing. I don't know how long it took me, but this is the way I learned how to read—kind of self-taught but influenced by my dad. That's when I started reading a lot.

When my sister passed away back in 1994, there was a friend of ours, our neighbor, and we were

Photo courtesy of The Cherokee Phoenix

talking about the past things we had done. She reminded me that she said, "You never played with us. You'd play with us for a while and then disappear, and we would go back to the house, and you'd be sitting there reading your books, reading your *Bible*." So I started reading as a relatively young person. I started reading in Cherokee at twelve.

Reading and writing are two different things. Reading is much easier. But when you have to write, you have to think what you're saying, what the letter looks like that has that sound, and then you finally find it in your mind, and you write it down. And when I was in Vietnam and was twenty-two years old, Mom would write to me in the syllabary. I'd read it, and I'd write back, written in English, and answer all her questions she had and told her about different things that were going on and things like that. One day, I said, "You know, I can read this stuff! I want to learn how to write it. I'm going to practice writing it." So I took that letter and began to answer it in Cherokee. It took about two hours to write just that much, but it was written by me. The next time I wrote another letter was a little quicker and a little longer. And so, that's how I learned how to write. So ten years later, I learned how to write in Cherokee.

Dad's full name was Jefferson Smith Feeling. Everybody called him "Jeff." My mom came from my family, the Youngdeer family. When I was seeking for my CDIB card, I had a lot of trouble because I had the information from my dad's side for a long time, and it was turning up I had information from my mom's side, but not enough. Every time they looked it up, it turned that I was half-Cherokee. I knew I wasn't. I went to Mom one day and said, "What's going on here?"

She said, "Why don't you look under Youngdeer?" And they had roll numbers they had to get you on the rolls and everything. I went back to Cherokee Nation and looked through the names and found the list of Youngdeers under Reuben Youngdeer, and that number that she gave me matched that. So that's how I got my 4/4 degree on my CDIB. We belong to the Youngdeer actually. Her dad was called Foreman. Somehow, they changed it from Youngdeer to Foreman, like they did lots of other Cherokees.

Continued on page 283

Clockwise from left: Durbin Feeling with his siblings. Euna Mae, Durbin and Russell, photo courtesy of artist; Chilocco Collage; Durbin Feeling, photo by David Fitzgerald

mask making 2007

"In all the traditions of masking among Native Americans, there are three distinct purposes for masks. The most important one has to do with spirituality, with healing. Has to do with the metaphysical and the mysterious. It has to do with the belief in a higher being, with spirits that control our lives. And so masks were used as visual images in lieu of actually seeing these spiritual forces."

—*Wendell Cochran*

"One of the things that the purpose that was really fulfilled with boogers and booger dancing was that it disarmed the angst and anger that the society felt toward a select group or individual."

—*Wendell Cochran*

"The masking traditions of the Cherokee are long and reach back to our ancient ancestors as represented in the archaeological record. Our ancestors utilized masks before colonialism and the forced removal to Indian Territory. Even after all the hardships placed on our people, we still used masks in our homeland and our removal homeland in Oklahoma."
"There are mainly two types of Cherokee masks—effigy and Booger masks. With the latter, the Booger mask term came about in the early Twentieth Century from anthropologists studying Cherokee mask dances. Before the Booger Dance was labeled as such, it was known as the 'Two-Can-Do' or 'Mask Dance.' While a Booger mask would fall under the effigy term, it is really representative of the ugly and mean human traits through satire and, thus, has its own category of Cherokee mask style and practice. Cherokee effigy masks include Warrior, Medicine, and animal masks that are distinct in their appearance and representations."

—*Roger Cain*

Pictured left: Oak carved mask by Clarence Downing, photo by Jeremy Charles; This page, left to right: Crooked Face Mask by Toby Hughes, photo by Jeremy Charles; Tsa-la-gi Ancient Village Booger circa 1980, photo courtesy of Cherokee National Archives; Cherokee Booger Mask by Roger Cain, photo by Jeremy Charles.

Photo by Will Chavez

eddie morrison

September 29, 1946
Tahlequah, Oklahoma

"I want to represent American Indian people with pride and dignity...my ideas and themes come from the philosophies of Native Americans about spirituality, family, respect for life, animals and all that is around us, and the Great Creator."

— Eddie Morrison

I was born in 1946 at Claremore Indian Hospital. My mother was Margaret Brackett. I was raised in Tahlequah by my Cherokee grandmother, Jane Batt Brackett. Some of my earliest recollections are of my grandmother and aunt crocheting and designing and sewing quilts, so I feel that art was a big part of my childhood. Other family members also did something with their hands—creating things—all the time. Of course, they were creating them for a different purpose than what I do now.

There was always someone doing something with wood in our community. I remember my best friend's father would sit, for hours-on-end, carving pieces of wood into beautiful traditional bows and arrows. I believe, as a child, I was more influenced—by him more than by any other person—about my feeling for working with wood. But I really didn't do anything with art when I was younger.

I attended Northeastern State University and started doing some painting back in the 1970s. My brother, Jesse Hummingbird, was a painter, and so his influence, and my own love for native art, started me painting. I got some paint, and the things that I needed to paint, and started to do some sketching and painting. Back then, they had a show of Indian art at the Philbrook Museum of Art in Tulsa, Oklahoma. I submitted some pieces and got two pieces accepted. I thought that was really something! That opened doors for me, so I continued to paint and started going to other art shows.

Above: Monument "Those Who Came Before," dedicated to Jesse Chisholm, who was half-Cherokee. Eddie Morrison statues. All photos provided by artist.

But then, in the 1980s, I started to realize that I just never felt completely comfortable with that medium. Painting was a struggle for me. I remembered my friend's father carving those bows and arrows, so I got my pocket knife out and got some wood and I just started carving. It came pretty naturally. I realized that carving was my artistic calling. After cutting the end of my finger off and having to have it sewn back on, I learned a lot of things on what not to do, but still, carving just felt natural. I don't know how to describe it other than the fact that I imagined a piece in my head and it would come out of my hands and into the piece. That's still the way I work today. I just look at the piece and go with the natural lines in the wood or the stone. I remember the carver, Willard Stone. His work influenced me, as well.

By then, I was in my forties, I wanted to learn more, so I saved up some money so that I could go to Denver for a week and enroll in the Art Student League of Denver. That week changed my life.

I had never carved marble before that. While there, I was deeply influenced by the great Chiricahua-Apache artist, Allan Houser, who was the guest lecturer and teacher at the Art Student League. I was the only Indian student that week, and he took me under his wing. Outside of being a great artist, Allan Houser was a great man. Just to listen to him talk—his philosophies about life, his respect for life and all that is around us — moved me. He encouraged me to continue my studies on a more advanced level at the Institute of American Indian Arts in Santa Fe.

When I graduated from IAIA, I was one of the older students, so I was really surprised to receive the Faculty Department Award for Outstanding Student in Three Dimensional Art. Being at IAIA opened so many doors for me. It was also life-changing because I got to experience a lot of other cultures in the classes. I learned so much. I never really liked to talk much in front of people, and we had to get up and talk about our art. We had to take a course called "The Business of Art" to know how to talk about our art—to market our work. That helped me a lot.

Continued on page 284

bill rabbit

December 3, 1946
Pryor, Oklahoma

Photo by Traci Rabbit

My personal experience goes way back to kindergarten. I was born in Casper, Wyoming, and I fell in love with painting. Then, in the fourth grade, I won my first award. My teacher sent my picture to Denver. It was a watercolor landscape. It won second (place) and eight dollars. I thought I had arrived! The fact is, I suppose I was an artist first because of where I lived. Russell and Remington were the artists everyone admired. At the time, my dad was a full-blood Cherokee, and we'd come to Oklahoma and visit. All my family on my dad's side spoke Cherokee. (That's when) I discovered my heritage. In Wyoming, Dad traveled. He was an iron worker. I was just another student in school.

Once I learned about my heritage, I thought, "Well, OK, I like to paint." I did a painting and took it to the Five Tribes Museum, and it was rejected, because it wasn't the flat, lined, traditional style. At that time, they wouldn't accept any blending of color; I had to go and learn how to paint traditionally. Then I entered, and it was accepted. That was a beginning. I believe an artist, depending on your background, you have to love what you do. I do, anyway. I spend way too much time doing it. But I think you can do both. In my particular case, I looked around and saw what the native artists were doing—they had multiples, reproductions, like any big company. So, I tried to do that. Why reinvent the wheel?

Bill Rabbit with daughter and artist Traci Rabbit, photo courtesy of Traci Rabbit. Photo by Larry Daugherty

"This is a piece I did years ago that's in black and red. On the right side, there's a heart, and the Indian is there looking out and he has his fingers cross. I titled it "Honest Indian." I suppose the statement was most people cross their legs or their fingers and say, "Honest, believe me." — Bill Rabbit

Early in my career, I caught a little flak from galleries and people. But, R.C. Gorman was my hero. He had something almost anywhere (in) a price range. I found out early in my career (that) you have to continually cultivate a new buyer. And that new buyer may only be able to afford a greeting card. But ten years from now, he may come and buy an original. So, I am an artist and an Indian artist. I walk in both worlds. It is very easy for me.

I consider myself an American first. I'm a veteran. In the '70s I was in Vietnam. I didn't have time to protest and do things like that. But for people who did, God bless them. I have never felt like a second-class citizen. My art has always had a life of its own. It wasn't there to shock anyone. The main thing I always wanted was to have someone look at it. Enjoy it! And share the moment they see what I'm thinking. That's what's important to me. I can do a painting with a flower, and I fall in love with that flower when I'm doing it. When I do a painting about our Cherokee culture, I fall in love with that painting while I'm doing it. But I know I've supported my family, put my daughter through college, and done my art full time— should be thirty years. That's my only source of income.

Now, I've kind of slowed down. No matter what you do, if you do your best, I think it will last. I think a young artist really has no idea what all is involved if they want to do it for a living. Now if they want to do it as a hobby or part-time, I just tell them,

Continued on pg. 285

Grandson Coming Home by Bill Rabbit, photo by David Fitzgerald

Photo by Jeremy Charles

ed fields

December 10, 1946
Wauhillau, Oklahoma

Some friends of Daddy—he was there in town at Stilwell by the courthouse—were sitting there on the lawn. A friend of Daddy wanted someone to translate the paper for him. And I would say what was in it in Cherokee for Dad. And Dad said, "Let the boy do it." And so Dad handed me the paper and I read it and I would tell his friend. Then I would read it some more and I would interpret a little more and he understood what was in there. I was pretty young. It was way back. We were living at Wauhillau. This was before high school, way back there. Eventually I learned some English because I was doing what he wanted—to read it.

Ms. Webb and also a guy by the name of Starr taught in the big room. That was after fourth grade. By fourth grade, I must have been doing pretty good or something because I had fellow students working on math, and they couldn't understand it. So I was showing them how to work it out, Then one of them (worked the problem) on the board so I could see how it was solved. So I wrote it on the board and solved it for him and things like that. When I was doing that, I wasn't really a mathematic genius, but I understood the math and I just solved it for him; he would copy that down and write that on paper. I guess it was OK with the teacher because he didn't say anything about helping out the student to understand the math problems.

There were Cherokee speakers who were patients who spoke Cherokee, and the nurses wanted me to translate what they said—I guess just to reinforce what they heard, if they didn't understand. I did the same for the nurses, too, to explain what the patients were saying in Cherokee. Because quite a few speakers, they were more at home in the language than in English. So, they wanted to talk in Cherokee. It's been several years ago, back in 2000 or 1999 since I had patients.

Online classes? I've been working at this for a little more than ten years, I guess. Started working in communities around 2000. And then about 2002, they started online classes, and they wanted some online volunteers. They selected us to work with them. There were quite a few of us originally. And each one taught a class. Later on, they all went to their other jobs, and they left me to do my class. Strange at first, you know. I was kind of nervous and didn't know what to say. When I started teaching the language or when I would run out of ideas of what to say, I got a little shy. I tried to interpret the meanings of words and what they were and how you might use it when you are speaking it. But sometimes I would get a little caught up in it and get shy, you know, so I would try and tell stories of how I grew up and what it was like when I grew up. I also got a little bit of animal stories, like traditional stories like that. They seemed to like that. To them, they would say it helps them to learn the language. So, I would use some words in the stories, like Cherokee words, so they could understand some of the stories—I mean not everything in the stories, but some words they could pick out.

Continued on page 285

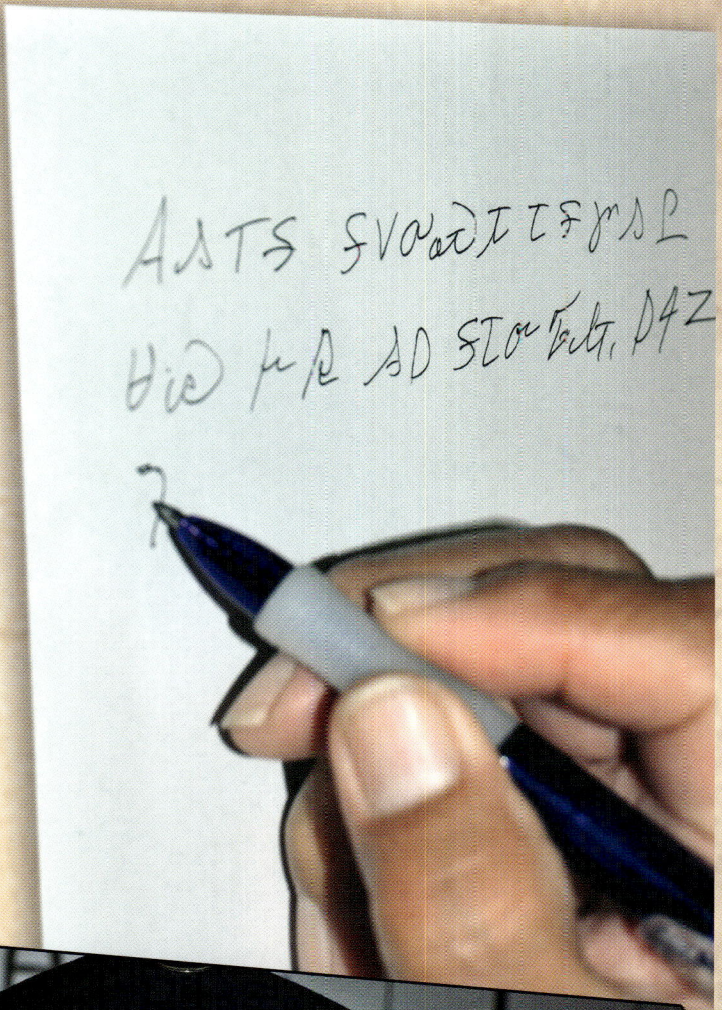

From top: Ed Fields composing in GWY syllabary, photo by Roger Cain; Ed Fields, photo by David Fitzgerald

vivian bush

September 27, 1947
Marble City, Oklahoma

I grew up in Marble City. I've lived in Marble City all my life. I was born here at Hastings over in Tahlequah. Cherokee has always been my first language. I had to learn English at school, and it wasn't very easy, but I guess we managed. Our school was called Henderson School back then. It was a one-room school house, and we had one teacher through the eighth grade.

At our school, I remember at one time there was like sixty of us in one room. And there was very few white children. At the time when we first started, we had this teacher; she didn't want you to talk Cherokee. So some of us would kind of sneak off and talk Cherokee anyway behind her back. And then, after that—after she retired—we got another teacher that come in, and from there, it gradually went to two teachers and three teachers. And somewhere down the line, our school consolidated with Marble City. So that's how Marble City come about. Yep, that's what happened. Eventually, the two schools merged. Instead of Marble City School being right there in town, it's over here where the Henderson School was. And then, they built a new school right there where it is. Not that big, just a long building—enough to hold three classrooms and cafeteria. Hey, we had modern bathrooms in there. From there, after Marble and Henderson were consolidated, well, they expanded the buildings.

I worked as a Cherokee bilingual aide at Marble City School for a few years. I've taught Cherokee (language) classes before. Then I went to regular classroom aide. After that, I took time out to take care of my aunt, my uncle, my mom. Then, I went back to work in the school system now. I cook for the Marble City Warriors!

My grandparents were Dave and Betty Garvin Bush. Everybody was from Marble City, and I guess we'll stay there. I was raised around my mom's family—the Bush family. The whole Bush family was just kind of in a cluster. I would call it Bush Community, myself. I still live in that area. Sam Ed (Bush, Cherokee Nation Tribal Councilor) was my first cousin. His dad was my uncle. My mom's name was Sally. Nancy was my aunt.

Back then, we had plenty of stuff to go look for. There was blackberries. When we were growing up, people raised strawberries, and you could go pick strawberries. Hey, that was a great deal because you got paid! I remember back then it was, like, seven cents a quart, and you had to stem them. I guess the lady—the wife of the man that had Baird's patch— I guess she thought I done real good, cleaning berries and stuff. So, if somebody came along and maybe wanted some strawberries with stems on that they wanted to buy, she'd ask me. And I felt real privileged because it was so much easier than to stem them—just break them off without stemming them. So, that was good. And eventually, I guess it went to ten cents a quart. We thought that was great! Eventually, down the line, I guess it went to twenty-five cents. But, I didn't do that. You know, you got a little bit of money. Proud of it, you know. The wild strawberries I've tasted, they were kind of small and sweet. I don't see those anymore, either. And then huckleberry was the thing, too. If people knew there was huckleberries somewheres,

Continued on page 286

Photo from top: Watercolor by Jamil Jaser, photo by Jeremy Charles; Vivian Bush, photo by Jeremy Charles; Turtle, photo by Emily Thompson

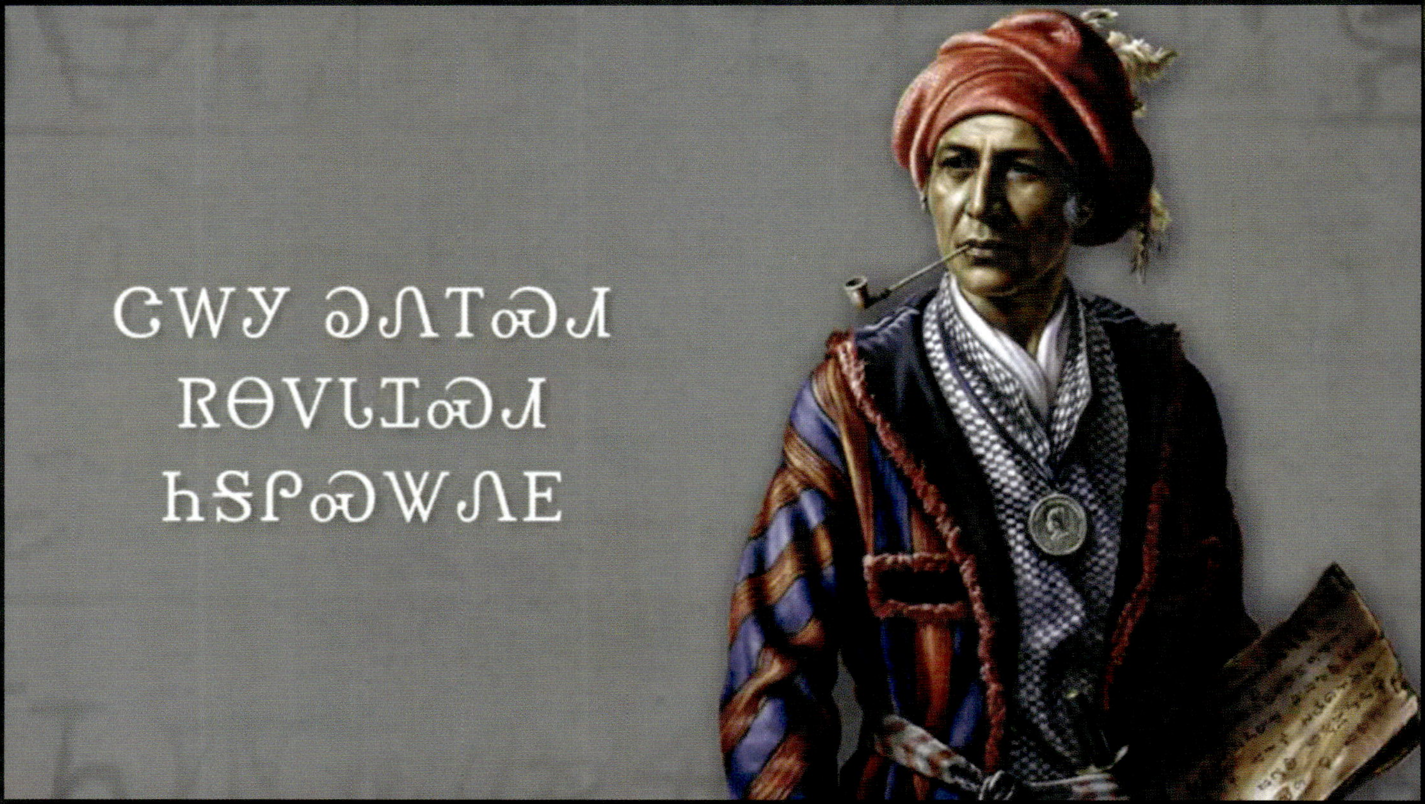
ᏣᎳᎩ ᎧᏁᎢᏍᏗ

CHEROKEE
WORD OF
THE WEEK

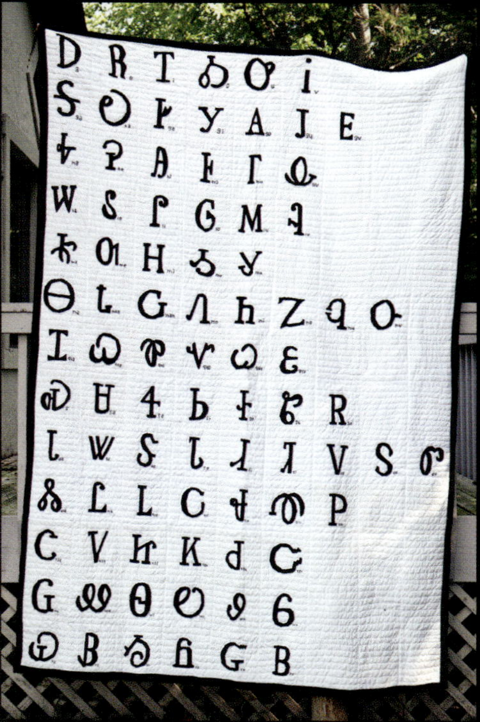

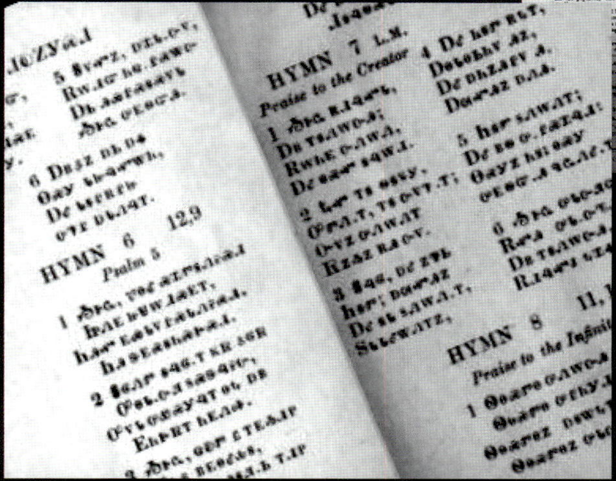
HYMN 7 L.M.
Praise to the Creator
HYMN 6 12.9
Psalm 5
HYMN 8

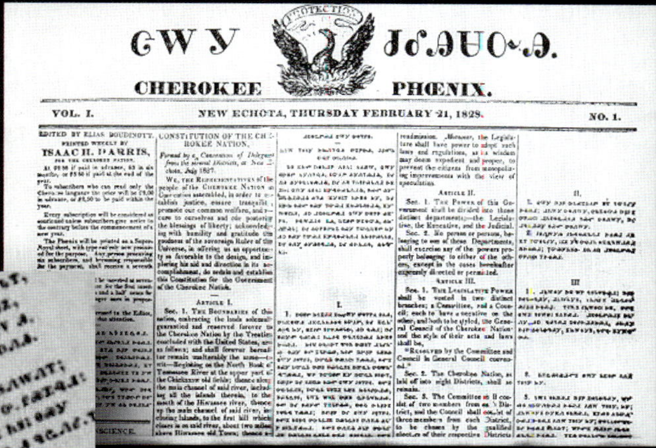
PROTECTION
CHEROKEE PHŒNIX.
VOL. I.
NEW ECHOTA, THURSDAY FEBRUARY 21, 1828.
NO. 1.
CONSTITUTION OF THE CHEROKEE NATION.

martha berry

June 10, 1948
Tulsa, Oklahoma

Photo by Dave Berry

For as long as I can remember, I yearned to know Mattie Eaton, my paternal grandmother. She left this world with five fine sons, but alas, she left before I was born. I grew up playing on our Cherokee allotment land and had lots of wonderful uncles, but I wanted to know what my female Cherokee ancestors were like. All of them had passed before I came along.

I longed to really know them. I wanted to experience their joy and their anger, to see them blush, to hear them giggle, to watch their hands as they kneaded bread dough. I wanted to know those things that you can never know about someone who has passed on. It left a hole in my heart, a space I needed to fill.

In the mid-1980s, when my girls were growing into women, I plunged into studying every book I could find about Cherokee history and culture, trying to fill the void that Mattie had left. I thought, perhaps, if I did something those women had done, I might be able to make the connection I so craved. If I could create a piece of beadwork that required hundreds of little decisions along the way, it would somehow bridge that gap and let me bond with them at last. So I bought a stack of how-to Native American beadwork books and hobby shop supplies and set about learning to bead.

I kept studying Cherokee history, though, and occasionally ran across a photo of a Cherokee beaded artifact or a portrait of a Cherokee wearing beadwork. None of the beadwork in those images looked anything like the beadwork in the how-to books.

I dug deeper and found that most Cherokees stopped producing beadwork at the time of the Indian Removal in the 1830s. Photos of Cherokee beaded artifacts—or old portraits of Cherokees wearing beadwork—were all dated earlier than 1840. Photographs of Cherokees wearing beadwork were all dated after 1920, and in every one I found, the Cherokees were wearing Plains or powwow beadwork. What had happened? How had our exquisitely created beadwork simply vanished?

Now, in addition to the void left by long gone grandmothers, I had a mystery to solve. Through research, I learned that our beadwork, although very similar to the work of the other Southeastern tribes, was quite different from the tribes of the Plains. The

Continued on page 287

From top: Berry Women—Christina, Martha and Karen; Bandolier Bags by Martha Berry; Sun Circle Mocs 2. Photos by Dave Berry.

Photo by David Fitzgerald

margaret wilson

September 23, 1948
Teresita, Oklahoma

My mother was the quilter in the family. I just picked it up from her. (When I was) a teenager, where we attend church at Johnson Prairie Baptist Church, the ladies got together on Wednesday. So we would quilt. And I would go with her, and that is where I started quilting. So I just picked it up from then on. Think I was nineteen. I would sew with the Elders, and we would have a good day on Wednesday and be with ladies and laugh and tell jokes. We would have one lady that would fix our lunch, and we would be there probably from maybe nine o'clock in the morning until maybe two o'clock in the afternoon. We wouldn't finish the quilt that day. We would all sit around the quilt and work on it. There was probably four, maybe five quilts at times being worked on. Work on the quilt and have a good day. I thought it was neat because I was the youngest there. We would have fun. Women would tell jokes about silly little things that they heard from somewhere, and we would all sit around the quilt. I did mainly listen because they were older ladies, and they talked Cherokee, and I didn't talk Cherokee. I could understand, but I couldn't really carry on a conversation with the ladies 'cause I didn't speak the language very well. Still can't at my age, but I can understand pretty good.

So from there on, I kept on quilting and picked it up. Now I have made many quilts and can't even count the quilts I have made since I started. A lot of my quilts are in different states—two out of the country. One in South Korea, and one in England. I have them in Texas, Tulsa. Also in North Carolina, but the ladies asked me if I could just quilt for them—the quilt toppings. I do that as well. Everything is done by hand. My husband wanted to buy me a sewing machine and said, "Wouldn't it be easier if you used a sewing machine?"

I said, "Well, it probably would be, but the sewing machine would just be in my way." I do everything by hand—cut the material by hand and everything by hand. I think they are just more unique that way. No machine quilting or anything like that. To this day, I do not have a sewing machine. And this is the only art that I know. I don't do any other type of art. I just don't have time. Right now, I am doing another quilt top, and it's

already sold before it's ever finished. I was told by a lady just recently she would buy every quilt I make. Got a thing going right there.

But, I do make some of my quilts as gifts—sometimes give them to my children as gifts and wedding gifts. To me, my quilts are just quilts. But others that see them, they can't believe that I do this all by hand. So it is a little work. There's probably some out there that do quilt, but do the machine quilting. And there is nothing wrong with machine quilting. But to me, I would rather do it all by hand. That's what I'm used to doing and am always going to do it that way.

I have one little grandson. He is six years old now. If I'm just sitting working on a quilt top, cutting my pieces out, he wants to pull a needle through the fabric and thinks he's quilting.

Continued on page 287

Top: "Mom and Dad," Eli Blossom and Sarah Blossom; Bottom: Margaret Wilson quilt, photo by Roger Cain; Margaret Wilson quilting, photo by Sammy Still

william cabbagehead

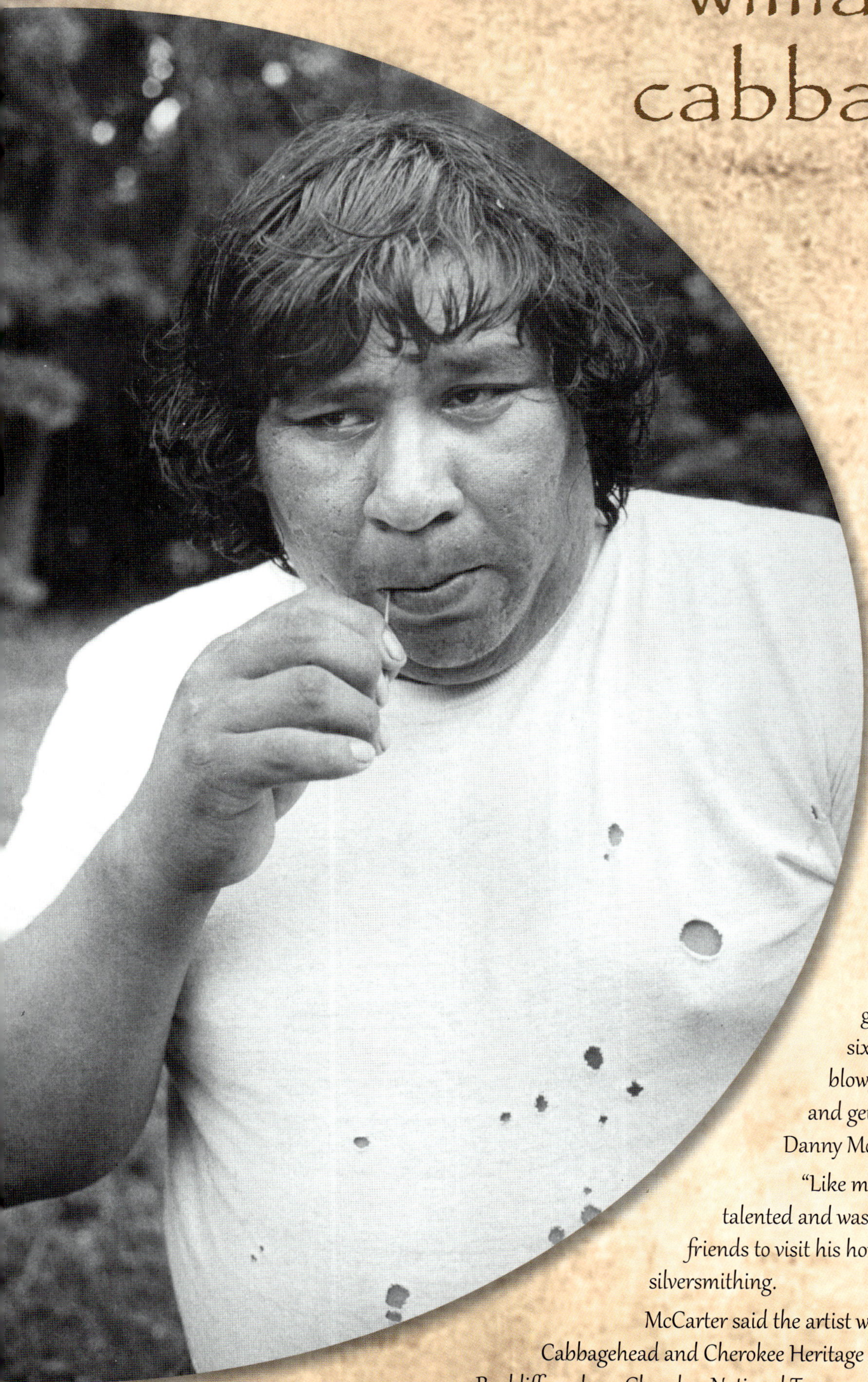

November 2, 1948
Tailholt, Oklahoma

By the 1960s, Cherokee craft making had dwindled as fewer Cherokee people practiced what their ancestors had carried forward. In the late 1960s while Vinita resident Anna Sixkiller Mitchell was gathering clay and researching the pottery work of her Southeastern ancestors, few Cherokee men were making bows and arrows or blowguns like their forefathers.

Later, Mitchell would be credited with bringing back Cherokee pottery to the Cherokee people, and she would be named a Cherokee National Treasure. Today, many of her former students are producing their own award-winning pottery.

While Mitchell saved pottery making, in the 1970s William Cabbagehead was instrumental in saving river-cane blowgun making for the Cherokee people. "He's really the man who is responsible for keeping the blowgun going because back to the '70s, there were only about six guys who shot the blowgun. He would give people blowguns just to try to get them to come out and shoot and get them interested in it," said current Diligwa villager Danny McCarter.

"Like many Cherokee artists, Cabbagehead was multi-talented and was also a silversmith," McCarter said. He would invite friends to visit his house in Grandview, north of Tahlequah, to learn silversmithing.

McCarter said the artist was always willing to teach others what he knew. Cabbagehead and Cherokee Heritage Center Tsa-la-gi Ancient Village Chief Scott Rackliff—also a Cherokee National Treasure—had a lot of influence on McCarter, teaching him how to make a blowgun and darts for the gun when McCarter worked in the village as a young man. Today, McCarter is an accomplished blowgun and blowgun-dart maker and also teaches others what he learned from Cabbagehead and Rackliff.

"You could always tell William's blowguns because they had big knuckles—joints on the river cane pole—on them," McCarter said. "He probably had the longest blowguns—10-feet long— I've seen around here. He was good-sized fellow, especially for a Cherokee guy." McCarter said he and his brother Rob would go out to Cabbagehead's house on weekends and have blowgun shoots with fellow blowgun shooters Chester Oosahwee and James Oosahwee.

"His wife was really nice. She would always fix something to eat. We would go out there and shoot on a Sunday," he said.

McCarter believes Cabbagehead learned his skills at an early age before he began working at the Ancient Village in the 1970s. McCarter also worked with him in the original Trail of Tears drama that was once produced at the Cherokee Heritage Center in the 1970s and 1980s during summers. "Cabbagehead would show off his blowgun-shooting skills—during the nightly drama and during downtimes for other cast members—by accurately shooting targets thirty to forty feet away," McCarter said.

From top: Frog bracelet made by William Cabbagehead (from the collection of Betty Frogg,) photo by Roger Cain; William Cabbagehead shooting blowgun at Cherokee Holiday, photo courtesy of the Cherokee National Historical Society; Blow gun made of river cane and blow darts made of Bois D'arc and Scottish thistle by William Cabbagehead

Cabbagehead made his blowgun darts from Bois D'arc and Black Locust trees. "He made the prettiest darts that you've ever seen. Black Locust is really what I remember him making them out of. They were light brown," McCarter said.

For his thistle, which is placed at the back end of the dart to help with its flight, McCarter said, "Cabbagehead tied two pieces of thistle to his darts while other

Continued on page 288

victoria mitchell vazquez

March 23, 1949
Vinita, Oklahoma

I was born in Claremore Indian Hospital and raised in Vinita, Oklahoma. My parents were Robert and Annabelle Sixkiller Mitchell. In my family there were five children—myself, three sisters, and one brother. Two of my siblings have passed on. There are three of us girls left now, and our lives are very different from one another. It just so happened that I am the only one of the five who had the desire to learn pottery. I feel very honored in that respect, that I am the Mitchell who's carrying this art forward.

I've worked in other employment positions, but in the late 1980s, I approached my mom to ask if I could apprentice with her. Really, it was just to spend some time with her and also to learn pottery. She was open to it and even happy about it. It really didn't happen until 1990, but it was a wonderful time. My dad was retired, both parents were in good health, and I was forty years old. I went to live with them in Vinita and, really, it was the first time that I had gotten to spend any time with my parents as an adult. It was wonderful!

Mom and I would go out and work a few hours every day. I also would sit on the back patio with Dad, who sat in the lounge chair and held his cat on his lap while we talked and looked out over the back of their ten acres. All you could see were trees and a pond and his birdhouses. My dad loved birds. There was a rock wall that Daddy had built, over the years, from rocks that came from the place where they built their home. It was also where Mom originally found the clay.

Daddy was a big part of Mom's pottery. I learned so much from him. He'd talk about the trials of helping Mom with the pottery and the travel. Then when Mom and I were together, she would just start talking as we worked in the clay. I wish I had recorded some of the things that she said. A lot of what she said wasn't even about the art, but stories about the family, her grandparents, my grandparents, and the events and people who had shaped her. We talked about everything. I just listened and soaked up all that I could. It was difficult to hear about her childhood, her life in boarding school. For me, those stories were heart-wrenching. It's hard to imagine how awful it would be, as a child, to not be able to live with your parents and then to be stuck away in some big building with a bunch of other kids. It was difficult to hear, but I'm glad I listened. I learned so much about her.

I spent a year with her and learned how to dig the clay, how to process it, how to wood fire, how to hand build and I absolutely loved it. That year of study and apprenticing with her was priceless. At the end of that wonderful year, I went back to Houston, Texas. I knew I couldn't make a living of pottery at that point in time, so I returned home to work in sales.

After Daddy died in 1998, I returned to Vinita to spend time with Mom, and then I decided to move back. That's really when I got serious about pottery. I guess I'm a mixture of both a traditional and contemporary artist, but it's hard. One of the things that I struggle with in the making of my art, is that I don't do it exactly the way Mom did. I still get the clay and process it like she showed me, and I still hand build. All of those things are the same. I use natural tools that are either found in nature or are handmade. The part where I feel challenged is that I don't have an outdoor firing facility at our ranch like Mom had in her backyard. So I do most of my firing in an electric

Continued on page 288

Photo by David Fitzgerald

Victoria Mitchell Vazquez and her mother, Anna Belle Sixkiller Mitchell.

Photo by Mesha Sanchez

painting 2011

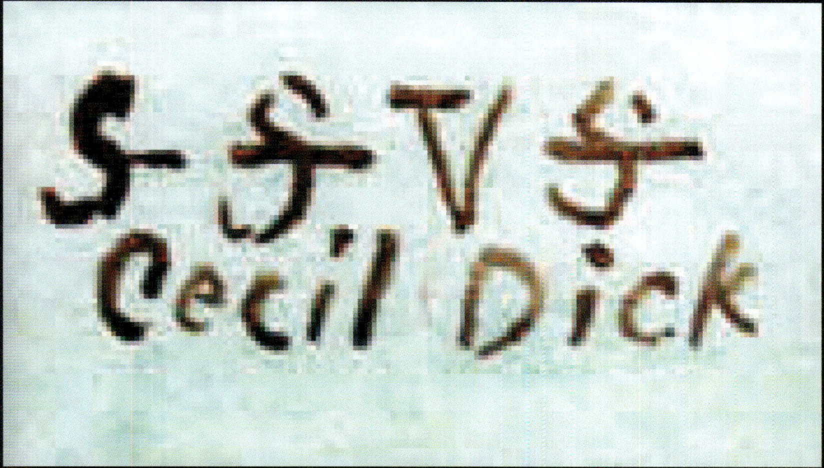
Cecil Dick

CHEROKEE SALINE COURTHOUSE

donald vann

October 22, 1949
Cherry Tree, Oklahoma

Donald Vann grew up in Adair County immersed in the Cherokee culture, thanks to his uncles and his grandfather, who took him hunting and camping. Those lessons and the places he would visit later in life became part of his watercolor paintings. For more than forty years, Vann has exhibited his work throughout the United States and Europe and has received numerous awards. In 2009, he moved from Austin, Texas, to Tahlequah, Oklahoma, where he set up a new gallery. He takes an occasional tour to galleries across the country, but most of his work is now showcased and sold online including originals, prints, and low-cost posters.

In 2013, Vann, now 67, was named a Cherokee National Treasure to honor his work that showcases Cherokee culture and history. "Of all the awards I have received throughout my career, receiving one from my peers and the Cherokee Nation has meant the most to me," Vann said. "I am honored and thankful."

His specialty is paintings using watercolors. He also adds "a lot of airbrush" to his paintings, which he said mixes well with watercolors. "I've been doing watercolors ever since I began. I've tried other mediums, but with watercolors I have better control, and it's a little more forgiving than other mediums," he said. "In doing watercolors, I believe it works very well with the type of artwork that I'm doing, which is Indian art. When I look at oil paintings, I think cowboy art or portraits and acrylics can go both ways—western art or Native

art. Also, it depends on the artist and how they want to go with it. It's open, but to me I believe watercolors really belong in the Indian art field."

Vann recalled the first time he made money creating his art. He was about ten years old and in the fifth grade. One of his teachers asked him to do a drawing of Christ hanging on the cross for the Easter holiday. He did the drawing and earned twenty-five cents. "It was just a black-and-white drawing, but twenty-five cents back in those days was a lot of money," he said "It went on over the years. People started recognizing my drawing ability, and one thing led to another, and an agent recognized my ability."

The agent, Nettie Wheeler, also operated an antique store in Muskogee called the Thunderbird Gift Shop. When he was about thirteen, Wheeler introduced Vann to Muscogee (Creek) artist Jerome Tiger, who was represented by Wheeler, and was getting attention for his watercolor art depicting his culture. "They were looking for people like me who might have the ability to continue and expand the painting of Indians. I'd never heard of Jerome Tiger at the time," Vann said.

Vann met Tiger to determine if Tiger could help him further develop his artistic talent. Tiger took Vann to an art store in Muskogee where they purchased drawing tablets, and Tiger asked Vann to "do a lot of

Continued on page 288

Clockwise from top: Donald Vann circa 1970, photo courtesy of artist; Suspicious Sign (left) and Evening Reflection (right), photo by Will Chavez; Lone Scout by Donald Vann, photo by Will Chavez

bill glass jr

March 15, 1950
Locust Grove, Oklahoma

My parents are Bill and Jean Glass. Dad, Bill Glass Sr. worked for the Bureau of Indian Affairs, and my mother, Ellen Jean Justice, was a nurse. After retirement, both were well known for their volunteer work for our tribe. Gregg Glass and Geri Glass Pearce are my brother and sister; they, too, have contributed in many good ways to the Cherokee Nation of Oklahoma. My contribution is through my art.

My art career began when I decided to attend the Institute of American Indian Arts in Santa Fe, New Mexico, in 1973-75. IAIA is just a two-year school so you can't really learn enough. Since then, I have continued on my own by researching, asking questions and experimenting. I am a contemporary artist who does sculpture, pottery, and design work. My primary medium is clay. I chose to work with clay because I am continually amazed by this natural substance that can be worked with your hands and be fired so hot that a metamorphic change occurs, making it impervious to water. I fire my work between cone 5 and cone 6. I take a scientific approach in developing many of my own glaze recipes, trying to create differences between glossy, matte, and various colored glazes and engobes. This addition has been something that has helped set my work apart from other ceramists all these years.

Our tribal heritage as Southeast Indians provides artists with a wealth of ideas to pursue. Design variations and quality of work are the keys in creating something new and exciting. Throughout my career, I have felt that the Creator has guided me and always provided for me during the many ups and downs of an artist's existence. In 2005, I successfully formed a group of Cherokee artists who were commissioned by the city of Chattanooga, Tennessee, to do a public art project, at what was formerly Ross's Landing, the point of embarkation for the Trail of Tears journeys.

The majority of the work was done at Glass Studio in Locust Grove, Oklahoma. This job led to my son, Demos Glass, and myself getting to work with internationally known architect Cesar Pelli. In 2007, we designed four, twenty-two-foot, southeast-style, terrazzo floor medallions for Tulsa's new events arena, the BOK (Bank of Oklahoma) Center. Since that time, my son, Demos, who is a metals artist, and I have continued to collaborate on several interesting Cherokee Nation-related public art projects, using a variety of mediums from ceramics, stainless steel, plastics, and powder-coated metal.

I believe in cultural preservation through the arts, whether it is of a contemporary or traditional style. Art has no boundaries if we as artists continue to have vision and confidence and strive to push the envelope further. Thank you to my family, friends, other artists, teachers, and collectors who have helped me pursue my career.

I am honored to be a Cherokee National Treasure.

— Bill Glass Jr.

Interviewed by Pamela Jumper Thurman

"Touch to Above"
A.I.C.C.M.
Oklahoma City, Oklahoma
13'6"x 10'½" x 2'

"Healer"
4' x 4'

"Sleeping Under Watchful Eyes"
Private Collection
17'3/4" x 13'3/4" x 13' 3/8"

"Mound Influences"
19 1/4" x12 5/8" x 12 5/8"
All photos provided by Glass Studios

Photo by Will Chavez

knokovtee scott

February 10, 1951
Marble City, Oklahoma

I am Cherokee/Muscogee Creek from the Marble City area. My mother is a Cherokee. Some of my first earlier pieces were of my Cherokee background. One of the basic designs I use is the Four Log symbol. After I came back from New York City at a show at the Museum of the American Indian, the Heye Foundation, I started thinking about my experiences up there. One thing I try to do with my artwork is to combine the old motifs with things that are very contemporary. I tried to incorporate those two concepts into one piece in which I carved the traditional design of the birdman flying over or through the city, to try to see what the city was like, to learn about it, then to come back and to bring that experience from his past.

I was taught if something good exists, it never dies. It just needs to be stumbled upon again. Maybe this was one way the old Indian people thought they could communicate with us here in the future. Indian people have been doing this for the last 2000 years. Now it's come full turn, and everybody is starting to look at these things again and realize the design importance and the impact it has. Even though the designs are very, very old, they haven't lost their vitality or freshness. They have so much strength and so much power to them that sometimes, in the art worl,d we want to incorporate that into our work somehow to give it strength, to capture that. So that's what I've been trying to do—continue that to capture that strength and vitality. And if other people can see this, they can feel it too.

Clockwise from bottom: Knokovtee Scott teaching at the Cherokee Art Center, photo courtesy of Cherokee Phoenix; Mussel Shell gorget and beads by Knokovtee Scott. Collection of (and photo by) Pamela Jumper Thurman; Mussel Shell Miniatures

I prefer to go and find my own materials, my purple shells. The purple mussel shells are rare and hard to find. When I can find one, it's a rare treat. It's like a gift from nature. I find it and take it back and use it and make something out of it, add a little bit of something to the beauty of it, then make it into something else somebody else can appreciate. From the beginning to the end, that whole process is important to me.

Once I've gotten the shell to the shop, I look for the things I can bring out in the shell as I cut it. The first step is to mark out the different parts that I want to cut out. I just pencil this on in straight lines. This will be my trim tracks, and these different sections of the shell will be used for different parts of my jewelry. The outer edge, the thicker lip part, will be used for the beads. The center part will be used for the gorgets. The lower end will be used for the crescents and also for earrings. Some parts of the shell sometimes has imperfections in it. These are blister pearls, and I try to save this part and incorporate it into some form of jewelry later. I also cut out the hinge area for earrings, and I'll save all this part later for beads. The next step is to go ahead and trim out the shell.

In 1972, I went to the Institute of American Indian Arts in Santa Fe, New Mexico. While there,

Continued on page 289

dennis sixkiller

Photo by Pamela Jumper Thurman

November 4, 1953
Jay, Oklahoma

I was born in Jay, Oklahoma, to Houston and Lillie Mae Davis Sixkiller. My dad's Cherokee name was *Ulogili* (Cloud) and my mother's Cherokee name was *Leli*. I was born in a two-room house that my dad and older brother built. We didn't have running water or electricity. Cherokee was the language that was spoken in our home. Dad talked to us in Cherokee all of the time. I was third to the youngest of my siblings. My older siblings went to school and brought English back into our home, so I learned from them. I think they had a rough time of it.

I attended Jay Public School and graduated in 1972. I played sports—a little baseball and a little football—but my best memories are of the times with my family and the time spent in our church. Our family went to Piney Baptist Church where they sang and preached in Cherokee. Back then, Cherokee was prevalent; you could hear it everywhere. Now, you don't hear it as much; to me, it sounds really good when I hear it. I don't really hear it very often, though.

As I grew older, I didn't speak the language as much as I should have, especially when I started school. I started to speak more English then. Even after high school, I just didn't talk it as much.

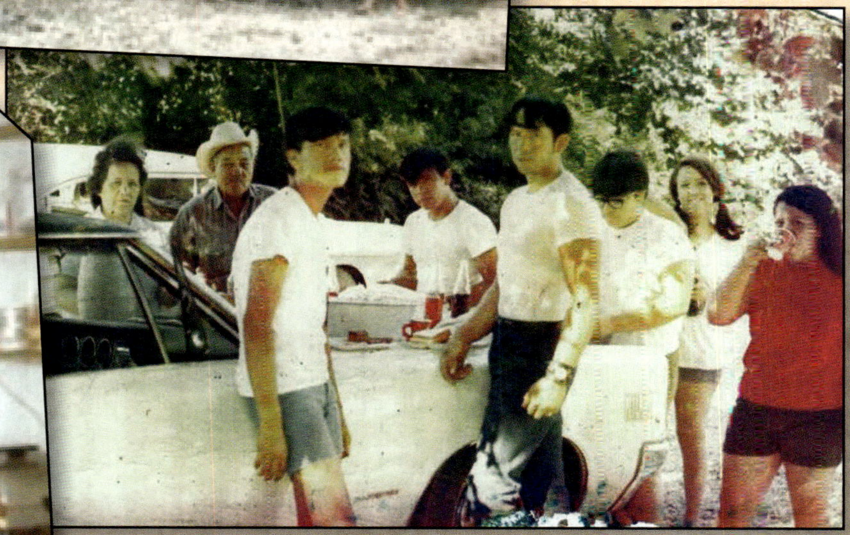

Clockwise from top: Dennis Sixkiller school picture; Dennis's dad, Kenny, Dennis's mom, Johnny, Josie, Dennis, Priscilla, and Sammy swimming at the creek; Dennis picnicking with family on Dennis brother's 1967 Lemans; Dennis at dinner at his mom and stepdad's place in Jay, OK.

I started working at the Cherokee Nation in 1991, twenty-five years ago. My first job was in housekeeping, where I worked for seven years. My second job was in the mailroom, delivering mail and going to the post office. I worked there just one week shy of seven years. Then I transferred to the communications department and started doing the radio show, *Cherokee Voices and Cherokee Sounds*, because of David Scott, who had been doing the show. We had talked quite a bit before that, and we always liked talking in Cherokee. He was leaving and asked me if I wanted to do what he was doing. I thought he was kidding. Then a few weeks later, he asked me again if I would be interested and that if I was, he would recommend me. So I said I would try it, and I I've been trying now for twelve years.

I had to go back and learn how to say some of words when I started working in the language program. Now I work the first half of the week in the communications department and the second half in education, or translation.

I was shocked to learn I was chosen to be a Cherokee National Treasure, but I was very honored, too. I believe that our language is the heart of our culture; it's our history. You have to practice it, just like when you play an instrument. You have to practice that instrument until it sounds good. Language is like that, too. Our language is the most important thing in our culture. An Elder I interviewed years ago said his Elder told him that the day we lose our language is the day we lose our identity as Cherokee. It's true. If you lose your language, you're just like all of the other people.

I think that I just took for granted that our Cherokee language would always be around, but I was wrong. A few years ago, there were twenty-four speakers who passed away in one month! That was really a loss.

Continued on page 290

beadwork

2013

richard shade

April 17, 1954
Fourteen Mile Creek, Oklahoma

I used to shoot a compound bow—recurved, laminated, fiberglass. I always wanted a wood bow. I basically knew how to make one, heard stories, and saw some of the older guys make bows. It was early fall, and I was bow hunting behind the house. Mom's old house. It's on restricted land there on Fourteen Mile Creek. I was back there hunting and I sat down by a tree for a sign—to see if a deer had been through there. I was thinking about a Bois D'arc tree and if I could find one around here. I looked around my feet and seen a horse-apple lying there. I thought, "That's weird; there ain't no Bois D'arc around here."

I sat there for thirty minutes and when I got up and got around, the tree I had been learning against was a Bois D'arc tree. It was a perfect Bois D'arc tree! It was the perfect diameter, about eight or nine inches. Straight for about eleven foot, and it just went crazy up there. That's the only Bois D'arc in that area. That was weird the way I found that. Then I left and I came back later on that winter, I guess it was in December, and I cut down that tree. I started making bows right there.

I knew it had to be done in the winter when the sap was down. Trees go dormant and sap goes down. I was just in a hurry to cut it and believe it was December. All the pieces made a good bow. Mom's dad was Looney R. Gourd. Their name was Rattlinggourd. (That was) their real name; they (had) shortened it to just R. Gourd. Anyway, he used to make bows. You know, after I found that tree, I was walking around that area. I found an old

Photo by Jeremy Charles

Clockwise from bottom: Richard Shade, photo by David Fitzgerald; Richard Shade taking a shot, photo by Roger Cain; Bows and Arrows hand-made by Richard Shade, photo by Roger Cain

log— an old Bois D'arc log—down there that somebody had cut. It had been laying there and had rotted. It had worm holes all over. Somebody had cut it a long time ago with an axe. The only person I knew around here was Looney. I actually picked it up and took it home (to) see if I could make a bow out of it. There really wasn't enough for a bow there. He was the one that probably cut that.

The tree that I found was a big tree, and after that, I heard that the old timers would bend down a tree—like a little sapling or a bigger tree—and either tie it down or break it down. What happens when it's growing down is the shoot will grow up and grow straight. Well, that tree that I found was like that. It had grown like that, and then it had shot up. I don't know if he did that or not. But if he did it, he made a real good stave.

I started making bows after that and I have ever since. I was in my twenties—I guess twenty-four, twenty-five, twenty-six—somewhere in there. You know what, I made a bow. I basically knew what a longbow looked like, and I just wanted to do a real good job on it. Make one myself.

Black Locust is a wood I use a lot. I've tried hickory. Hickory is kind of a soft wood,. I don't really like it for a bow. It is good wood if you dry it out right. Some guys make nice bows out of hickory. But Black Locust is a good wood.

Continued on page 290

john ross

February 16, 1955
Greasy, Oklahoma

I was reared in the rural Cherokee community of Greasy in Adair County. Cherokee language was very important to me in my early childhood years. Cherokee language shaped me into who I am today. I am bi-literate in the Cherokee language with English as my secondary language.

Cherokee was the only language spoken in our home because my parents spoke very little English. We, the children, were not required to speak only Cherokee. It was just natural to speak only Cherokee after school.

My world is surrounded with my language; I work with it every day. I work forty hours a week with the language, and I do freelance translation from home for clients. I am working with the language eleven to twelve hours a day. I think in Cherokee, and I have to process the English language in Cherokee before I speak in English. I got started translating the Cherokee language by chance. I was the official language translator and interpreter for Cherokee Nation Community Services. When a job announcement was issued for a translation specialist position, I jumped at the chance and applied for the position in the Cherokee Nation Education Services Translation Department. I was really fortunate to be selected for the job.

My mother, Nancy Augerhole Ross, started teaching me to read the Cherokee Bible when I was twelve years old, and I never stopped learning. I have been working with the Cherokee language for over forty years. It is gratifying for me to be working with my first language. Now, it is very important to create many different ways to teach the language by publishing books, translating books, saving the spoken language by audio and video, and creating a computer language that will be viable for Cherokee use.

JOHN ROSS HOME

My biggest breakthrough working with the language has been decoding Sequoyah's numeral system. Not many people know that Sequoyah invented Cherokee numbers. However, the Cherokee Nation Tribal Council never adopted the number system. Sequoyah created numbers from one to a million, and I created numbers zero—important in any number system—billion, trillion, and quadrillion. I was able to decode Sequoyah's old number system, and I have created a tutorial book to learn the number system and a calendar.

The most difficult aspect of working with the language would have to be translating the Cherokee writing our ancestors left behind. We just don't have enough translators to do the work. We will never be able to translate the numerous documents in museums, which will take many years and more translators. I have heard people say we have 10 to 20,000 fluent speakers. That's just not the case. I wish that was true. We will be lucky to have 1,500 to 2,000 fluent speakers left, and that's counting the Eastern Band of Cherokees! We are losing fluent Cherokee speakers every year. In my opinion, the speakers in our communities will have to take the lead in saving our Cherokee language and start teaching the children and our grandchildren.

As a nation, we can start daycare centers in the heart of our communities, where the speakers are still prevalent, and teach the babies and our young

Continued on page 291

Clockwise from top left: John Ross standing next to his ancestral home in Georgia, photo courtesy of artist; UKB Chief John Ross standing next to portrait of his ancestor, Cherokee Nation Chief John Ross; John Ross as youth in Adair County, photo courtesy of artist

JOHN ROSS HOME

betty christie frogg

Photo by David Fitzgerald

August 7, 1955
Wauhillau, Oklahoma

Like most Cherokees around here, I was born in Tahlequah, Oklahoma, Hastings Hospital, August 7, 1955. I think my parents were both born at home. Dad is Lacie Christie. Mom is Louise Christie—Louise Ross. She was born in Salina. Wauhillau Community, Adair County, is where I am from. I was raised right down the hill across the creek. Dad bought ten acres off of my grandpa, Bill Christie Sr. This is originally allotted land that he had. Yes, and I'm trying to hang on to it. If I could put my land back in trust, I would. I hear that it can be done, but I don't really know the process. If I knew the process, I would do it. I would put it back. So, I pay taxes on this land. I try to pay taxes on the whole ten acres Dad had. I had to fight for this place. I fought for him (brother) and it didn't turn out even though this house was on our land. It didn't work out for him. He said, "I'm tired of fighting." But I ended up with it, because I fought for it. I didn't want anyone else to have it because it was on Christie land!

First memories of school? Aha, Seneca Indian School, Wyandotte, Oklahoma. In fact, my brother, my older brother, went first, which I didn't know. It was like one day, I didn't have an older brother around.

Betty and Mom at Stilwell Court House, waiting on the bus to Seneca Indian School; Calvin, Harvey, and Betty Christie, Wauhillau Community; White Oak Basket with black walnut dye, photo by David Fitzgerald

And then, when it came time for me to go to school, they sent me to Seneca Indian School, too. That's where I found my brother! I had no idea where he was. They didn't talk about things like that. They didn't say, "Your brother's at school." I guess they thought it wasn't any of our business and wouldn't affect us in any way. I spent two years at Seneca Indian School. My dad told me not to cry. He said, "Don't cry." He said there's nothing he could do. Nothing we could do. "Don't cry." I never cried while I was there.

They used to take us to the courthouse in Stilwell, and they'd put us on this bus. And, we'd end up at Seneca Indian School. Well, this one year, they didn't do that. They took us to Wauhillah School, just a couple of miles down the road here, and enrolled us there. I was in public school ever since. Seneca Indian School was a total experience. I didn't speak English. I didn't even know there were other people around besides Cherokees. And we weren't allowed to speak Cherokee up there, because there were all other tribes represented at that school. I had no idea when I learned it. I know I learned to speak English at Seneca Indian School. I learned a lot of things. I actually got to watch "The Wizard of Oz." That scared the crap out of me! It was the flying monkeys. I didn't know what to think about that. I was little, and I'd never seen anything like that before, you know.

I learned to speak English at boarding school. But, when I came back here and they enrolled us at Wahillau, Dad would always say, in Cherokee, "Don't speak English to me." Even though he could understand it, he said, "Speak Cherokee." He would say I would use it one of these days. He said always talk to him in Cherokee, *"Jalagi squa tla no he di esdi."*

"Speak to me in Cherokee," he said." There's no sense in speaking English to me." I thought all that stuff was normal, I guess, because this is what we were taught. But it wasn't until after I was grown when I realized (that) what the boarding school was (meant to do) was to take the language away from the people. And that's why I

Continued on page 292

tonia hogner-weavel

September 16, 1956
Hardesty, Oklahoma

Photo by Jeremy Charles

Sewing began, for me, with embroidery. My mother taught me embroidery stitches and ordered pillowcase and tea towel kits for my practice. I always enjoyed needlework. I grew up in Hardesty, Oklahoma, a small farming town in Texas County where I showed lambs as my 4-H project, helped Dad with the wheat crop, drove the truck as my brother bucked bales and learned to work hard. I grew up in an artistically bland world. There was little theater or music and certainly no Cherokee culture. But I craved it. My mother fed my thirst by introducing me to dance, piano, and voice lessons.

We vacationed every summer in the Fairfield Community, Adair County, where my granny, Katie Hogner, lived. This was my dad's home and, being one of eleven children, I had plenty of cousins to pass the summertime. For a long time, I thought everyone vacationed in Stilwell, Oklahoma, because that's the only vacation place I knew. In the early days, my dad's family would travel to the Panhandle to find migratory work, and on these trips, they would play baseball. The Indian boys from Stilwell could really play ball. Natural gas companies in the Panhandle began to form baseball teams and would recruit players by offering them a job to work for their company. My dad was recruited as a pitcher for Panhandle Eastern Pipeline. He retired from that same job thirty-eight years later.

My maternal grandmother literally went to the Panhandle in a wagon. She was born in Kiowa-Comanche-Apache Lands, although she was not Indian. My mother was born in Hardesty and met my dad while he was working and playing baseball. I was born in Perryton, Texas, but I am truly a child of the union of Oklahoma Territory and Indian Territory which formed the state of Oklahoma. My history ranges from one side of the state to the other.

During my teenage years, I had the pleasure of being in the *Trail of Tears Drama* in 1974 and 1976. This was during the heyday of the drama when the cast was eighty strong and the 1800-seat theater was filled six nights a week. Exposure to acting and dancing only fueled my desire to be a part of the performing art world. After graduating from Oklahoma State University in 1979, I moved to Tahlequah to find employment. I was hired by Cherokee Nation in 1980 and have worked for the tribe off and on since then.

I learned to sew in home economics class at Hardesty Schools where I attended all twelve years. I never liked to sew as a teenager and had a task master for a sewing teacher. However, all those basic skills she taught me have lasted a lifetime. My introduction to the Cherokee tear dress came when I competed for Miss Cherokee in 1982. Ruth England—now a Cherokee National Treasure—made my dress. She was my first teacher and probably doesn't even know it. I turned that dress inside out and measured every piece. I tried redoing everything as she had done. The first tear dress I made was for my friend's young daughter. Fifteen years later, I made that daughter an adult tear dress to compete in Miss Cherokee. That was a circle completed and a proud moment for me.

All I know about tear-dress making was learned from my mentor, Wendell Cochran. I call him the "Father of the Tear Dress." I learned so much from him. He hired me to make three dresses—I'm sure, to test me. He then proceeded to tell me all I had done wrong. I have never made those mistakes again! He is a bright and intelligent man, and I have immense respect

Continued on page 292

Clockwise from left: Cherokee Tear Dress and Jacket made by Tonia Weavel, photo by Jeremy Charles; traditional and contemporary Cherokee clothing by Tonia Hogner-Weavel; Tonia with sons Parker and Wrighter Weavel, photo by Jeremy Charles

flute making 2013

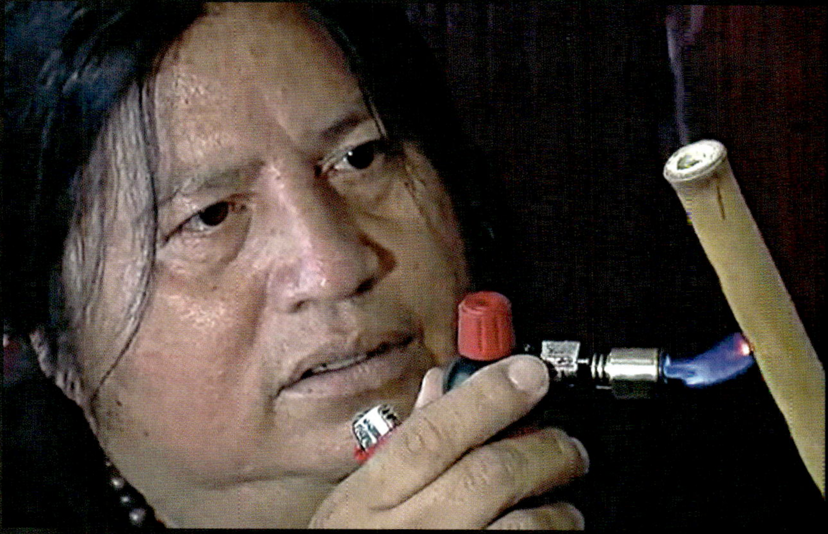

In 1990, I got hired at the Cherokee Heritage Center, Tsa-la-gi Ancient Village. That's where I learned about river-cane blowguns and flutes. One day, my buddy, Jay Yahola, and I started experimenting on how to make a river-cane flute. After we learned how to make them, I kept making them, and blowguns, too. After a year of making flutes, I learned to compose my first song. I still make river-cane flutes and perform for my tribe, the Cherokee Nation! I always appreciate my parents and ancestors for the beautiful Cherokee heritage I've been raised in and live my life as much as I can with pride and honor. ***Osda!***

—Tommy Wildcat

***Pictured left:** Completed river cane flutes, photo by Tommy Wildcat; This page, left to right: Healthy river cane, photo by Roger Cain; Tommy Wildcat flute making, photo by Kristen Dickerson; Harvested river cane, photo by Roger Cain*

david scott

February 14, 1957
Rocky Mountain, Oklahoma

Photo by Will Chavez

I get my talent from my dad. I used to watch him carve things. He was kind of a perfectionist. He made a lot of stuff—canes, bows, that kind of stuff. I was influenced by my dad as far as the art, and I was influenced by my dad as far as the language.

He always encouraged us to speak the language, especially at home. When we got back from school, English stopped and Cherokee began. We knew that rule, and if we didn't follow it, we got in trouble.

Reading and writing Cherokee is another thing he stressed. I don't know how many syllabary charts he made in his lifetime; it was quite a few. Every spare time he had, he was making charts for one of us kids or all of us. In the end, some of us retained it and some of us didn't.

When I was growing up, I thought every family was the same as far as the language. I thought every parent did that for their kids, but as I got older, I found out that wasn't true at all. I found out later on parents, based on what (they had) experienced, didn't want their kids to learn to even speak (Cherokee), let alone read and write it. I guess in the end, we were the exceptions. And that's the same thing with our culture. I always thought every family was like that but come to find out, we were the exception.

If I had my preference, I would rather get it for the language rather than my art. I think there's some people out here in these communities that are far more deserving. I know one lady; she never had any ties with the Cherokee Nation, but she always taught the language, and that's the kind of person you're looking for. She never wanted anything from the Nation. She just done it on her own. To me that's who is more deserving of winning an award.

Me, I was involved and have been fortunate enough to be involved in making videos. That's how I got involved. It was kind of like an accident, really. I was just there at the right time and right place. We got to make some videos that were in Cherokee. Some of them are still around, and there are some publications where my name is (listed) that I helped with. There are even some movies that I've helped with. I've had people call me off the set about the right way to say things.

As far as the Nation's concerned, we've made some strides, but I don't think we've gone far enough. My thinking about the language is there's got to be a way to teach

Continued on page 293

Clockwise from top left: David Scott, photo by D. Fitzgerald; Gourd Carving by David Scott, photo by D. Fitzgerald; Gourd Mask by David Scott, photo by Will Chavez

Rosie Chewie with basketry wall hanging, photo by David Fitzgerald

rosie chewie

February 17, 1957
Little Kansas, Oklahoma

Rosie Chewie was born on February 17, 1957, in Claremore, Oklahoma. She is the daughter of Cherokee Treasure Marie Proctor. Rosie loved to carry on her Cherokee tradition through making Native American baskets and blankets. She also enjoyed watching World Wrestling Entertainment. Her favorite wrestler was The Rock.

Rosie always liked spending time outdoors, and she especially loved to go fishing. Family was important to her, and she always looked forward to family time and cherished each moment that she had with her children. She was a caring and loving mother to her sons.

Rosie was chosen in 2000 as a Cherokee National Treasure for her artistry in traditional buck brush Cherokee basketry. Rosie and her mother, Marie, are an example of the tradition of passing down cultural knowledge to other family members. Marie taught her daughter the art of basket weaving. Like her mother, Rosie used traditional materials and natural dyes for her artistry. She created her baskets from both honeysuckle and buck brush and used walnut and bloodroot as her traditional dyes. Rosie was also a quilter and made lovely quilts for family and friends.

Rosie had three sons—William, Michael, and Jonathan.

Obituary information
Courtesy of Shipman's Funeral Service, Pryor, Oklahoma
Compiled by Pamela Jumper Thurman

Clockwise from left: Rosie Chewie, photo courtesy of family; Rosie Chewie receiving National Treasure award; ; Rosie Chewie double-wall, lidded basket, photo by David Fitzgerald

Photo by Jeremy Charles

vivian garner cottrell

May 24, 1959
Tahlequah, Oklahoma

I was 13 years old when my mother, Betty Scraper Garner, taught me to weave Cherokee double-wall baskets. I was in eighth grade at Briggs Elementary School at the time. We used commercial reeds and dyes to weave our baskets at first. The material was purchased, and it was easier to handle for me as a youth.

As my weaving abilities grew, I would sell to area gift shops in the surrounding counties. One day, my mother told me to take my baskets to a gift shop located across from the tribal complex. The owner would buy my baskets at 10 cents an ounce. I watched him as he placed each basket on a scale and marked down the weight. He did this for each one, and when he finished, he calculated the price and he wrote a check to me for my baskets. When my mother asked how much I received, she was not pleased. When I was ready to take more baskets to the shop owner, Mom told me to wet the baskets first and let them air dry a little while before taking them to sell. When I returned, she asked how much the owner had paid. She was happy at the amount of the check that day. Mom didn't like anyone being taken advantage of. She thought the work it takes to weave baskets was worth more than 10 cents an ounce.

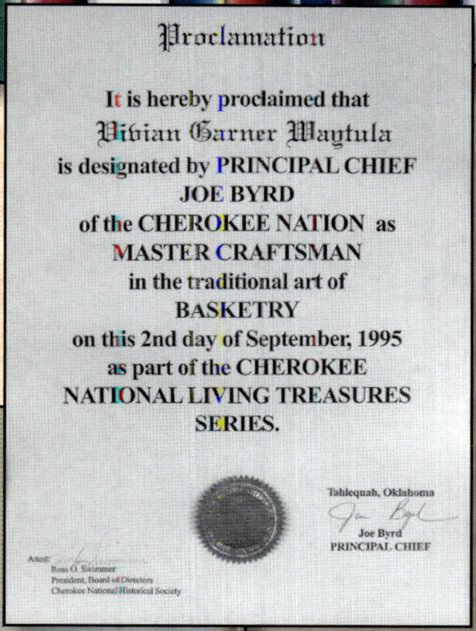

Proclamation

It is hereby proclaimed that
Vivian Garner Waytula
is designated by PRINCIPAL CHIEF
JOE BYRD
of the CHEROKEE NATION as
MASTER CRAFTSMAN
in the traditional art of
BASKETRY
on this 2nd day of September, 1995
as part of the CHEROKEE
NATIONAL LIVING TREASURES
SERIES.

Tahlequah, Oklahoma
Joe Byrd
PRINCIPAL CHIEF

From top: Vivian with her mother at Red Earth Art Market; Vivian Cottrell Cherokee National Living Treasures Proclamation; Vivian Cottrell (picture provided by artist)

Most shops would purchase each basket (according to) size and whether the basket had a lid or not. At that time, I was paid $5 to $20 for each basket. I tried to weave and sell as many baskets as I could during high school. I was trying to save to buy my first car.

Over the following years—from the 1970s through the mid-1990s—Mom and I began weaving honeysuckle and buck brush. We gathered, prepared the runners, and gathered the natural dye materials together to weave traditional baskets. We stopped using commercial materials. My dad had closed in our garage. We displayed our baskets in the den. During the summer season, Mom would get calls from gift shops in town to see if it was OK to send tourists to our home. Mom and I would sell our baskets from our home for many years.

I was honored as a Living Treasure in Basketry in September 1995. My mother was in attendance to see me receive this acknowledgement from our peers. We learned from each other. She and other weavers had encouraged me to develop my own weaving style. I weave a buckeye in the knobs of my lids. I begin baskets with the traditional start—12 ribs (6-over-6), but I also begin baskets with a multiple

Continued on page 293

Photo by Jami Murphy

richard fields

August 7, 1959
Kansas, Oklahoma

Cherokee Nation citizen Richard Fields first learned to make handcrafted bows and arrows from a family member in the late 1980s, but it wasn't until later that he found his true potential in carving a business out of being a bowyer.

"I used to travel around building restaurants all the time, and when I come home (I) didn't have nothing to do. My older cousin said, 'Hey how'd you like to learn how to make your own bow?'" Fields said. "I said 'I don't know, I don't got enough patience for that. I started then."

Fields said he was originally from Catoosa, and then moved to Kansas, Oklahoma, where his father's family was from. Growing up, he said, he didn't know much about making bows.

"It's all new to me you know, back then. I learned a lot of things just through my family. I was more the type of kid that just liked to run around and do things you know," he said. "I wasn't into this stuff, and that's what's wrong nowadays. Not very many kids get interested in this stuff. We almost lost it for a while."

He said he began selling bows in the 1990s, and chose to work it as a business around 2012. That was at the suggestion of a student to whom he had been teaching bow-making skills.

"His name was Tom Nave. He was wanting to learn how to make a bow, so he come to my house to learn, and he said 'Man you ought to sell these things,'" Fields said. "I said 'I sell one once in a while,' and he said, 'Man, you make

fantastic bows.' He said, 'You ought to get into business.'"

After that, Fields said he sought out the Spider Gallery in Tahlequah and began teaching bow-making classes, as well as selling bows and arrows.

Fields uses seasoned Bois d'arc wood to make his bows. A long bow with an arrow rest whittled into the handle costs nine hundred dollars. A flat bow or "D-bow" and a regular-handled bow costs five hundred dollars. He sells his arrows in a set of three for forty-five dollars.

"Here lately I've been selling them all—the flat and regular—just for five hundred dollars because the economy was going down and not very many people can afford that," he said. "In order to keep business going, that's what I've done."

A bow, on average, takes Fields about forty hours to complete.

About twenty years ago, Fields said, he asked to take part in an Elder camp where they taught cultural lessons. He asked a Cherokee Elder what it would take to make a bow for himself, and the response he got was, "You've got a long ways to go."

Clockwise: Hand-made bows by Richard Fields, photo courtesy of artist; Richard Fields shooting at the Cornstalk Shoot, photo courtesy of artist; Richard checking wood to make staves for bow making, photo courtesy of artist

"He said, 'You're not a bowyer until you got some years underneath your belt.' I finally figured out what he was talking about because it don't matter who you are or how good you are, there's always going to be a busted bow," Fields said. "Not everything is perfect. The Indian has never been perfect."

—Richard Fields
Interviewed by Jami Murphy
Courtesy of Cherokee Phoenix

digital design

2015

Daniel Mink is the first and, currently, the only Cherokee National Treasure distinguished for his artistic skill in Digital Design.

At an early age, Dan Mink said, he liked to draw and because he didn't have art supplies, he drew things on the back of his homework sheets with pencils and ink pens. He didn't study color in art until later. "At first I was drawing on walls, but that didn't last very long." He said his first interest was creating contemporary settings for drawing Indian people he saw or knew at that time. He incorporated airplanes and cars into his art; he wondered, "If an Indian artist drew only contemporary Indian people, was it still Indian art?"

Dan Mink said he is most proud of the graphics he created for a 2005 Seven Cherokee Clans poster, which often can be seen in tribal offices. He designed a Southeastern-style border for the artwork he created for each clan. "It (clan art) took off. I really didn't expect that kind of response from people."

Creating the main design for the Cherokee Nation Holiday has become something Dan looks forward to every year. He said he is pleased with the Southeastern-style designs he created in 2014 and 2015. The designs are used in advertising, for the holiday T-shirts, and in the official holiday program. "I appreciate this administration allowing me to do what I was trained to do," he said. "I'm always up for a challenge."

—Will Chavez

Pictured left: Long Hair Clan; Bird Clan; Wild Potato Clan; Blue Clan; Deer Clan; Wolf Clan; Paint Clan. All tiles by Daniel Mink.

Photo by David Fitzgerald

perry vanbuskirk

December 4, 1959
Rocky Ford, Oklahoma

It really wasn't so much getting into it. I think it was actually, as a person would say, almost like it's bred into you. So it came through the family. 'Cause if I look at it, what do I have? Five people in my family that's National Treasures; that's including aunts and uncles. It's almost like we've been exposed to it all of our life. And I'll tell you, and this is just a fact: until I came to work at the Cherokee Heritage Center, I didn't think anything of it, because I just thought, "It's all just part of, I guess, where we grew up at Rocky Ford. It was just all part of it. "Like, OK, you know how to do this, and my thinking—even back then—was, "OK, all of these Indians know how to do this."

But, you know, then, as I got out—because growing up, we didn't get out any; I mean we just didn't travel anywhere or go anywhere, so, it's just like in your thinking with being taught all of that—well, (I thought) everybody is getting taught this. And then I come out—almost like you'd say, into the world—and I thought, "Man, I'll tell you what, there's so many Indians that don't even know this, and don't even know their culture because it isn't taught to them." But, I'll say this: I'm thankful and fortunate that my family was one that believed in passing down culture, tradition, and stuff like that.

So we grew up almost as you'd say, in a traditional home. Tradition is made by you do something all the time in that same method or pattern or whatever. And it becomes tradition because you don't break it—because you know that's how it's set. So, to me, that is how tradition is set. Everybody is like, "Well, you're traditional." Well, everybody can be a traditionalist in their home if they've actually done this through—as we'll say—through generations, through life and stuff. That's how I got into it: just seeing my family—aunts, uncles, (and) my mom.

I hear all the time, "How do you know how you're traditional or not?" Well, who's to say what tradition is. Tradition don't mean that you walk around with a bow and arrow all the time. Tradition means, "This is the way your family lived, and this is the way you lived so you're living traditional because this is what's been passed on to you."

For example, my grandpa lived right next to us. Believe this or not, he lived in an old log house that didn't even have a wood floor in it. The floor was actually dirt. Through the years, where it had been stepped and walked on so much, it was hard as concrete. My granny would actually sweep the floor

Continued on page 293

From top: Bone Carvings by Perry Vanbuskirk, photo by Jeremy Charles; Cedar Flute made by Perry Vanbuskirk photo by Jeremy Charles; Perry Vanbuskirk at Tsa-la-gi Ancient Village, courtesy of Cherokee National Historical Society.

Photo by David Fitzgerald

lisa smith

May 4, 1961
Vian, Oklahoma

Cherokee National Treasure Lisa Smith is always on the lookout for yard sales or places to buy used, leather cowboy boots for her turtle-shell shackles. She attaches the shells to the boot tops, which allows women to fold the leather around their shins and tie the shells to their legs. She said it is getting tougher to find used boots made of real leather and not manmade or synthetic leather. She also searches for leather for leather strips that she uses to tie the shells together and for wire she uses to fasten the shells to the boot tops. "And then we're always picking up rocks and the right kind. They can't be flat and not too big (about a half inch)," she said.

During stomp dances, women and girls wear Lisa's shackles under traditional Cherokee skirts. The women and girls dance counterclockwise around a fire keeping the rhythm with the sound of the pebbles in their shells as men lead the dance and sing traditional songs. At fifty-five, she no longer dances and hasn't in about ten years, she said. When she was young, she decided to learn how to make turtle shell shackles because she wanted a pair of her own. Before that, she had to borrow shackles from other people to dance, so that was another reason for wanting her own.

"That's why I started, because I wanted a pair, and I didn't want to buy them. I had to make them," she said while laughing. "I've been making them a long time."

Clockwise from bottom:(from bottom right) Lisa's brother Joe, sister Sherry, Lisa and her sister, Sandra; Turtle Shackles made by Lisa Smith, photo by David Fitzgerald; Lisa Smith with her mother, Nancy with her great granddaughter Sophie, photo courtesy of Lisa Smith.

By helping make her own shackles with her mother, she was able to pick the turtles she wanted and how many shells she wanted on her shackles. She said cleaning the turtles didn't scare her off. She recalled she used to watch her mother, Nancy Smith, and Eva Smith, both Cherokee National Treasures, clean the turtles and prepare them for shackles. In the summer, she recalled, she and her mother would gather all of the turtles they could and then clean them on the weekend so that the shells could dry out during the week. "After they get dried out, you can put them together anytime," she said.

She said she usually sells her large shackles, with approximately thirteen shells per shackle, for four hundred dollars. "Baby ones," with maybe four shells per shackle, are sold for $50, but it can vary.

Making turtle shell shackles is not the easiest job, but Smith said she enjoys doing it because it allows her to spend time with her mother and sister, Diane, who also makes shackles.

"Usually we clean them in one day and then drill them and put the rocks in them and hang them up (to dry). And then, maybe two or three weeks later, we put them (shackles) together if somebody wants a pair."

Continued on page 294

kathy vanbuskirk

Photo by David Fitzgerald

May 8, 1961
Rocky Ford, Oklahoma

In 2004, nearly twenty years after she was introduced to basket making, Kathy Vanbuskirk was named a Cherokee National Treasure. She was introduced to basket making when she began working at the Cherokee Heritage Center in 1986 and saw the women working in the Ancient Village making baskets. "Anna Sixkiller worked there at the time, and she showed me how to start a basket. Just watching them make their baskets, I just kind of picked it up and learned," she said. "Really, starting them is all you can teach a person, and then where they take it from there is all up to them."

Kathy said from that point she became interested in basket making and has made them since. She worked on baskets in the village and made baskets on her own at home. "And then, through the years I just kept making them in every shape and size. I sold a lot through the gift shop," she said. Kathy said it didn't take long for her to be confident enough to sell her baskets because she picked up basket making "really well, right away. It's like in my mind. I thought, 'this is how I want to make this one,' and 'this is how I want to do this one.' So, it's like you get it in mind and you just do it; you make it. I did a lot of experimenting," she said.

Kathy has sold a lot of baskets in thirty years, but it took her longer to feel good about entering area art shows with her baskets. It was

just about ten years ago when she began entering her work. "I would think, 'I don't know if mine are show quality.' I would always think that, so I just didn't (enter). And then when I did start entering, I started winning the art shows, so that gave me more confidence to keep entering," she said.

Her first entries were medium-sized, traditional Cherokee baskets made with round reed using honeysuckle and buckbrush reeds. "Once I did so many baskets, I wanted to do something else with the reed because you figure out you can twist it and turn it so many different ways. I did turtles, angels, ladybugs, and spiders. I just started doing different shapes—oblongs, purses, just experimenting," she said.

Today, she sticks with honeysuckle and buckbrush, and she said if she can "sit under a willow tree" she likes to make willow-tree baskets. She said people usually know her from her turtle baskets and a spider she wove from reed. She has also woven a swan from reed and wants to tackle weaving a turkey next. "I have to get it all worked out in my mind on how I'm going to do it before I sit down to do it. Once I have it in my mind and figured out, then I can make it," she said.

Cherokee National Treasures are chosen, in part, because they choose to share their knowledge with others, which Vanbuskirk has frequently done in thirty years. "Oh, my goodness, I have probably taught thousands over the years. We used to travel to the schools, and the schools used to come there

Continued on page 294

Clockwise from top left: Large round reed basket by Kathy Vanbuskirk, photo by Will Chavez; Kathy Vanbuskirk holding her Spider Basket, photo by Will Chavez; Fancy Reed Basket with loops. Previous page: Kathy Vanbuskirk, photo by David Fitzgerald

dan mink

February 28, 1962
Candy Mink Springs, Oklahoma

Photo courtesy of Dan Mink

Daniel Mink grew up near Rock Fence Community but lives in Candy Mink Springs in southern Adair County. He received his Cherokee National Treasure award for incorporating designs, motifs, and borders from mound-builder pottery designs. "I wanted to have a cultural identity apart from what we usually see with Plains or Southwest motifs. It took some research. I guess like many, I wasn't aware of our cultural background." Mink uses a couple of books for his research, which are *Sun Circles and Human Hands* and *Hero, Hawk, and Open Hand*.

"It's really interesting stuff. I didn't realize such a culture existed before contact. It was a huge complex Mississippian culture," he said.

Mink also works to incorporate the Cherokee syllabary in his artwork and designs that are created mostly for the Cherokee Nation. His work can be seen on T-shirts, posters, and advertising throughout the Cherokee Nation. After his coworkers nominated him for the Cherokee National Treasure award two years in a row, Mink said he was still surprised to receive the award in 2015. He said Principal Chief Bill John Baker personally called to inform him he had received the prestigious award. "It took a little while to sink in. I didn't really ever expect to get that. Just seeing my work around the (Tribal) Complex was reward enough for me," he said. "I'm just thankful and honored to be recognized. It's my job to make the tribe look good visually."

From his upbringing, he remains "quiet and humble" and said he is proud to be listed among great Cherokee artists like Anna Mitchell or Donald Vann.

At an early age, he said he liked to draw, and because he didn't have art supplies, he drew things—with pencils and ink pens—on the back of his homework. He didn't study color in art until later. "At first, I was drawing on walls, but that didn't last very long."

He said his first interest was creating contemporary settings for drawing Indian people he saw or knew at that time. He incorporated airplanes and cars into his art and wondered if an Indian artist drew only contemporary Indian people, was it still Indian art?

Mink wondered where his art fit in just as someone suggested he consider enrolling in a graphic-design program. He chose Oklahoma State University Institute of Technology in Okmulgee, Oklahoma. He said he learned quickly that graphic artists work under strict deadlines, have to "switch gears on the fly" a lot, and must be prepared to put in long hours to complete assigned jobs. He said the experience he received working outside the Cherokee Nation helped him when he landed a job with the tribe in 2005. "I was excited to apply what I had learned to my culture to contribute to what the Cherokee Nation was trying to do here to get a uniformed look to all their printed material," he said. "I really didn't like the

Continued on page 295

Photo from top: "Untamed" by Daniel Mink, photo courtesy of artist; "The Clans" by Daniel Mink; 2016 Cherokee National Holiday design by Daniel Mink

storytelling

2015

I had watched a number of storytellers—Jake Chanate a Kiowa storyteller and educator at Northeastern State University, Hastings Shade, former deputy chief and a Cherokee National Treasure for gig making, also a wonderful storyteller, Choogie Kingfisher, and Will Hill, during the Trail of Tears drama seasons; as well as Sequoyah Guess, a noted Keetoowah storyteller and Wisdom Keeper. Gayle Ross, Sammy Still, Janelle Adair, and Woody Hanson are all well-known Storytellers I've enjoyed listening to over the years.

—Robert Lewis

Pictured left: Robert Lewis telling a story, photo by Will Chavez; This page, clockwise from top left: Robert Lewis telling a story, photo by Will Chavez; Sequoyah Guess telling stories; Story telling by the fire , photo by Pamela Jumper Thurman

Photo by Jeremy Charles

roger cain

April 5, 1963
Briggs, Oklahoma

I always felt I was lucky because I had three grandpas and everybody else had two. I always wished they had Indian names. In fact, I thought my Cain name was Indian, as in river cane. I didn't know it was my dad's side, and an Irish name, until much later. That's when I realized my Cherokee grandpas both had Cherokee names. One was Pumpkin and the other was Batt. My grandma, Agnes Christie, had my mom with Richard Batt. But a few years later, she married George Pumpkin. By the time I was born, Grandma and Grandpa Pumpkin had been married a long time. So, I was raised with three grandpas. One was full-blood Irish, and the other two were full-blood Cherokee.

My mom is 31/32 Cherokee; 1/32nd more and she would be a full-blood. That is a crazy number. We come from Watt Christie who was half-Cherokee way back in 1839. That is the only documented white man or woman on my mom's line. My dad is a white man. His nickname was "Chalk" because he was so white. But he sure believed in Indian medicine! I grew up around a full-blood, Cherokee-speaking family where I was the only white-looking boy in the bunch. I never could really understand Cherokee much. That's why I followed around my aunts and uncles. I have uncles younger than me, and we used to play together all the time when we were young. I loved it.

Clockwise from left: Roger's grandmother, Agnes Christie Pumpkin,with Roger's mother, Florene Batt, "My grandma, Agnes Christie Pumpkin, with my mom, Florene Batt, one year before she was forced to attend Sequoyah Vocational School at the age of 5. My mom is now a Sequoyah Schools alumnus and holds a Master's Degree in School Administration from the University of Oklahoma."; Roger in first grade with cousin, Gary Smith; "Booger Dancer," copper sculpture and wooden mask, photo by Jeremy Charles

I've always played in cane breaks from the time I was a little kid. I still do. I remember going to stomp dances all my life and being called *Yoneg* (White) because I wasn't dark enough and *Gunage* (Black) because of my curly hair, but it didn't bother me too much. It made me tough and I was having fun. And my grandma said it didn't matter because they didn't know what they were talking about. I sure loved my grandma. I was her first-born grandchild. I used to beg my parents to let me live with her on the creek down there at Briggs. I got to go there a lot! I sure was happy being with Grandma, Grandpa and all my aunts, uncles, and cousins. Now that my grandparents are gone, we don't get together like we used to. I sure miss those days.

Cherokee art became important to me in the 1980s when I realized there was more to being Cherokee than language and stomp-dancing. I was teaching out in New Mexico. An Acoma Pueblo man was asking me about our art, and all I could tell him was about stomp dances, language and the syllabary. That's how it is, sometimes, when you are right in the middle of it. As Shakespeare said, "You can't see the forest for the trees." So, I started researching and asking around. It wasn't long before I started playing with different art forms. I was a welder at the time, and I started cutting out metal shapes of the *Uktena* and rattlesnake motifs. My family thought I was crazy! Then I met my current wife. She didn't think I was so crazy and encouraged me to explore more art. That's what gave me the confidence to enter my first show. She bugged me to do it.

Continued on page 295

robert lewis

October 10, 1965
Salina, Oklahoma

Robert Lewis is an award-winning Native storyteller, author, and artist of Cherokee, Navaho, and Apache descent. He was born in Claremore at the Claremore Indian Hospital to Yazzie and Lou Aline Lewis. Robert is of Navajo and Apache descent on his father's side, and his mother is Cherokee.

From Robert Lewis

"My father grew up in Chinle, Arizona, next to the Canyon De Chelly, and my mother grew up in the Kenwood area of northeast Oklahoma. I grew up in Salina, Oklahoma, a very small town next to Lake Hudson. I have three other brothers in my family—Phillip, John Mark, and Paul. At the age of seven, I heard my first traditional story, and it came from my father, Yazzie Lewis, on a family vacation. We had stopped at a rest area, and he brought our attention to the night sky and started telling about the creation of the Milky Way and why the stars are scattered across the sky. I had stories read to me by my mother, Lou Aline Kingfisher Lewis, from books, but to hear an explanation for the universe, while looking at the starry sky, was an extraordinary experience, and I never forgot it.

"I began telling stories at the Cherokee Heritage Center while working in the Cherokee ancient village. It has since been removed, and a new updated village is in operation there. I started storytelling to keep a restless group of school children entertained until it was time for the tour to begin. This was sometime in the fall of 2003. After I had finished, the school group left to take their tour, and Barbara Girty, who was in charge of group tours at the time, had seen me and remarked that she didn't know I was a storyteller. She began to

Clockwise from top left: "Check the Ears." Robert Lewis; Robert Lewis at the Cherokee Heritage Center; Robert Lewis telling stories at Gilcrease Museum in Tulsa, Oklahoma

offer storytelling to groups coming to the museum. My supervisor at the time, Perry Vanbuskirk, a National treasure for Bow making, told me to go out and gather stories. So those two individuals are instrumental in starting me on this path of becoming a storyteller.

"I had watched a number of storytellers before—Jake Chanate, a Kiowa storyteller and educator at Northeastern State University; Hastings Shade, former deputy chief and a National Treasure for gig making, (also a wonderful storyteller); Choogie Kingfisher and Will Hill, during the Trail of Tears drama season;, as well as Sequoyah Guess, a noted Keetoowah storyteller. Wisdom Keeper, Gayle Ross, Sammy Still, Janelle Adair, and Woody Hanson are all well-known storytellers I've enjoyed listening to over the years.

"My particular way of involving the audience with the storytelling is different than those mentioned above. When I gave tours through the ancient village, I would interact with my groups, physically involving them with what I was telling them. If I described the clans, I would pull someone from the group, and they would become part of the narrative I was telling them. Subsequently, when I began storytelling, I continued to do the same thing, except the person pulled up and into the story acted out the part of the Bear or Turtle or Rabbit.

"I enjoy the experience in seeing others become transformed by the story. I am telling the story, and they are playing the parts. Initially, those individuals called upon to be part of this storytelling experience sometimes surprise others and me with what they bring to the story. I am told, from time to time, by teachers and parents that an individual I had chosen surprised them with the performance they gave or that the one who is normally a shy person suddenly opened up and gave more than what they thought that person would do before they walked on stage."

Continued on page 295

shawna morton cain

October 5, 1966
Stilwell, Oklahoma

Photo courtesy of Shawna Cain

I'm a Stilwell gal—well, an Adair County gal. Growing up in a little town like I did, I always had aspirations of moving away to the city. I tried that a few times when I was younger and never lasted a full year. I longed to come home every time. I know I will never leave this place I've called home all my life. What I couldn't see as a teenager, I can now see. I love my hometown. I was born to Patsy Lynn Eads Morton and Warren Neil Morton. I have one big sister, Camille, and one little brother, Nason. I've helped raise more than a few kids, but the two that claim me are my boys, Jamil Jaser and Reuben Cain. (She laughed.)

I was raised in a household dedicated to Cherokees. You learn these things early in life, sitting at the dining room table. Our table was busy with adult talk related to Cherokees one way or another. Dad worked for Northeastern State University and Cherokee Nation at different times, and my mom was a tribal council member from the time I was nine until I was 21. All my life that's all I ever knew was going to Cherokee Nation or just Cherokee events, programs, activities, and that kind of stuff. In my head, I lived and breathed Cherokee. I've always been proud to be Cherokee...and Irish!

As far as being a basket weaver, that kind of went along with my love for the woods and plants. I really became a basket weaver because it allowed me to go to the woods and gather the materials for weaving and for dyes. I used to take my little boy out with me when he was in preschool to gather all we could along country roads and in the woods. My first teacher was Thelma Forrest; I can only imagine what a pain I must have been to her. One summer when I was about ten, Mom would drop me off at a summer craft camp that Thelma was teaching over in Tahlequah. I don't remember anyone from that day camp but Thelma! She was just so good to me and made me feel so special about weaving baskets. I guess, because I had a natural interest in it, I just took to it quickly. My first baskets were small, and I gave them to family members as toothbrush holders. My sister, Camille, used hers for years.

I've said many times that it is when I am in the woods gathering that I really feel a purpose. This purpose is to continue a tradition that was one of my ancestors and of all of our ancestors. Basketry is so much more than just weaving a basket. To know how to truly make a traditional Cherokee basket, one must learn multiplication, the seasons, the phases of the moon, the weather, the companion plants and a respect for reciprocity. I know that when I pluck that root from the ground, if I take it all, there won't be any left for next time. That line has ended. Over time, I have learned that

Continued on page 296

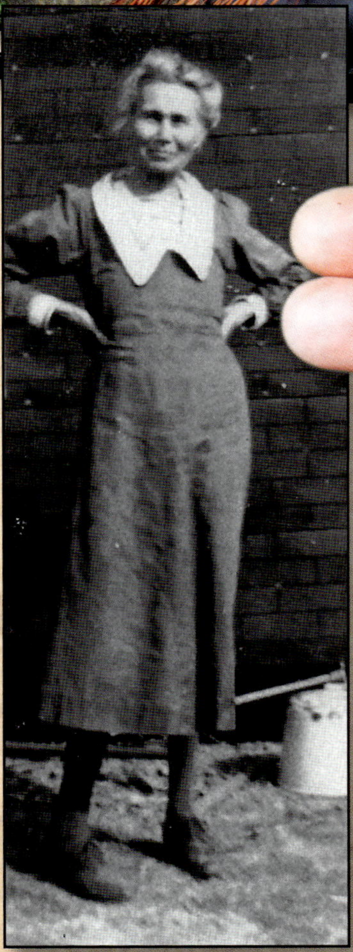

Clockwise from top: Shawna Morton Cain displaying basketry at home on Twist Mountain, Adair County, photo by Jeremy Charles;Shawna holding bloodroot in late Spring, photo by Jeremy Charles; Penelope Ross Eads, Shawna's great-grandmother, Dawes Roll #2231

noel timothy grayson

December 24, 1966
Tahlequah, Oklahoma

Photo by Jeremy Charles

Well, it all started when I was just a child growing up, being raised in a native family. Me and my brothers all played "Cowboys and Indians" but it was more like Indians and Indians as the cap guns of the day didn't fare too well against actual bows and arrows that we had made ourselves. We would shoot at each other—me and my brother Web.

Web, he is a pretty well accomplished artist in his own right. He's a good bow maker, too. We would try to make our bows; you know, we were just little kids. My arrows wouldn't come out real straight. He would try to make his nice and straight. My brother, Sean, was a good artist. He would throw things together. His arrows wouldn't be straight. His feathers wouldn't be straight. When that arrow would be coming at you, it would be coming like a bee flying at you or something. And you couldn't dodge it! You just had to turn your back and hope it didn't hit you. Web's were a bit easier. When Web shot his arrow, it come at you and you could pretty much dodge it. Just move. But we never shot at each other from real close.

I feel that I must tell you that these bows were strong for us as we didn't want a bow that "only spit" an arrow. We wanted a bow that would "shoot" an arrow. This game consisted of actually shooting at each other with these bows, not as dangerous as it sounds because we took safety precautions in the form of using the foam seating of our oldest brother's Austin Healy. (Sorry, Joe Jr.; it was Web and Sean's idea.) My oldest brother, Joe, had it parked behind my dad's house. He was crazy about working on cars. He and my dad. That was their thing. They both liked to rebuild cars. We used to sneak up on John Jr.'s Austin Healy. That's back when they had foam seats. We'd reach in under there and grab a handful of foam and rip it out, and we'd tie that on the end of our arrows, like that was gonna do any good. And that's what we shot each other with. We tore that thing up. But, it was fun. It seemed to be a good one at the time though—foam on the end of arrows to "cushion the blow." Yeah right! It still had a good sting to it but, hey, it was better than not getting to play at all. We were always looking to improve our game so as we would have an idea, study on it, and try to get it. Eventually, we struck on "skins."

Being kids we were limited to what we could shoot—squirrel and rabbit mainly, as deer season only came once a year. Lots of trial and error went into figuring out how this worked, as we were limited on any books to look up the subject. Gotta remember! No computer to "Google" any of this. We relied on Elders telling us, so any info we heard, we tried. But eventually, my brothers grew up and quit playing which left only me—not as sad as you would think; it was around this time that I learned how to sharpen arrows with a pencil sharpener! I wasn't giving up my childhood toys so easily. As time went on, I continued to make and play with my childhood toys and eventually got my brothers back into making bows and arrows.

You have to learn to speak that language. And that's something all of us artists have in common. We know what's going on. And it's conveying it into our own language. That makes it ours.

Continued on page 297

Clockwise from left; Noel Grayson with his handmade bow, arrows and textiles, Adam's Corner, Cherokee Heritage Center, Tahlequah, photo by David Fitzgerald; Noel Grayson flintknapping at Lake Tenkiller, photo by Jeremy Charles; Handmade arrow by Noel Grayson, photo by David Fitzgerald

metalsmithing 2016

"Through the relationships that I embrace—between ancient America and the present—I am inspired to create contemporary forms that represent my cultural artistic identity. The technical challenges of mixed media allow me to create interaction among different materials working together as one."

- Demos Glass

Pictured left: Osiyo, Voices of the Cherokee People, "Bill and Demos Glass, Art for Everyone"; This page, clockwise from top left: Osiyo, Voices of the Cherokee People, "Bill and Demos Glass, Art for Everyone"

tommy wildcat

May 3, 1967
Greenleaf Lake State Park, Oklahoma

O*siyo!* Along with my twin sister, Tammy, I was born at the old Hastings Indian hospital in Tahlequah, Oklahoma, in 1967. We were raised in the southern region of the Cherokee Nation by Greenleaf Lake State Park near Braggs.

I grew up with five siblings, and our parents raised us in the old stomp-dance customs of our Cherokee heritage. It was a household where Cherokee speaking, ceremonies, and cohesiveness of our Cherokee culture was observed, and I appreciate the education I was given in our old ways. Being raised in the old customs of respecting traditions, it was always my honor to be involved in promoting, teaching, and sharing our Cherokee heritage.

I always loved my heritage since I was a little boy, and I admired my father, Tom Webber Wildcat, for his cultural knowledge. I am humbled to have learned so much from him and my mother, Annie Sue Wildcat. She has become my Elder and teacher after my father passed.

I started making blowguns when I got hired at the Cherokee Heritage Center in 1990. I was hired as a stomp-dance leader and was learning to teach and be taught about the broader perspectives of our Cherokee heritage. It was known as the Tsa-la-gi Ancient Village, and it is where I learned how to make blowguns, darts, and clay beads.

Photo courtesy of Tommy Wildcat

In 1993, I began to make my first river-cane flutes. I would travel around to small shows, promoting our Cherokee heritage through dance and river-cane flute playing. Two years later, in 1995, I came out with my first river cane-flute recording. The CD was recorded with a river-cane flute that I had made, and I believe it was the only one of its kind recorded nationally. The CD is utilized on the Occonluftee Island Park in Cherokee, North Carolina, as a music background while visitors hear the story of the Cherokee and the Great Smokey Mountains. My second album, *Warrior Flutes,* has always been my best seller since it came out in 1997. It has outsold all five of the musical recordings I've produced over the last two decades.

continued on page 297

Clockwise from top: Tommy Wildcat accepting his Nammy (Native American Music Awards) for Cherokee flute music, photo provided by artist; Tommy with his mother and inspiration, Annie Wildcat, photo provided by artist; River Cane Flutes made by Tommy Wildcat, photo courtesy of artist

david comingdeer

February 6, 1972
Spade Mountain, Oklahoma

David Comingdeer was named a Cherokee National Treasure for his stickball stick making in 2014. He has crafted his handmade sticks for twenty-two years from hickory wood that he cuts and then shapes, using heat.

Comingdeer was born to Tanya Comingdeer in February 1972 before the Indian Child Welfare Act was passed. His mother was just fifteen when she had him. He was kept in Oklahoma City until he was two months old before he was adopted by Colonel Jim and Lisa Rabon. His adopted father was the commanding officer of Ft. Sill in Oklahoma.

He grew up on several Army bases until his father's retiring in 1978.

"We moved to his home state of South Carolina where I went to school and played football. I graduated high school in 1991. As a teenager, I worked in Charleston for Palmetto Carriage Works for the Doyle family. I was a barn hand, and cared for about ten teams of mules used to pull carriages—loaded with visitors—to the historic district of Charleston," he said. It wasn't until 1990 that David contacted his birth mother, Tanya, and, after finishing high school, he moved back to Tahlequah at age nineteen. "I became a federal firefighter and a carpenter for the Cherokee Nation," he said.

Comingdeer's family has lived in both Adair and Cherokee counties since arriving in Indian Territory, he said. His cousin, Chooch Christie, was the first to introduce him to ball stick making when he was nineteen.

"He made my first pair of sticks. That's when I became curious about making sticks. So I helped Chooch make a few pair for our Ceremonial Ground," he said. "As I learned more about stick making, I started cutting logs and trying on my own. Victor Wildcat was also very influential in those first few years of stick making. Victor shared much information about stick making, and he is very knowledgeable. Other stick makers influenced me over the years; all of them have passed away. Those are the men that taught me the old-time way of stick making—with drawknife, fire, and steam. I had seen a need for sticks in my community, so I started making sticks for the younger guys. Over time, I got better at it and made sticks for men of all ages and tribes."

Comingdeer said that his two most memorable moments in regards to stickball were at the Echota Ceremonial Grounds and seeing his son complete his first pair of sticks. "There was a stickball game going on, and as I looked around, I saw that

Continued on page 297

Clockwise from top: David Comingdeer finishing up a pair of ballsticks; David Comingdeer turning ball sticks; Stickball Sticks demonstrating various webbing styles by David Comingdeer. All photos courtesy of artist

demos glass

June 6, 1976
Locust Grove, Oklahoma

I was born on June 6, 1976 in Tahlequah, Oklahoma, and grew up in Locust Grove, Oklahoma. My earliest art memories began when I was young, tagging along during one of the high periods of Native American art in Oklahoma. Being the son of an artist, Bill Glass Jr., was very inspiring. It allowed me the opportunity to be exposed to many diverse forms of Native American art. As early as I can remember, I continually wandered through art shows and Indian art markets trying to expose myself to as much art as possible. I would spark up conversations with different artists and discuss their art and techniques. These discussions and interactions became relative as I continued into my own art research. The friendships I made in my childhood would motivate me throughout my lifetime. Throughout the years, I've been inspired by many artists and their artwork. I'm still motivated when I see a new art technique. That's what I try to do today—create contemporary, cutting edge art that will be inspiring to others.

My grandparents, Bill Glass Sr. and Ellen Jean Justice Glass, were very influential in my art career. My grandmother would encourage me to fabricate paper with glue and scissors. This is still some of the preliminaries I do in my art today. My grandfather was an inspiration to me because I would watch him weld and see him create beautiful pieces of jewelry later in his life. Many of the techniques that I enjoy as a metalsmith today I had seen growing up, admiring the way my grandfather had rigged things. His work inspired me to replace the existing Miss Cherokee crown that he had made with one of my own creations in 2004 and then again in 2013.

High school wrestling led me to Southern Illinois University Edwardsville, and I was immediately drawn to the art department. This is when I realized how much I had absorbed throughout the years by my exposure—*from* a young age—to art. In college, I learned sculptural *fabrication* techniques and studied metalsmithing under Paulette Myers. My cultural influences were present throughout this period, (during) which I felt different from the other art students, who were in constant search for their conceptual premise. In 2005, I became part of a team of Cherokee artists who were commissioned by the City of Chattanooga, Tennessee, to do a public art project at what was formerly Ross's Landing, the point of embarkation for the Trail of Tears journey. This job led to many public art commissions for Glass Studio and has allowed my father and I to collaborate on several Cherokee Nation-related public art projects, using a variety of mediums from stainless steel, ceramics, plastics, and powder-coated metal. I'm very proud of the public art that I have been part of and see the power that it has to transform the perception of all who encounter it.

I feel blessed by the circumstances that have led me to this particular point in my career. The basis of my work today is influenced by all these experiences. Thank you to my family, friends, teachers, who have helped me to pursue my art career.

I am honored to be a Cherokee National Treasure.

— Demos Glass

Interviewed by Pamela Jumper

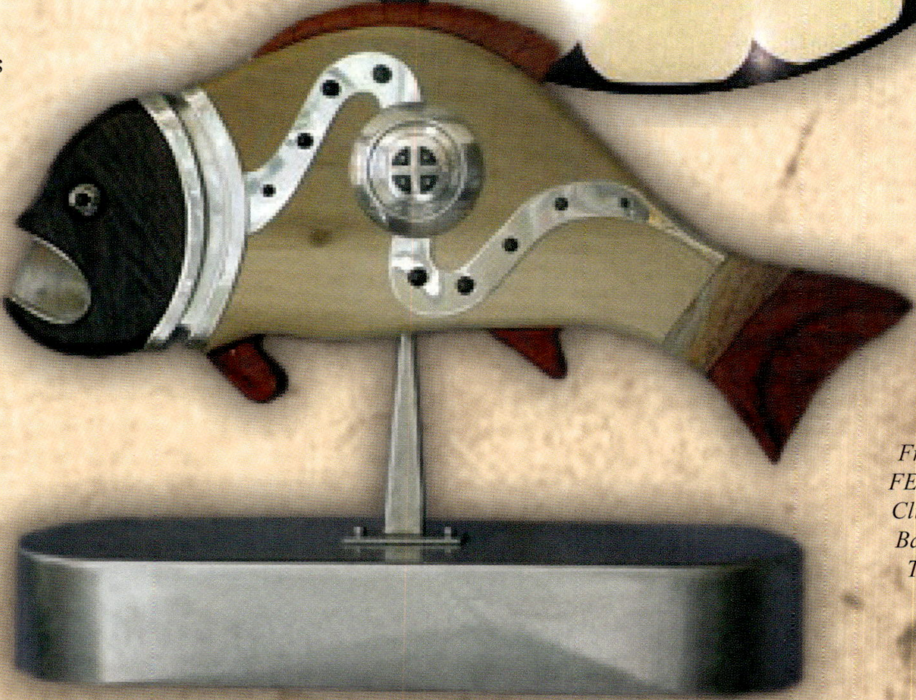

From top: "PRAYER FEATHER" Sallisaw Clinic; Upper Realm Bank of Oklahoma—Tulsa 22' Diameter; "Fish Dreams" Demos Glass

rachel dew

November 26, 1981
Tahlequah, Oklahoma

Photo by David Fitzgerald

Cherokee Heritage Center: Rachel, tell us a little about when and how you began making baskets. Who taught you?

Rachel Dew: I've been around basket makers most of my life, but it wasn't until I was about ten years old before I really started wanting to learn. I used to watch my aunts and other ladies in the village make baskets, then try to mimic what they did. I asked lots of questions and experimented a lot. Sometimes it worked. Sometimes it didn't.

CHC: How do you feel about being the youngest person to ever be named a Living Treasure?

Rachel: Just to be nominated is such an honor, and to be recognized at such a young age as having the qualities and attributes it takes to receive such an award is beyond incredible. It is very humbling.

CHC: You are also developing quite a reputation as a potter. Which do you prefer? basketry or pottery?

Rachel: Basketry, just because I've been doing it for so long. But I do enjoy the challenge of learning something new.

CHC: Where do you learn about traditional techniques?

Rachel: Asking questions from people who actually go out and do it.

CHC: Have you ever created your own design, or do you stay with traditional patterns?

Rachel: I have made an elephant, a woman, and a canoe. I have also made a baseball bat and several baskets with my favorite MLB logo on them.

CHC: Finally, How do you think being named a Living Treasure will affect your career?

Rachel: I can't even begin to imagine if or how it will affect my career.

World's Tallest Cherokee Basket on Display

ICTMN Staff

June 07, 2012

The Cherokee Heritage Center in Tahlequah, Oklahoma, has welcomed a very big visitor—a Cherokee basket measuring over eight feet tall. The basket, woven over a four-month period and consisting of more than a mile of reed, exists to promote the Cherokee Baskets: History Woven in Art *exhibition, which opened a few days ago and runs through August 19.*

The weavers were Cherokee National Treasure Rachel Dew and Donnay Leach of Tahlequah. "Baskets have always been an important part of our Cherokee culture," said Dew in a statement released by the Heritage Center. "My ancestors were renowned for their basketry skills, and I'm just doing my part to keep that part of the culture alive."

Leach added, "My ancestors were excellent in basketry skills, and that inspired me to do the same. I am just trying to make them proud."

—Rachel Dew

Courtesy of: Cherokee Heritage Center/"Columns" publication, September 2006

Newspaper article: Courtesy of ICTMN

Clockwise from top: Basketry lesson with students; Honeysuckle Basket; Rachel demonstrating basketry at Cherokee Heritage Center. All photos courtesy of Cherokee National Historical Society

alex england

continued from page 29

betting and eating and, of course, they'd all have food and it was just a big celebration (that) lasted all day.

Mr. England said that the night before they had the Cornstalk Shoot, all the leaders (would) have kind of a medicine man (who was) leader of the group. And all the Cornstalk Shooters would go to some secret place and spend the whole night there. It would be on a Spring Branch or something like that, close by. And they would go there and they wouldn't sleep all night long. And Mr. England said there were all kinds of things they did. He told me a bunch of different things I can't tell you about. But, for example, he said they would take a cornstalk spike and they would put it down in the water and—this was after dark of course—(he) said (when) the crawdad came out, it had certain meaning to it. He also said (the shooters) would smoke tobacco and they would blow this tobacco up in the air. It would go across and come down where the other team—the opposing team was "hid out." (The smoke) would come down among them and just blow up like a bomb. They had some kind of little beads, I guess they were some kind of little plant seeds or something. They colored them. You'd take these and you would put them on the water and however many of them floated and how many of them sank would tell you which team was going to win the next day. That was another thing they did among all kinds of things. And Mr. England said, "The next morning, all over your arms would just be power."

— Interview with Alex England, July 25, 1988
Courtesy of Lost Arts Program

george fourkiller

continued from page 33

and push it out and pull. I just watched him. The few chances I did watch him, I did pick it up. For the white oak, we would get white oak the year around, but he would get hickory in the spring time. And he did make stickball sticks, but he didn't make them that much.

I really don't know what he did other than (work as a) farm hand. I heard that he worked for the railroad for a while, and when I was growing up, he would get on broom-corn harvest around Colorado Springs and wouldn't get home until around Christmas. And some people told me (that) while he was on broom-corn harvest, he would cut (the) hair of people there with him. And when he finally settled down and couldn't go on the broom-corn harvest anymore, he would pick strawberries, green beans, and tomatoes. After tomatoes, school would start, and I don't know what he picked then. He always tried to have a really big garden and would supply vegetables to neighbors around here and gave (vegetables) to the church to give out to people. So he was kind of glad to show where vegetables come from. One time I came down here, and he was growing tobacco for himself.

His Indian name was *Wasvndv.* Don't know if that is pronounced right or not but everybody called him George Washington. His birth certificate said George W. Fourkiller. He was ornery and liked to tease. He cared a lot about his grandkids and great-grandkids. We always called him *Walosi* (Frog) and told everyone that was his Indian name. He was kind of short and had a big belly—kind of like a frog. He would always be squatting; (it) never failed. And he always enjoyed having kids around, and every Halloween he would get an old-man mask and have fun with them at church with it. All the kids at the church called him "Grandpa" 'cause he was old. It would be snowing, and he would be walking to church to fire up the stove to warm it up for church services. No matter what time we got home on Saturday night, he was always up early the next morning and on the road to church.

He always liked playing jokes on everybody. Daddy had one brother and one sister. I did meet his one brother, Felix. I met him one time and didn't get to know him very much. He has about fifteen grandkids and about twenty great-grandkids and one great-great that we are raising now. Dad just had two kids—myself and James. I'm the oldest. And he had two stepkids—Beverly Proctor and Levi Sunday.

He was a very spiritual person in both Cherokee and Christianity. He liked to travel. He worked at the Stilwell Canning factory at Wauhillau and would bring damaged cans home. After Wauhillau, he went to Seneca Indian Boarding School, but he didn't graduate. When we moved back here, we were teaching him English. He was married to Ruth Swimmer, my mom, from Adair County. He was a character to be around.

He liked music. If someone wanted him to sing, he was ready. He always liked to sing bass. He mostly sang in Cherokee. He used to sing with Red Fourkiller and the Chieftan Quartets. His favorite song was "Orphan Child" in Cherokee. When the Chieftan was around here, they would always ask him to sing bass for them, and he didn't need a microphone. His voice would carry that much for a little man, but you could hear him in the back of the church. He surprised me when he would be playing bass for the church, and I didn't know he could play the guitar. It never surprised me on what all he could do. He was so religious he would not hold grudges and would say, "The Lord knows.

—J.C. Fourkiller, son, and
Tashina Whitebuffalo, granddaughter
Interviewed by Shawna Morton Cain

stella livers continued from page 35

she was making quilts—sewing quilts and piecing quilts. She was proud of all the baskets she made."

In 1990, she was given the National Treasure award by Principal Chief Wilma Mankiller during the Cherokee Holiday. Her baskets won many awards over the years she was alive, but she was excited to know that former President Lyndon B. Johnson purchased one of her baskets. She also has a letter from Senator David L. Boren thanking her for the beautiful basket his wife received from the Democratic Women of Adair County in 1983. She would make about thirty baskets a year. Making one usually took her only a day. The highest price she received for a basket was two hundred dollars.

—Brenda Lawrence Partain, great-niece
Interview with Carol Sanders, daughter, and
Imogene Duncan, granddaughter

willie jumper sr. continued from page 39

Tribute to Willie Jumper
Cherokee
3/31/1911 – 8/22/1977

Willie Jumper, a long-time resident of Tahlequah and Cherokee County probably had no equal in the scope of his knowledge of traditional medicinal practices, which he spent a lifetime studying and perfecting. It is notable that historians such as Anna and Jack Kilpatrick considered him to be an authoritative source of information in Cherokee lore.

Willie was born March 31, 1911, in Delaware County, Oklahoma. He and his wife Minnie had fourteen children, eight boys and six girls. Many of his notes and observations, written in Cherokee, are preserved by the family.

With the passing of Willie Jumper, on August 22, 1977, the Cherokee and the country lost a vast repository of knowledge and traditional philosophy, sadly, a good deal of it gone forever.

The Cherokee Bilingual Education Center staff is proud to dedicate a calendar to the memory of Willie Jumper, Cherokee Medicine Man. He was respected and beloved by several generations of Cherokees, near and far, who sought his company and services. His knowledge and wisdom was a sustaining force in the lives of many Indian people throughout his life. In the waning years of his life, he expressed a philosophical view that he believed his talents were a powerful gift to be shared.

In a fatherly way, Willie Jumper was counselor, teacher, healer and friend as he practiced the use of ancient Cherokee Indian Medicine. To his followers he possessed a rare insight to life. His passing breaks a vital link in Cherokee culture and tradition. And so, it is with great appreciation for his lifelong work, that the staff of the Bilingual Education Center, in profound gratitude for the heritage he gave us, proudly remembers the late great Cherokee Willie Jumper.

— Courtesy of the Cherokee Bilingual Education Center

rogers mclemore continued from page 41

building, he would stop and watch the women craftsmen as the brightly colored yarn was woven into blankets.

"After they left for the day, I started weaving. They didn't find out for a long time." He lets out a high-pitched laugh again. "Then they put me to work." Lucille says sometimes Rogers can be found asleep in a chair early of the morning. "Sometimes he can't sleep at night. He'll come down here at two o'clock in the morning and weave 'til he falls asleep."

At one time, ten weavers worked in the business. The sound of the creaky looms could be heard in unison. One by one, the women left for other jobs—just as they did in the other community projects. Lucille has just returned to weave after working elsewhere for four years. The business started on its own road to decline; it was not caused by a lack of demand for blankets but from a lack of interest from the trained weavers. While U.S. 62 was once the main highway through the area, construction of Interstate 40 and the Turner Turnpike have rerouted tourists, says Jody Dreadfulwater, chairman of the board for the Sequoyah Weavers Association.

Since the tourists have disappeared, Rogers no longer makes blankets to sell in the store. He works on request and nods to piles of yarn stacked on a shelf. "I'm behind," he sighs. He has over two dozen orders waiting to be filled. Dreadfulwater said a few years ago, Neiman-Marcus, the department store in Dallas, Texas, put in an order for several thousand blankets for its Christmas catalog. The order had to be turned down. There weren't enough people to make that many blankets. "We figured out it would take Rogers 162 years to complete the order," he remarked.

Rogers also made more than one hundred saddle blankets for the Cherokee Nation this summer. His requests come from as close as "Tulsie" to as far away as "Newbraske."

"It's a good operation," remarked Terry Combs, tourism director for the Cherokee Nation. Combs said the tribe would like to repair the building and try to interest the community. He said mass marketing the blankets to Chicago and New York is also an idea.

There are not many left with the skill, Dreadfulwater noted. "It's becoming a lost art. If there isn't some interest generated, weaving is going to be a thing of the past."

"The younger generation doesn't seem interested in it," says Lucille. Rogers taught a class of seven students this summer. He said a couple of the children seemed interested. "Some of them, all they're after is money."

"I'm getting old," he says, commenting on thoughts of retirement. He sits on one side of the loom, Lucille on the other. There's another

Continued on page 262

rogers mclemore *continued from page 261*

lengthy period of silence after Rogers is asked what will happen to the store when he leaves. "I don't know. Everybody quit I guess."

Muskogee Phoenix "Insight" *November 14, 1978*
Text by Nancy Mathis
Photos by Mary Urech

To those responsible for recognizing my father, Rogers McLemore, along with my four brothers; Grover (deceased); George Robert, nicknamed "Dugam," Tahlequah; Sammie Leon, Briggs; and Edwin Lloyd, Wetumka. Dad never met a stranger. He was always eager to help anyone in need...an avid churchgoer, fluent in his Cherokee language, "Oochaled" is what he was named. As well as a gifted weaver, he was a wonderful cook. What I wouldn't give for one of his cobblers. I feel so fortunate to have had the greatest father who sacrificed so much for all of us. I can recall how he and I would jump in his little blue pickup truck and travel to Cedar Hollow to gather heating wood. I feel so fortunate to be left with all kinds of good childhood memories.

—Sara Leona McLemore Wofford
Interviewed by Shawna Morton Cain

cecil dick *continued from page 43*

"Fine," I said to Cecil, "Let me put you on the plane to Tulsa. You can go to a Creek wild onion dinner there. And get your son to come over from Tahlequah to pick you up in Tulsa and take you to another wild onion dinner in Tahlequah."

"All right," he said, "we'll do that tomorrow." And we did. I bought him a one-way ticket to Tulsa, took him down to the San Antonio airport, and said goodbye. I then drove to my office at St. Mary's Law School. Later that day, the phone rang at my office. I answered. The voice on the other end asked, "Are you Dr. Strickland?"

"I guess so, but who is this?" I answered.

"This is the FBI," the voice on the other end of the line replied.

"Oh," I responded.

The FBI agent went on, "We have someone who claims to be Cecil Dick. He has a one-way ticket to Tulsa."

"Well," I said, "since I just dropped Cecil Dick at the airport, the odds are that the person who claims to be Cecil Dick is Cecil Dick."

"Well," the FBI agent explained to me, "this person who claims to be Cecil Dick fits the profile of a Cuban hijacker. He has a one-way ticket and he is...."—there was a pause and the FBI agent continued—"an ethnic."

I responded, "You mean he is a brown person. A person of color."

"Yes, and he speaks with an accent, too," he added.

I'm not sure that Cecil spoke with an accent, but anyway, they said he did. And then they came to the point of the call. "He claims you can identify him. Would you be willing to come out to the airport and identify him?" he asked.

So I went out to the airport to identify Cecil Dick. I took four or five books with me that had pictures of Cecil with his paintings. When I arrived at the airport, the FBI was there, the airport security was there, and they had Cecil in their custody. They had stopped Cecil at the check-in counter and taken him into a back room. I identified Cecil. Showed them the pictures of him and his paintings and explained why he had a one-way ticket to Tulsa.

"We understand, Dr. Strickland, but you know, there are radicals and revolutionaries everywhere. We've got people coming from Cuba and everywhere. They're very dangerous. We thought Mr. Dick might have been a radical or a revolutionary, not just an artist," they concluded with obvious contempt.

Eventually, Cecil and I were allowed to leave. As we walked away, Cecil turned to me and said, "Don't they understand? Artists are the real revolutionaries."

lizzie whitekiller *continued from page 49*

We can't count them all—about sixty-five—but then my grandson had a baby and your grandson—that's about seventy. It's a king size.

Working on Next

Lizzie: I got one I'm quilting for my daughter. I'm not going to make any more tops. I'm just going to sew for my kids whatever they give me. My pastor, I made a summer quilt for him personal.

Ella: I'm doing a top now; it's called the "Eight Pointed Star." It's yellow and blue set on a white background. We don't sell them; we give them to family and donate them to fundraisers. It makes us feel better to do that.

Lizzie: If you go to the Cherokee Nation Gift Shop and look at the quilt, a lot of them got long stitches on them and not quilting; they tied. I gave the chief one, when he got in office. I don't know what the name of that was.

Ella: I don't know any (young people) making quilts.

Continued on page 263

lizzie whitekiller

continued from page 262

What Could Cherokee Nation Do?

Ella: I think (what) you need to do is start smaller children—only 6 through 12. Get two or three to start and get a certain place. It has to be like in town, probably, but through the summer, I'm sure the parents want their children to be there to have something to do. Young, young children. I think Janie (Jane Osti) does a wonderful job. It's just that wasn't me, but I loved all her art—all her pottery and things. Other than starting a sewing class for younger children—and that would be good for their hand-eye coordination—and getting them involved. It's just fun for us. If you enjoy it, it's going to be a lot easier to do.

— Margaret Raymond

From an interview with Margaret Raymond, July 2006

todum hair

continued from page 51

that box. As he got each piece out, he began to put them on—one-by-one—to show us the complete outfit. I can't say how special I felt watching him pull his "parade clothes" out with pride and accomplishment, telling stories of all of the different parades he had walked or ridden in.

Needless to say, as we pulled out of his driveway later that evening, we left Todum Hair's home both gifted and appreciative of him and all the old timers and their ways!

As always, Todum's medicine worked!

—By Roger Cain
Cherokee National Treasure

lucille hair

continued from page 53

She always wished that Cherokee Nation would do something to fix up the weaving shop. The building and looms are in such a state of disrepair. It used to be twice the size, but literally half the building collapsed. That never stopped or discouraged her. In the heat of the Oklahoma summer, she would be up there weaving away—windows open and fans going. The only source of heat was an old cast-iron wood stove. If she had winter or Christmas orders, she would go up and get that baby cranking. It would heat up the shop enough to make it bearable. The looms that she used were constantly breaking. She would take parts off one to fix another. I went up there one time when she was well into her '80s and found her on the floor, on her back, under a loom, working on one of the pedals.

In her later life, she would express worry that once she was gone, no one else would carry it on. For a long time, she was the only one weaving continuously. She taught several people to weave, including my cousins, Shirlene Dreadfulwater Proctor, Katie Ross, and myself. I learned to weave wall hangings the winter of 1989. I was in my fall semester at Northeastern State University and needed money for Christmas. I was wondering what I was going to do to come up with some Christmas cash, and Granny suggested that we go up to the shop and she would help me put up a warp and thread a loom. That time that we spent up there is invaluable. She would tell stories about all the other weavers who used to use that shop. I'm glad to see that people are picking it up again. Dorothy Ice has been weaving more these past few years, and Kathy Moomaw is in there also.

My grandmother was a very humble person. She never did it for the recognition or awards. She often wondered what all the fuss was about and would have just preferred to stay under the radar. She was more proud of the fact that she was the oldest living member of Cedar Tree. She was from a different time of being Cherokee than the rest of us. She was "old way." Grandma could read and write Cherokee. She loved to read her Cherokee Bible and sing Cherokee hymns. She always had something on the stove, just in case someone stopped by. Her legacy to us was to put God and family first.

—Aaron Lamar Hair, grandson

william foster

continued from page 61

Cherokee was spoken at home. In fact, that's the only language that my granny spoke. Both grandmothers spoke Cherokee.

I try to carry on his crafts; I do some woodcarving and can make wood products. I speak Cherokee, and I guess I'm sort of "craftsy." One of my favorite memories with my dad was working on cars and cutting firewood. We had lots of interaction then.

He loved to tease Mom. They'd play cards till 12:30 at night. Their favorite game was rummy. They would go get ice cream every evening at 6 (o'clock) except on Sunday. Sunday was church day, but every other day, they headed to Stilwell for ice cream.

Dad was recognized as a Cherokee National Treasure for bow making. He was a pretty good wood craftsman. He had an imagination. He made covered wagons, tables, bows and arrows, (and) river-cane flutes. He didn't get back into bow making until later in life—maybe in his sixties. He picked it all up on his own. He might have picked up some from Grandpa—I'm not sure—but he sure liked to make things. For his bows, he used the wood from Bois d'arc trees. He also made those whirly gigs and would paint them in good colors. One of the last pieces he ever made was a wooden airplane. He often gave his art to family members.

— Kenneth Foster, son

Interviewed by Pamela Jumper Thurman

david neugin

continued from page 63

Maxine: Levis Mose was the medicine man out from that area. And (Levi) was William Cabbagehead's brother- in-law.

Katherine: William also taught us how to play stickball. He knew how to use them.

Katherine: My brothers—when we worked at the village—made arrowheads, and Dad had to teach them how to make flint arrowheads. Dad knew how to do all that. He was the one at the village who taught how to make arrowheads 'cause he was the only one that knew how to make them with deer antler. My brother, Bobby, was a flintknapper at the village, and Dad taught him as well. It all got passed down.

Maxine: Even that marble making: no one knew how to make marbles, but Dave did. Your dad did.

Katherine: I don't think anybody knew about marbles and the game of marbles.

Maxine: Kathy, you should have brought your marble. She has a marble that came over the Trail of Tears. It belonged to Rebecca; she gave it to her dad. Then Dad made marbles.

Bryan: He (David Neugin) single-handedly saved the game, the craft, and the tradition. He taught a few people, and it went out from there.

Katherine: Up until Dad started teaching—and he taught two or three people—no one had heard of marble making.

Katherine: He made his bow string out of groundhog hide. Me and Mom used to really get aggravated at our dad 'cause when we were driving and we saw road kill, he would make us turn around.

Rebecca: Yeah. One time he made us turn around right after a coyote got hit. We were scared it was still going to attack us.

Maxine: She, my granddaughter, was named after Rebecca Neugin.

Katherine: I think Dad's bows were shown at the Smithsonian.

Rebecca: That is why he went to Washington.

Maxine: Yes. It was in the mid '90s.

Katherine: And at Gilcrease Museum, they showed his bows, and (at) Five Civilized Tribes Museum, too.

Katherine: Dad was raised by his grandparents,Turn and Alice Neugin.

Bobby Neugin, son: This point here is my dad's. He made it. That is a Cornstalk Shoot point and those are goose heads. One day, Dad come up and said, "Can we make eighteen bows by Saturday?"

And I said, "You make nine, and I'll make nine."

Dad said, "No you make all of them!"

These bows were going to Albuquerque. But we made the deadline. They were all Bois D'arc.

Katherine: He used to run around everywhere looking for Bois D'arc.

Bobby: Here are pictures of Dad stretching groundhogs out for strings. He would soak the hide in ashes, and after he finished treating the hide and getting the hair off, he would cut it to make a circle. Then he would cut a 1/8" strip all the way around it to make his bow strings. He would use two of them and twine them up together with loops on each end, and put weights on it to stretch the skin. He would use the back of the ground hog. The belly is too thin.

Bobby: Here is a picture of one rattlesnake he brought in, but he brought home a bigger one. Dad would bring rattlesnakes home to skin. One snake he brought home was twenty-two inches across and was seven feet eleven inches after squaring it up. Never saw a rattlesnake that big. He told me to go out and get the snake out of my truck, and it was as big as a stove pipe and was still wiggling when we was unloading that thing.

Katherine: This area is called High Grounds, but when Dad grew up, it was down close at Fourteen Mile Creek with his grandparents. He was telling me a story about when he was about nine years old. His grandmother got sick, so his grandpa sent him to his dad's mom and dad, who lived on the other side of High Grounds, at night. I said, "Dad wasn't that scary?"

And he said, "I had my lantern. I hunted all the time anyway." To him it was alright, but to me it was sad, a little boy going out so late at night.

Bobby: Dad said there was no brush around like it is now. So this land doesn't look the same as it did back then.

—Maxine Neugin, wife
Katherine Neugin, daughter
Bobby Neugin, son
Rebecca Neugin, granddaughter
Bryan Shade, nephew
Interviewed by Shawna Morton Cain

sally lacy

continued from page 65

together to make quilts, and my grandmother would sit at those long boards and sew, along with Jennie Sapp and some of the other Cherokee basket makers, weavers, and quilters. She would go to a church out on old Highway 33 and make jewelry with turquoise and metal. I had a ring she made. I'm kind of like her, I like making different stuff and so did she."

"Grandma made baskets for as long as I can remember. Whenever she needed money for us, she would make a basket. I remember her making a big hamper with a lid on it for a nurse at Claremore. It took her a month to make it but it was something!"

Sally would gather buckbrush and honeysuckle near her house, set a fire, and boil the vines for hours. The grandchildren would help her strip the bark off of the vines. She used natural dyes for dying the reeds and walnut was one of her favorite dyes.

Theresa grew quieter as she said, "She believed in family. She took care of her uncle who had cataracts. Her taking care of us is my favorite memory of her. She was my Mom. I miss her. Sometimes, I sit and wonder how I would be now if she were still here. She was a good person (and) very talented. She lived at Big Acorn Hollow until she got sick. She passed on around Labor Day in 1980. They gave my dad her Cherokee Treasure award after she had passed away. They had the singing at Kenwood, and we had the funeral after Labor Day. She's buried in Kenwood."

Story told by Theresa Buck, granddaughter
Interviewed by Pamela Jumper Thurman

john ketcher

continued from page 71

So being one of the first—they had one class started just ahead of me—they didn't change me again. But then I started to think, "Is this the only thing I'm going to be able to do?" I began to think, "Will I be able to get a job doing this?" That became a question, so I stayed with it 'cause my other option was to work on a farm, and I didn't think I wanted to be a farmer 'cause my family was always farming, and they didn't get too far in life. So, I thought I might do something else. Anyways, Mr. Ames came to Sequoyah around 1938. Well, we learned how to weave at Sequoyah. This was all I had.

But the years went by, and after four years, I was able to finally be ready to go home somewhere. I was halfway through the tenth grade when the war came, and was fastly coming on to eighteen. Because the war had conscription and I became nineteen years old in the midterm of my eleventh-grade year, I didn't want to take that chance. I decided to join at my choice so they wouldn't draft me and put me where I didn't want to go. 'Cause I know I couldn't dig a foxhole fast enough, but I could swim! There were four or five of us guys who were the same age, and we told our teacher we were going to miss school and join the Navy. We left out for Muskogee—putting thumb up in air like a hitchhiker. The recruiter told us they had filled their quota and to come back later. As we were walking out, the recruiter stopped me and said, "I have one spot if you're interested, but you will have to leave your buddies." I replied, "To be honest with you, they just tagged along with me."

During World War II, I was assigned to the U.S.S. New Orleans. It was a heavy cruiser. I became a gunner and first loader on the U.S.S. New Orleans for my remaining time in the war.

After the war—I think I was probably at my Aunt Katie's at that time—somebody knocked on the door. She said, "There's some man out here asking for you."

I said, "Do you know who it is?"

" I think he said his name was Ames," she said.

I said, "Oh yeah, I know him! That's my teacher at Sequoyah. He's the one who taught me weaving at Sequoyah." I went to the door and asked him in and introduced him to my aunt. We visited a while. And he said, "You need a job?"

I said, "I sure do!" Everywhere I go, they say everyone's already coming back from the war; jobs were being soaked up real fast. I said, "What ya' got in mind?" You know, because of the war effort and everything, everybody was gone, and they all went off to the war plants so now they are all coming back, taking all the jobs they can find.

Mr. Ames told me the Indian Bureau just sent him a letter from them saying, "We want to start up the crafts and the weaving in the communities for supplemental income. Teach them how to do that, and then we'll help them try to sell it—as they make them and they are saleable (and) good enough to sell."

I said,"Well, we can do that can't we?"

He said, "Yeah, I'm over all the five tribes now. I have to start everything in all the tribes." He said, "You can work in the Cherokee Nation since you know most of these people. We'll start here." And so he said, "Come on down. I can't pay you much starting in."

I said, "Well if it's just enough to keep me in tires and gas. Right now, I'm staying with my aunt, but I'll move over to Tahlequah, and I won't have to travel so far to my job."

He said, "That's good. Meanwhile, I'll try to get more money for you on contract."

That's the way I started out. I had a contract, and he said, "I want you to start first out here at Briggs. It's close by, and that will be your baby." He said, "I'll be working some of these others I've been working with until you get these started, and then we'll put you in different places." OK, that was, I guess, in 1947—something like that—or late '46 or so.

He took me out there and introduced me where he had started in a church. That's where they started. They had room for about two looms, and that's where they were when I took them over.

Continued on page 266

john ketcher

continued from page 265

Meanwhile, we begin to look around; if we were going to teach quite a few people, we needed a bigger place. I guess he had read in the paper this Army camp over by Braggs would begin to close down when they got all their soldiers out of there. They said they were gonna sell the barracks and all the things there because they were closing down. Being a government facility, anyway, we were able to get one. We had to go get it and set it up. They cut it in half—two sections. Government trucks hauled it back in two pieces. They took it out to Briggs, and this lady, Ms. Hair, and her family owned all that strip in there. They allowed Mr. Ames to build that on their land. We used again our carpentry shop people. Our electrician boys learned how to wire it up, and we had electricity. Only thing we didn't have was water, 'cause there were no rural lines in those days. So we dug a well right on the east side of there. I don't know how good that water was 'cause sometimes you dig a well, you get sulphur or salt or something. Anyway, they threw a bunch of pills of some kind to clean it up. I guess they used it for a while; I carried my own water.

It's important to keep all this stuff going. It can get hard or discouraging at times, but you just have to keep on going, plugging away. It will pick up again. I like to see people like your group here bringing the weaving up again. That's how it should be.

—John Ketcher
Interviewed by Roger Cain

mildred justice ketcher

continued from page 73

Mildred was born to Reverend Walter and Freddie Justice on their allotment land in the Green Community, Adair County, on the banks of what I grew up knowing as "Ben Night Creek." In a two-room cabin, she grew up with siblings, grandmother and "Uncle Walter,", an orphan child that the family had taken in to raise as their own. She attended Green Church, a structure that her father helped to construct and in which he served as a deacon. The family donated a portion of their allotment for the cemetery, and the church is still active today. On their allotment land, the family farmed and raised livestock, while her father also worked on the railroad. For a time, her father served as Deputy Sheriff in Adair County, an effort which allowed him to side the log cabin with clapboard that was painted white and to purchase a mantel clock for his wife.

Moving to Tahlequah from Green Community, Mildred attended Bagley School, which was located on the Northeastern University campus. She spoke fondly of her participation in the school's drum and bugle corps and of her pride in traveling to represent her school and town. Following graduation, she attended Haskell Institute, now Haskell Indian Nations University. Graduating in secretarial studies, she worked for Douglas Aircraft, the Tulsa bomber plant, during World War II, and later, at various Indian agencies in Valentine, Arizona, Philadelphia, Mississippi, Muskogee and Concho, Oklahoma. She also worked at the original Housing Authority of the Cherokee Nation and at Haskell Institute in Kansas.

Following the war, she married John Ketcher, and they spent their lives together, working on behalf of the Native tribes.

— Gary Ketcher, son
Interviewed by Pamela Jumper Thurman

jennie sapp

continued from page 75

Annie said "Whenever I think about that, I wish we had taken a picture of it because it was so amazing. Each side of the fish had eyes, just like a fish would." What's really amazing is that Jennie was pretty much self-taught on the crafts that she made and stayed busy making them all of the time.

Jennie was also a teacher; she taught people how to make baskets at places like Rocky Ford and Bull Hollow. At Rocky Ford, there was a loom, and Jennie could weave on the loom. She was a very gifted woman, and whatever she decided to do, she excelled. She was part of the Women's Church Club at Steely Baptist Church. The women would meet there and quilt on Wednesdays.

Jennie could also bead. Back in the 1980s, there was an arts and crafts store that sold supplies. Nita Underwood owned that store. That was where Jennie would buy commercial reed. Nita was holding a political event and requested that Jennie make an eagle, a donkey, and an elephant. Jennie did so. When Nita passed away, her niece contacted Annie and gave those baskets to her, along with some duck and swan baskets. Annie kept the eagle but shared the donkey, elephant, duck, and swan baskets with other family members. One of Jennie's wire turkeys is in Har-Ber Village in Grove, Oklahoma. It's been there for about twenty years. In fact, it was one of the first turkeys that Jennie ever made. Jennie also has a basket in the Smithsonian in Washington, D.C. When Chief Wilma Mankiller was invited to White House, she took one of Jennie's baskets to present to President Ronald Reagan, who then donated it to the Smithsonian Institute.

When Jennie taught at Rocky Ford, she taught some people who were really dedicated. She always knew if they showed up

Continued on page 267

jennie sapp

continued from page 267

every time, they were dedicated. Sanford Cummings was one of her students. He went on to make a lot of baskets. He excelled in basketry as well and was starting to make hats out of baskets. He also made vases. A Cherokee treasure who learned some weaving methods from Jennie was Mary Foreman. Jennie also taught Ella Mae Blackbear—another Cherokee Treasure and Jennie's relative—how to do some things with basketry.

Jennie taught high school students at both Jay and Grove public schools. The schools would invite artists in to teach various arts and crafts, and Jennie went several times. She was an amazing teacher because she explained things so well. Annie recalled, "She would tell us what to do and what not to do. She would get me started on making something, then tell me to make it the way I wanted. She might finish it up for me and have me watch her so that I would know how to do it later".

Another skill that Jennie taught herself was how to repair rocking chairs that were woven. She would cut and split the oak herself, a very hard task. The oak strips have to be sliced really thin, and she would soak them for days to get them limber enough to use on the chairs.

Annie said Jennie always made their holidays and birthdays special. Jennie raised a couple of her grandkids and babysat others. She still had time to do housework and cooking, would always save time to go see her mother and sisters, and always went to church. For the most part, Jennie made her crafts in the evening times, after supper, then worked with them until midnight. She would get up at 5 in the morning, have everybody fed by 7 a.m., and if she didn't have anything scheduled, she'd work on her crafts. She cooked three meals a day. However, Jennie would never make anything on a Sunday. That was her day of rest.

Annie said, "She loved to tell us stories about things that she and her sisters did. It was hilarious to hear them talk. They spoke in Cherokee. We weren't supposed to listen to the grown ups talk, but I understood everything they said and I would laugh along with them".

Talent runs in the family. Jennie's younger sister, Marie, a Cherokee Treasure, mentioned above, made baskets. (Her) niece, Leona Tiger, does beadwork. Rosie Chewie, another Cherokee Treasure, and another niece also made baskets. Jennie's son, Billy Joe Sapp, carries on his mother's tradition of weaving animals. Weaving animals is becoming a lost art among the Cherokee. Billy also makes very large baskets and weaves baskets around glass jars. Annie makes baskets when she has time.

Jennie passed away December 6, 1955. Annie said, "She was a treasure even in her family's eyes. She was a gem and well-loved."

—Story provided by Annie Sapp Loy, daughter
Interviewed by Pamela Jumper Thurman

betty scraper garner

continued from page 83

Betty was diagnosed with a terminal illness in 1992, but that did not hamper her spirit in educating those interested in basketry. She continued to teach others when she could and always had a positive word to say to those who came to see her at her home.

Betty was honored as a Living Treasure for the Art of Basketry in September 1993. She sat, as she always had, in her lawn chair on the square during the Cherokee Holiday, watching the parade and then turning toward the stage to hear the Chief's Speech during the State of the Nation address. When Deputy Chief John Ketcher announced those who had been chosen to receive the National Treasure's award and her name was called, it was one of her proudest moments. She was unaware that she had been selected to receive the honor, and the expression on her face was priceless.

She continued to weave with her daughter, Vivian, until she lost the strength in her hands to hold the weavers. Even though she could not weave, she would admire the baskets and hold them when finished and would always say, "This is a good basket. It feels so good!"

Betty succumbed to her illness in June 1997.

—Vivian Garner Cottrell, daughter

clesta manley

continued from page 85

get married instead. She did take an accounting class and worked at the courthouse in Mayes County for a year. During that year an election for county sheriff was held. Laughing, she said, "That was when I saw what really happened was not always what made it in the newspapers."

She says she has had some interesting jobs. Her great uncle was a tailor and taught Clesta and her mother how to sew and to use a tape measure to make their own patterns. She worked for the Cherokees making western pants. They put her on a machine that sewed the pockets and zippers. Square dancing was popular so she worked long hours sewing square-dance dresses, too. She was at the bank one day,

Continued on page 268

clesta manley

continued from page 267

and they asked her if she wanted a job. Clesta worked at the bank in Pryor and retired as an assistant vice president, after twenty-three years, when her children graduated from college. Her son is an engineer, and her daughter is a teacher.

Her dad had a place by the Grand River, and she wanted to build a house out there, but her husband did not want to live that far out, so they settled on a place about five miles west of Pryor on Highway 20. She built a shop on that property, and at her grand opening, several artists like Bill Glass, Bill Rabbit, Ben Harjo, Knokovtee Scott, and Ben Shoemaker attended. "I enjoyed it so much; it was just like a big play house. I really enjoyed it and was there about seventeen years. Then they decided to widen the highway and took our place."

Clesta taught some art classes to people who moved to Pryor due to the industrial park. She met people from other countries during that time. Some were from China and some from England. They were very nice people and bought several paintings from her. "It was so much fun teaching," and she is glad she listened to the friends who encouraged her, as she feared no one would be interested.

Since she discovered drawing and painting, Clesta has painted in the evenings and whenever she can make time. She took all the art classes Rogers College offered, and they sent her to the University of Tulsa for a class in Art History, then to Italy to study for a month. She remembers when she arrived in Italy, there was not even a road going up the hill to their hotel. A young Cherokee man in the art group carried her luggage up the hill for her.

She has taken all the workshops she could, even in Old Mexico, Santa Fe, New Mexico, and the Ozark Pastel Society. She was invited to enter works in the International Pastel Society and won a category where the award was given in art supplies instead of money.

Clesta Manley no longer has the van she used for years to travel to art shows, but she is still a very active artist. Her eyesight is not as good, but she is in a support group that meets monthly, and through the group. has a large magnifier that she uses for reading and painting.

— Clesta Manley
Interviewed by Susan Gilliland, vice-president
Indian Women's Pocahontas Club

mary foreman

continued from page 93

for basket making were the runners that were found on the ground. The vines were then boiled for several hours and stripped. Mary also used buckbrush for her baskets and always used natural dyes. Bloodroot was one of her favorite dyes, but she used walnut, from time to time, for darker color. Louisa has been making baskets ever since Mary taught her.

As the story came to a close, Louisa smiled and recalled that Mary said, "Don't ever do anything different, because this is the Cherokee way to make baskets. When you look at the basket at the bottom, you start out with twelve sticks, then you add two." Mary said that's the way they're supposed to be if they're Cherokee-made.

—Information provided by Louisa Soap, sister
Interview by Pamela Jumper Thurman

anna mitchell

continued from page 95

like a hundred years ago. They were the first Indian Market—Indians who started selling things to the public. And I admire them for it. They are great potters. They're sort of "sliding out of (traditional) ways," the elder's told me, when I was out there. (They told me) "Don't ever change your ways. Our younger people are making molds. They are doing this and they are doing that." So, I took their advice.

My husband was truly my partner. If I needed to go eat lunch, he was there to help me. The first year they (the Santa Fe Market) were so strict, I was scared to death. And when I came back from lunch, there was these two big old Pueblo guys standing in my booth. I was thinking, "Oh my gosh, they are going to kick me out of here." They were converging on my husband. And, of course, he had already told them about me going to (Seneca) Indian School. And so, they told us they would send somebody around to inspect our work. So, I went up and introduced myself to them. Immediately, they started telling me Indian jokes. So, I was in—never again to be questioned. And we had the same language because we went to Indian school.

I was a seamstress before I was ever a potter. I've always been a seamstress. I've sewed for people. I was a stay-at-home mom. I sewed for people and altered clothes and all of that—even designed my own kids' clothes, sometimes. Well, actually, I learned to sew at school when I learned how to read patterns and that kind of thing. That was good. But I built upon it after I started having children. I decided I needed a sewing machine, so that's what we got. I decided that I'd have to learn how to get those patterns out and use them and learn how to make clothes for my kids, which is what I did. That was what I was before I

continued on page 269

anna mitchell

continued from page 268

became a potter. I was a stay-at-home mom and did all those kinds of things the first part of my life. And the last half has been as a potter, I guess you would say.

I don't think you ever quit learning. I don't think you ever quit living. Because to begin with, you've given, before you've even started being a National Treasure. You can't be a National Treasure unless you've given. You're going to be asked to continue to give. A lot of times, the rewards are not in money, but they are just in whatever you're willing to do or are able to do. But, yes, I still continue to try to help when I can.

Anyway, that's my story.

—Anna Mitchell

Interviewed by Shawna Morton Cain

lee foreman

continued from page 97

The tradition of marble playing continues today with the use of billiard and pool balls. On nearly any night of the year, summer and winter, the Foreman brothers—Lee, Edward Charlie, and Andy—along with many other family members, will be playing marbles at the Cloud Creek Marble Field.

Lee Foreman was born October 19, 1928, in Delaware County, Oklahoma, to Richard and Sally Birdchopper Foreman. When he married his wife, Minnie, she had four young children—Dale, Opal, Dennis, and Jewell. To this family, another son, Amon, was born. Lee worked at various jobs while his children were young, even moving the family to California for a short time. But he knew the best place to raise them would be back home in Delaware County. The last years of his employment were spent in a job requiring the trust and care of the community as he drove a Colcord school bus transporting children to and from school and to school events in other towns. Lee Foreman's kindness and generosity in teaching others of Cherokee tradition have touched many lives.

— Cherokee National Treasure Nomination Letter by Phyllis Fife

Northeastern State University Bilingual Education Center

Cherokee National Holiday Committee

albert wofford

continued from page 101

The hard work would enable him to be among the select few when jobs like the railroad companies would want him. His work ethic would take him to the State of California, where he went to make a living for his family—staying for a while and even having a daughter born there—only to miss the wooded areas of northeastern Oklahoma, to where he and his family moved back, this time permanently. He gave his talent of hard work to different companies until finally coming to Phillips 66, where, even after retiring, the company still asked him to come back.

His artwork makes me think of his commitment to his God. His mom and dad would raise all their children in a church called Little Rock Indian Baptist Church. This church would become the family church.

The religious upbringing would also allow my dad to learn Cherokee songs and hymns. Having been raised in a home where only Cherokee was spoken, our dad would not learn to completely speak English until about the age of 20, understanding that a changing world and a necessity to support a family required a new language in a changing job market, but like Cherokees, our dad always learned to adapt.

The strong messages from Cherokee preachers like Smith Grass, who baptized him at age ten, would help to strengthen his belief, mold his life, and later his art.

The artwork of our dad can be seen in the way he served his country and his church. A U.S. Army Veteran, he talks about the many places in the Pacific he saw and how he hitched a ride home from California back to Oklahoma when his tour was over. When the decision to serve his church was settled, Dad was responsible for helping the Quarterly or "Two-Day" meetings that would happen at Little Rock. Dad wouldn't get the fatted calf, but the fatted hog, and help boil the hog meat, (completing the job) just in time when all the Cherokee preachers had finished their all-day sermons (and needed to feed) to a hungry congregation. The fellowship that took place was great; my dad loved the people coming together and would often recall when he was a child—how families would show up in wagons and camp out from Friday to Monday, all in preparation for Cherokees coming together.

His art would be tempered by a wonderful partner who also truly represents the Cherokee way. In 1949, he met a young Cherokee girl named Lena Scuggins, our mother.

Our mother, along with her two sisters, Nellie and Lorene, and her older brother, Curtis, lived at the Sequoyah Orphanage School in Tahlequah. Our mother's mom, Allie Galatcher Scuggins was a midwife in the community of Eucha, and my mom would often

continued on page 270

albert wofford

continued from page 269

recall how she would hear a knock on the door as a neighbor would be looking for help from her Mother to deliver a baby in the middle of the night. She would harness up the horse and wagon to go and be of service. Unfortunately, her mother would pass away when she was a child. Their father, Grape Scott Scuggins, was an engineer and brought the kids to the school to receive a proper education. Curtis would leave Sequoyah when World War II came along and join the Navy. Our mom graduated from Sequoyah in 1951, and on that bright sunny May Day, our dad was there to pick her up; later that year, they were married. Together, they would raise six children. Later, they would be blessed with 21 grandchildren and 15 great-grandchildren.

Our mom was instrumental in developing Cherokee Government representation in Mayes County in the 1970s, when Native American Tribes were beginning to re-establish their sovereignty, attending the first Cherokee Nation Council meetings of the modern era. Our mom was also helpful in developing the local Head Start Education Program in Mayes County in the 1960s, which culminated in (both) my sister and her meeting President Lyndon B. Johnson in 1966, when he visited Pryor, and giving the First Lady, Lady Bird Johnson, a scrapbook of the Head Start program, as well as a bouquet of roses.

Our mom encouraged our dad to pursue his art.

Growing up, our mom taught us to say "goodnight" to each other. When we would say goodnight to our dad, we would always see him reading his Cherokee New Testament. Dad not only can speak Cherokee but was raised to read and write it as well.

When I look at our dad's art, I think about all the strength, care, hard work, and, most of all, love that can be seen.

There are many true Cherokee Treasures since the time God created us to be Cherokee, but I need not look any further than our Cherokee dad to know that we have truly known and seen one.

— Gerald Woffard, son

ella mae blackbear

continued from page 103

Now, I'll have a basket and someone will come knocking at my door, and they say, "I was visiting a friend who said you might have a basket." It's already been asked for. Now that's hard. And I feel sorry for them. And then I have to turn this basket loose and then make another basket for the other lady. That's when I get disgusted, and I just feel like quitting. It was like last night,. I called a lady and said, "I got your basket ready." I thought she'd come in that weekend and pick them up or after Thanksgiving. She said, "I'm leaving right now." And I still had the rim to do. And my daughter: I said, "Charlie, I'm in a mess." And I had that basket done about 10 minutes before she got here. It was still damp. I said, "Never again will I do that." That was a close call!

I'm not really after that big money. I just get by. I guess you could make a lot of money. But, I'm not for that. I like to keep friends and make them happy. When they're happy, it makes me happy.

I think they (the younger generation) can do a lot better if they take interest in it. I hope that my daughters can continue as they get older. They think it's for older people. Guess they think it's for people that sits around and doesn't have nothing to do. And I know if they really take interest in it, they can do a lot more than I can.

— Ella Mae Blackbear

Excerpts from *"Native American Master Artists Video Series"*
by Full Circle Communications
Ella Mae Blackbear: Cherokee Basketmaker

kathryn kelley

continued from page 105

over his head, and we'd have to wash our faces so many times. You're familiar with that, right?

My mother was non-Indian. She spoke perfect Cherokee. My dad's two cousins taught her. And she helped them with their English. I am half-Cherokee.

How did I get started making baskets? I saw in the paper or somewhere they were having a class. And I thought, I'm going to go to that class and see what it's like. Well, I just fell in love with it. And then there was a lady who lived there, and she had a shop, basket materials, and supplies. She just kind of took me under her wing. She and I became great friends right off. She'd call me sometimes, and she'd say, "What are you doing? Come on out and let's weave." I'd go out to her shop, and she taught me just about everything I know about weaving. She's still living. She's real old. Martha Featherston is her name. And I got started weaving with her, really. It was after I retired from teaching that I began to weave baskets.

Well, I claim to speak Cherokee. Maybe I could if I had to. Yes, it was the first language, really, in my home. And like I said, my mother spoke it, too. I never did read it. Of course, at church, it was always in Cherokee. Did I say that my daddy was a preacher? He preached in Cherokee. Baptist—I'm half-Baptist.

When I married Bob, he belonged to the Christian Church. I could not get him into the Baptist Church. He had more excuses.

Yeah, Daddy preached in Cherokee around the Rocky Mountain area. He had a church down toward Sallisaw, south of Stilwell somewhere, that he had for a long time. Yeah, he preached in Cherokee—long and loud! I always liked it. I really respected my daddy being a preacher. Yeah, I spent a lot of time sleeping on the church bench when I was real little.

—Kathryn Kelley

Interviewed by Shawna Morton Cain

betty bean smith

continued from page 107

Mr. Hagerstrand was over that. I jumped into making anything—basketry, pottery—and I was just a villager then until I started going up and getting acquainted with more of the Cherokee work we were doing there. And it had to be traditional— which was hard to keep accurate—because you couldn't use modern tools or anything like that. He wanted it to be a living museum, as he called it. No metal knives, no glasses, no eating modern food in front of the tourists, talking Cherokee, and it was hard. You wouldn't think it would be just to do that. Once in a while, somebody would get caught with a knife.

We started with the training program before anything was opened up, even the village. See, the village was just him (Colonel Martin Hagerstrand) and "Chief" Boyd's idea. We took our training at Sequoyah in one of the rooms there. For eight weeks before the village opened up there, we had to learn basketry, pottery, buckskin clothing, arrowheads, bow making, and the story on how the fire came to Cherokees. That had to be part of the story. So that's how that was born. That's a better word for it—"born." I guess about twenty, give or take, did the training. We had to learn what they made the arrowheads out of—flint, (and using) deer horns as hammers. I mean the whole raw materials. Hagerstrand thought it was unusual that I took up on Cherokee history as much as I did. He said, "You were kind of shy when you first started."

I said, "No I wasn't. I was just sizing you up!" I found it interesting because history was my favorite subject in school and I guess it just stayed with me.

I was approached by Bob Carlisle, and I can't remember the second person. It might have been Ross Swimmer. I don't know. They asked if I was interested in running for Cherokee Tribal Council and I said, "Oh, I don't know. That's too much responsibility."

They said, "No, we'd like for you to run. We think you could win."

And I said, "Well, let me talk to Columbus (her husband) about it and see what he thinks." And I talked to him.

I was kind of excited about them to ask me about it, and Columbus said, "Well, I think you could if you have the heart to do it."

I said, "Well, let me think about it for a while." And Carlisle gave me about a week to think about giving an answer. So, I finally decided to go ahead and run. It's been very interesting going around campaigning, you know. It was like all at-large; I went through all the counties campaigning. I found it very interesting and rewarding to be representing the Cherokee People. Columbus went with me. He'd go out into the crowd and talk to the people that talked fluent Cherokee—explain to them—and they'd ask him why he wasn't running. He said, "Well, I'm not good with the public." He said, "She can do it. She has any questions, and I can help her out." So from then on, I got on the Council after that.

Well, I think about Cherokee history being born to Tahlequah. I don't care what anybody thinks or says. I think we opened up the history for the Cherokees with the Tsa-La-Gi Village. Because a lot of them didn't know what you were talking about whenever they said, "We're going to train for pottery. We're going to train for basketry, arrowhead making. But, everything's going have to be traditional."

No, they didn't know what that meant. We didn't go by the books; we lived it. We trained with it. I didn't know what clay pots were until we started working with it. No modern clay at all. Flint for arrowheads. Cane for blowguns. Anything. And we didn't have children in the village the first few years, and then after that, we begin asking, "Weren't there children in the village?"

"Of course there was!" So, we were allowed to start bringing our children. They ran around there just like they were at home. It made it seem more authentic than modernized. And the kids weren't allowed to talk to the tourists. They'd shy away from them. But after a few years, they just got used to it. They didn't let the tourists bother them. At first, they were kind of standoffish. Then later on, it was like they weren't even there. They were just living their own lives. They didn't even wear moccasins until, if they wanted some made, the Cherokees made pucker-toe moccasins if they wanted them. The kids went barefoot. Well, the adults did too after a while. Somebody complained about our running around there and not having shoes— moccasins—on. Mr. Hagerstrand tried to get us to wear moccasins. We stood up to him and said, "Well, they didn't wear moccasins in the summertime! Maybe, in the wintertime." So, it made it normal. After that, if you wanted moccasins, you learned how to make the pucker-toe moccasins.

Almost all of my kids worked in there. I think I had one daughter—she didn't go because she was too young; of course, I had to hire a babysitter. One was a guide, and the rest of them worked inside the village. They learned arrowhead making, blowgun making, thistle for the darts; everything was handmade. And they could make them look pretty. They grew up there. We were always together, all year around.

— Betty Bean Smith
Interviewed by Shawna Morton Cain

vyrl keeter

continued from page 111

"When I pop a large stone and it splits open—showing the beautiful color—and make a nice arrow point, it causes the youngsters to want to know more and study the Indian culture and history," Vyrl said. "I suppose I shall never stop teaching the art of knapping."

His skills and teaching the art of flint knapping gives him satisfaction that he is helping to preserve the traditions, skills, and customs of his ancestors, the Cherokee people.

—Vyrl Keeter
Interviewed by Jami Murphy

maxine stick

continued from page 113

We would travel to numerous places to sell her baskets. She, for the most part, had her regulars. Selling her baskets was her means of income. I remember there were days, when she would take one basket into town, sell it, and then buy groceries. People always came to our house looking for baskets, and she always had some on hand. She would always say how it would be a disappointment (for them) to come so far and not find what they were looking for.

I love going to a place and seeing her basket displayed. I enjoy hearing people say (that) they own one of her baskets and how she was the sweetest person they met. Or meeting someone and then finding out that they used to buy baskets from her. I often look at her awards and letters of thank you that she received throughout her life. (She was sent a) letter of thanks from Ronald Reagan for receiving one of her baskets that Wilma Mankiller presented to him. (She was also sent a) letter of recognition from the Smithsonian Institute when they put her basket on display. Recently, I became excited when I viewed her basket on display at a local museum.

I can only hope to be half as great as she was. I talk to her when I begin weaving and even though I do not have her chair, I have her scissors and her knife. So every basket that I make still has a part of her.

—Stephanie Stick, daughter
Interviewed by Jami Murphy
Courtesy of Cherokee Phoenix

sue girty thompson

continued from page 165

attended Haskell Instit\ute and took some classes at Northeastern State University.

When I came to work at the Cherokee Nation, Durbin Feeling was teaching a class in Cherokee. That's my job now, a certified teacher of Cherokee literacy, in the Cherokee Teacher Enrichment Program. We include the history, the culture and the language. We teach a lot of people. We go out into the communities to teach, and we teach in the public schools. We have flash cards, and we teach them the syllabary. My knowledge of the Cherokee language enabled me to teach Cherokee language classes at adult education sites in the Cherokee communities during the early years.

I met Jerry Thompson, my husband, while working at the Cherokee Nation. We were married on June 28, 1968. He passed on November 24, 2002. We have one son, Scott Thompson, and two granddaughters—Taylor and Taryn.

In 1995, the Johnson O'Malley Program initiated the Cherokee Challenge Bowl for students in grades K-12 to expand their knowledge of Cherokee history, government, and culture as they competed in academic competitions by teams. I was instrumental in helping to develop the 450 Cherokee words and phrases list that is currently being used in the CCB manual. Then, in 1998, the JOM Program initiated the Cherokee Language Bowl for students in grades K-2 to engage them in academic style competition as a team, testing knowledge of the Cherokee syllabary and use of the written and spoken Cherokee language. My knowledge of the language was helpful in selecting words and phrases for accuracy pertaining to the Cherokee language. I was also instrumental in typing the syllabary and phonetic sounds for the Cherokee Cultural Competitions Cherokee Words and Phrase List. This year, we'll offer creative writing. The kids can write a story in Cherokee. It keeps the language going.

I think the Cherokee language is special; it's what makes us Cherokee. Speaking Cherokee is fun; we can always throw in something funny. It makes you feel special to be a speaker. Cherokee is a lot different from English; it's more personal. If your grandma gets after you and she tells you that you'd better not do that, it hurts more to be told in Cherokee.

Being a speaker is something I grew up with; it made me special, and it's what makes me Cherokee. Some people may say they're Cherokee, but they may not have lived like a Cherokee. It's different. It's our culture. It's the things we do, like the stomp dance. Next year will be my fortieth year here at the Cherokee Nation. It is not work. It is a privilege and an honor to serve my tribe.

—Sue Girty Thompson
Interviewed by Pamela Jumper Thurman

lorene drywater

continued from page 117

As the rest of us grew older, we learned different things. Jobs were hard to get for my daddy. I remember I seen him get up hours before daylight. He always carried a cross-cut saw and old axe on his shoulder. And Mama, she went on with her chores, keeping house, doing the laundry when she had soap to wash with. It was one of her wash days that I decided to cry for a doll. Before that, I was thinking, "All my cousins have pretty, store-bought dolls. They cry when they want something." Then, too, there were grandparents living with them. They bought dolls, food, clothing for the family. But there were no grandparents living with us. We had to go visit kinfolks for a few days at a time. I believe that was my parents' way of getting us kids food.

Anyway, the day I cried, thinking that I might get a doll, Mama was walking down a path that led to the creek where she did her wash. She was carrying a sack of laundry over her back. I was walking behind her. I couldn't see too well because my eyes were full of tears. She stopped

continued on page 272

lorene drywater

continued from page 272

and bent down. I bumped into the sack. I fell backward. She said, "Here pull up this weed. Come to the creek bank and wash the dirt off the roots. I'll show you how to make a doll." That's how I learned to make Buffalo Grass dolls. I've improved a lot. Then, it was all grass—nothing added on. Cows will not eat this grass, but they will chew it. That's how I used to lose my dolls from my playhouse. Cattle roamed free then.

Some people donate (material), and I still have another box coming in from Bartlesville where she said her niece got that (material) from somebody. They just come over and hand it. They say, "Here's a box." I used to get my scrap material from, let's see, I think it was called Bacone Resale Shop. It was on First Street in Muskogee. My daughter, Susie, was just a little bitty thing. And I just started taking us to that resale shop, and I would find skirts big enough to make my little girls' dresses, whatever they needed. And I didn't have to buy new material. I got white shirts for my doll's slips and just whatever I could find, and then after I'd get it home, I would go back through that and choose which one I'm going to use for my babies' dresses. Now, this is what I was doing, putting my children through school. Altogether, I have seven children. It's fun to raise children.

I pray a lot—I still do—to let me work on my dolls until my last day on Earth.

— Lorene Drywater

Interviewed by Shawna Morton Cain

marie proctor

continued from page 121

sister of the late Jennie Sapp, who was designated as a Master Basket Weaver in 1990. To have four Cherokee National Treasures in one family speaks to the talent in these women.

In 2006, Marie Proctor was also the recipient of the Keetoowah Cherokee Tradition Keepers award for her skill in basketry. This award is designed to honor Keetoowah Cherokee craftspeople, artisans, and elders who are committed to education and cultural preservation. Primary emphasis is given to crafts or arts produced in the traditional manner, using Native materials.

Marie, like all other elders, has begun having health issues. She hasn't sewn in over three years, and the last basket she weaved was a year ago. It was a wall-hanging basket made of reed. This basket hangs above her bed. Her daughter and son-in-law have since passed, so getting natural material is impossible.

She still attends the same church, but now she catches a ride. She still finds things funny. She says she wants to try to sew again, and maybe with her new glasses she will be able to do so. But for now, she keeps busy watching her chickens and gathering their eggs.

—By Stephanie Stick, Interviewer,
and Pamela Jumper Thurman

eva mae pigeon smith

continued from page 123

She was very particular about teaching how to shake the shackles. Ellen Murdoch, Eva's daughter, recalled that she and her cousins would practice in the yard, and Eva would instruct them. She was constantly making a new pair or repairing a pair for family or friends. Ellen also said "I learned how to use an electric drill by watching Mom drill holes in many, many turtle shells." As long as her health allowed, Eva never missed a stomp dance. She would shake shells from the first dance of the night until the last dance the next morning.

Sadie Ringgold, Eva's daughter, said that her mom gave her turtle shells and told her to keep one (shell) in the house because it would keep her home safe from storms. She told her to point the shell toward the oncoming storm, and the storm would turn away from the home.

Eva Mae Pigeon Smith passed away on December 28, 2004, at her home near Vian, Oklahoma. She was preceded in death by her husband, William Lee Smith, both of her parents, Sam and Easter, brothers Dewey Pigeon, Sie Pigeon, and Watie Pigeon, and one great-granddaughter, Sierra Hornbuckle.

—Story provided by daughters,
Sadie (Smith) Ringgold and Ellen Murdocch
Eva's words courtesy of KJRH, Channel 2, Tulsa, Oklahoma, documentary,
Spirit of the Fire, by Sam Jones
Interview by Pamela Jumper Thurman

lena blackbird

continued from page 125

new one. But when I was there, I remember we were really busy. There were kids around and everybody was like family. Everybody enjoying each other when there was time to do that.

Lisa: We'll be out and see others—people from the village—and they are still real close.

Lena: Sometimes the village was so hot. Sometimes people would say, "I don't see how you can stand it out there." There were trees and a lot of shade. I never knew how hot it was until we came out of the village. Then I knew how hot it was. It seemed like there was always a breeze blowing. I met somebody on the tour from Pennsylvania. Another one too was from Wisconsin, I lost touch with her later on. We talk and they ask me something and then get started talking and we fall in love.

Some of the younger girls was learning to weave. They also would come ask me how to do this and how to do that. Some of them

continued on page 274

lena blackbird

continued from page 273

would get it right away, but some didn't have that natural ability, I guess. It was funny one time when we was making baskets there, they would send them upstairs to sell. The young girls, they really didn't know how to sometimes get theirs right. And one got hers rejected, and they sent it back. We just thought that is what we had to do—whatever they told us to do or make in the village. Those were sent up to the shop to be sold.

Lisa: We used to set up booths at almost every show—Cherokee Holiday, Five Civilized Tribes in Muskogee, Saline Creek, (and) Broken Arrow.

Lena: It was Chester Oosahwee who nominated me for Living Treasure. I guess to me, traditional would go back to our ancestors, and it's about all they used back then. They used to go split them splints. I think this is why we still want to use those things. Of course, we can't just go out and cut trees. Lisa still uses honeysuckle when she can find it and get it.

Lisa: We talked about this. It almost feels like and looks like people aren't caring enough about the traditional anymore. To us, we do! I mean, everything around us changes, but we still have that traditional way of life. There's more to us than just commercial. The colors they use weren't (like the colors)— nature colors—found way back then. Staying with the traditional colors and natural dyes is important to us too. She taught me not to mix the commercial dyes with the natural reed. I agree with that—for us, anyway.

We're all proud Mom has taught us all—even her grandkids—how to make traditional baskets. She is a really good teacher and has taught a lot of people.

Lena: And I loved doing it, too.

—Lena Blackbird
with Lisa Forrest, daughter
Interviewed by Shawna Morton Cain

clarence downing

continued from page 131

Indian associated with the recording by singer Hank Williams, made for a Grove restaurant.

"I ain't too high on 'em," he said of his prices, ranging from about $65 to $500. "I want everyone who wants one to have them when I leave here." He said he often gets his ideas as he sits down at his workplace. "First I get it in my head, and then I know what it's going to look like." And he tries to finish before leaving from the mound of shavings, "unless I get stopped by snow or rain."

Clarence's artwork is on display throughout the world, including Japan, China, Rome and the Vatican. For fun, he also enjoyed playing bingo, fishing, and hunting for crawdads.

— Jami Murphy
Courtesy of The Oklahoman

dorothy dreadfulwater ice

continued from page 135

I don't know how many times we stopped. They were wooden spokes. It was a model T 1928. I've been working on cars ever since.

I started dancing when I was three years old. I started with Jig, which I don't do anymore. And then it switched over to Charleston—Charleston to Jitterbug to Two Step to Square Dance. And they're not doing the same Two Step that I did. It's different now. And I clog now. Matter of fact, shoes are down at the shop. I've got to pick them up tomorrow—getting them fixed, changing out the taps, putting louder ones on.

There used to be country home dances, country square dances. They would move all the furniture out of the living room—put it outside, pull up the rugs, or whatever they had on the floor. And about 10 p.m., the ladies around there would cook and sell sandwiches. Maybe have ice cream and sell an ice cream cone for a nickel. People of all ages! The instruments were a fiddle, two guitars, no electric. It was not electrified. The lights were "kool" lamps. It was fun. Now it's all electrified. It's loud. You don't enjoy it as well. It's different. Fiddle and guitar is all I like, really. We danced all night and then sometimes, they'd hang quilts on the window to make it dark at dawn. As long as there was somebody there dancing. I mean, there were always a lot, a lot of people. They walked about seven miles, some of them did. Some of them had cars. Some came on horses. It didn't matter. Whoever wanted to participate. It was mostly those who wanted to dance and wanted to learn, and it was all ages. The elders are the ones I used to like to dance with 'cause they knew how. I already knew how because I started when I was about two or three.

Then I started Stomp Dancing. I started Stomp Dancing when I was pretty young. I didn't start wearing shells until I was eight. My Grandma Dreadfulwater would do her ritual thing. When she finished hers, she would tell me to come sit down on that old log, and she'd put them (shells) on me. She'd get me up and push me out there. She put tow sacks around my legs first and then put the *daksi* on. The tow sacks were like you now put towels on the legs for *daksi*, keeping them from falling or rubbing blisters on you. I would finish the night out wearing those. I didn't have to adjust them, 'cause Grandma knew how to put them on. I would dance the rest of the night at Chewey; I think they call it Long Valley. And then later, I switched over to Red Bird. It was back in 1990s, I guess.

I go there now. I don't Stomp Dance as much as I did because my back is bone-to-bone. So I just do what I can. But I enjoy it. I dance all night. I went last month in June, and I spent the night in my little car. I enjoyed that. Listening to bugs.

—Dorothy Dreadfulwater Ice
Interviewed by Shawna Morton Cain

al herrin

continued from page 135

were things that had been traditionally used by Cherokees, handed down, and just about to become lost because all the old bow makers, for example, were just about gone and no young Cherokees were learning it. I had learned how to make bows and arrows from older Cherokees, like I said, and Colonel Hagerstrand asked me to work with him on this in the bow-and- arrow part. For example, Hastings Shade was working on marbles, and other people were working on other things. Different people worked on trying to preserve these arts.

In all these years I was on that committee that selected the National Treasures each year, and I was the longest serving member on it when I resigned in 2015.

Around 1958. I got my bachelor's in chemistry at Northeastern State University and then I got my master's degree in biological sciences from Oregon State in 1967. I got my Ph.D, in science education from Nova Southeastern University in Fort Lauderdale Florida in 1972. My thesis was on how cultural differences—like (in) Indian and (in)non-Indian kids—affect the learning of science. So I came back from Florida and did my data collection at Sequoyah High School and Tahlequah High School. I analyzed those groups and found out all kinds of factors that affected learning experiences.

For example, you would think Indian kids who were traditional and who lived back in the hills might have more superstitious beliefs and, therefore, have difficulty learning science because of that. I found that there were things that did affect the learning of science. And of course, I made recommendations on how these (findings) could be used to better educate Indian kids, how to adapt the program to them and their methods of learning.

I wrote my book, "*Cherokee Bows and Arrows: How to Make and Shoot Primitive Bows and Arrows*," as part of my work on that, and then I started teaching people how to do this. For that work and for preserving the making of bows and arrows, I was named a Cherokee National Treasure in 1991. I had always wanted to write and, when our kids got grown and left home, Frankie and I were both teaching. I told Frankie that I had always wanted to write and I wanted to stop teaching and write, and she said, "OK." That's when I wrote the Cherokee Bows and Arrows book and *"Cherokee Calling."* I did a lot of other newspaper articles and chapters in other books. I started a newsletter called the *White Bear Newsletter*. It was basically about Cherokee culture—hunting and camping and outdoors kind of things. It is published about four times a year or more. I'm still writing—still working on things every day.

I've been married to Frankie for 57 years. We started going together when we were juniors in high school. That's where—in the English class where we first met—I developed my desire to be a writer We've been together actually 63 years. Together, we have four children, 10 grandchildren and four great-grandchildren.

What I'm doing now is teaching. I teach with the mentorship program created by the Cherokee Nation where I give the knowledge in bow making I've gathered over the years to further the art of bow-and-arrow making. This book, "Cherokee Calling," deals a lot with Cherokee history and culture and spirituality. I am a firm believer in the worth of Cherokee culture and Cherokee spirituality. Both have had a big effect on my whole life. I have a very close connection with nature and with the animals and the plants. I very strongly believe in many of the beliefs of the ancient Cherokees,. The spirits and nature have done a great deal in guiding my life.

—Al Herrin

Interviewed by Jami Murphy

nadine wilbourn

continued from page 137

would drive all the way from Locust Grove to the Cherokee Heritage Center in an older car with no air conditioning. In the summer it was really hot, but Nadine didn't mind the heat. She worked at the village for approximately ten years and really enjoyed it.

Darrell recalled, "It was pretty neat when she started making baskets. We lived in Muskogee for a while, and I think she may have learned how to make baskets in Tahlequah. I'm not sure. I just know she made them for a long time. She would make her baskets and do beadwork, and we kids would sometimes go with her to sit at the booth while she sold her arts. I never learned how to make baskets; I thought it was a woman thing," Darrell laughed. "My sister might have learned a little. Mom was a good basket maker."

Nadine would show her arts at Arkansas and Fort Smith a lot and stayed very busy with demonstrations and orders. She married Verlon Wilbourn in 1980. Nadine Mankiller Chuculate Wilbourn was named a living treasure in 1997 by Chief Wilma Mankiller for her basketry skills. She also received honors for her honeysuckle baskets at the Five Civilized Tribes Museum and received other awards and honors as well. She was well-known for her use of natural materials as well as for her split-oak basketry skills.

Granddaughter Patricia Thomas learned basket weaving from Nadine and was fortunate to work with Nadine at the Cherokee Heritage Center. Nadine taught her granddaughter beadwork and taught her how to speak the Cherokee language.

In the telling of this part of the story, Lorene laughed and said she once asked her mother, "Why didn't you teach me all of that?"

Nadine's response was, "You wasn't ever still enough for me to teach you anything."

Nadine spent her later years in Locust Grove but continued her zest for life. She was learning to read Cherokee. The world lost quite a treasure on April 13, 1999, when Nadine passed away in Locust Grove, Oklahoma. She is buried in Barber Cemetery.

—Darrell Chuculate, son, and Lorene Chuculate, daughter
Interviewed by Pamela Jumper Thurman

bessie russell

continued from page 141

were scared to get up and bat against my pitching. I liked that. Their coach told them, "Just choke up on your bat., Choke up on your bat!" I'd get up there to the plate, and they'd get up there, and, instead of doing what "choke" is in baseball or softball, they would just grip that bat really, really tight like they were choking it. Oh, that was crazy! One game I remember, I struck out fourteen, I believe it was.

I married three weeks before I turned seventeen. My mama had to go with me and sign. I met my husband at a ball field. They used to play baseball back then; it was always baseball. There used to be a ball field where I said the blackberry patches were—up there on the hill. This one day, we girls went to the ballgame after church. I really can't say I met Chief up there at the ballgame, but that's where it all started. We got married about a year later on May 28, 1955. We were married for 47 1/2 years. We used to say, "What are we going to do for our 50th anniversary?" We never made it. Two-and-a-half years is all we missed it by.

I am a traditional basket weaver. To be able to call yourself a traditional basket weaver, you need to gather your own material. Go out and get your own reed and process it the way it needs to be processed. Even if you know how to get it, there's a difference in knowing how to get it and then doing it yourself. That's the way I feel about it. I feel like I can totally say I am a traditional basket maker if I go out and get my own reed and dye. I would say that you have to go out and get the honeysuckle, and you do all the necessary steps to make a basket, and dig your own blood root or whatever color you want or you are going to use. To me, that is a traditional basket—knowing what to gather, the best. You know you can gather anything, but it should be the best kind you can find. When you talk about honeysuckle, people will say, "Oh there is a lot of it down here." And to me, what they're looking at is what's on the fence or trees or whatever. You can use some of it. Most of it is so twisted and curled, you can't take that out. It's permanent. I don't care how long you soak it, it will just not straighten out. It takes knowledge and skill to know where to get the best honeysuckle runners to use for basketry.

My daughter, Teresa, is a basket maker, and I try to encourage her to keep it up. One of these days, I won't be able to do it. And I want Teresa, Vicki, or somebody to carry on. I think they will.

—Bessie Russell
Interviewed by Shawna Morton Cain

richard rowe

continued from page 143

well but she couldn't recall just how many people he had taught. Madonna said that Richard liked teasing friends and family. She shared the memory of Richard teaching someone to carve an eagle head, but when the man showed the family, he was not aware that Richard had already instructed them to say, "That's a really nice rooster!" The family laughed at that memory.

Friend Joe Byrd, past Chief of the Cherokee Nation and current Cherokee Nation Tribal Council Speaker, recalled meeting Richard in 1995. He described Richard as a traditional, language-speaking, spiritual man who came into his office. "I recall that he had a slight limp. He congratulated me in the Cherokee language on my election as Chief and warned me that it would be a tough road. He said that they would come at me from every side, that I would be like a tree—almost uprooted and turned in every way—for the next four years. He was from the Moodys/Teresita area. During that visit, he said that he had to go back through Phoenix and up to Seattle (and) then (to) Alaska, where he was helping some tribes. He had one sample of the knives he made. He only stayed thirty or forty minutes, but you can always tell if someone is genuine, and he was genuine."

Joe said that Richard was a knife maker, a carver, and a gig maker. He used springs out of older cars—no older than 1949 though—and made gigs and knives. His knives are owned by some very famous people. One is in the possession of former-President Bill Clinton; another is with Governor Frank Keating, and another(is) with Senator Kelly Haney.

Joe said that Richard came back some time later and said, "I told you (that) you would be all right." Joe said that he had an old bag, kind of like a tow sack. He said that he needed some help. He had some health problems that were going to cost about six thousand dollars. He said that the knives in the sack were all that he had. "We set up a contract to pay him for the knives and cut a check so that he would be able to take care of himself. I remember that he seemed to take care of everybody else. There were lots of people who depended upon him. He was a real humble person of soothing demeanor, a good spiritual humble man. He was special to me."

Friend and relative David Cornsilk said "Richard was well-known in the community for his fluent Cherokee, and he gave many children their Cherokee names when other family members couldn't. He was a very funny man with an easy smile and a kind word for anyone who met him."

Richard was honored in 1996 as a Cherokee National Treasure for his skills in carving.

Richard Rowe, the adventurer, the artist, left this world on February 3, 2004 while living in Sacaton, Arizona. He was buried with the Olympic medal that meant so much to him. The family has kept the last project that he was carving— a white buffalo. Though another carver offered to complete the carving, the family has chosen to leave it as it is.

Story from family members, Madonna Rowe Ritchie, niece;
Thurman Ritchie, nephew; Jamie Ritchie, grandniece;
and Joe Byrd, friend
Interviewed by Pamela Jumper Thurman

ruth england

continued from page 145

Brendalee: How did you learn how to make baskets? Did you learn from your mom and dad?

Ruth: No. Oh that old man, George Fourkiller taught Bob, and Bob taught me, I guess you would say that. That was oak—oak splints.

Brendalee: Well, I remember when I was younger, Grandma and Grandpa making stick ball. I remember they had the leather machines. I'd get into it and get in trouble. And basket weaving.

Ruth: I've done baskets, too.

Brendalee: I remember you sitting on the front porch and Grandma and Grandpa would be out there making the flat oak baskets.

Ruth: I hadn't done them round ones. I did that flat kind, though. We used to go teach basket classes way up at Pocola, Oklahoma, somewhere. Me and Bob. He'd teach and I'd teach the beadwork. I do the beadwork, too.

Brendalee: Then your first tear dress was when Mom was little? Mom said that was in 1975. That was over thirty years ago. Did your mom used to make tear dresses?

Ruth: My mom was already gone by that time. My mom's been gone over fifty years. I learned off that guy—Robbie Robinson—at Tahlequah. He showed me. I used to take it over there and ask how to do it. I used to go up there and ask if I'm doing right. Come home. Do some more. "You doing right!" he would say. That's where I learned.

Brendalee: How did you learn to make dolls?

Ruth: (I made) my own. Practice. I used a pattern, but I just changed the pattern. And I had five of them big ones, too. But now I don't use them no more. I used to cut them out of rags.

Brendalee: How about on your quilts? Were you taught how to do that?

Ruth: I done it myself. I learned it myself.

Brendalee: I remember working on the quilts and handsewing them with you. How old was you when you started sewing? Did your mom sew a lot?

Ruth: I was pretty young. I was used to making doll's clothes. That's when I learned to sew. I done it on my own. Well, they did sew. They used to make my dresses. I don't remember them. But, Mama did. Those flour sacks.

Brendalee: Your dresses were made out of flour sacks?

Ruth: Yeah. That's been a long time.

Brendalee: How long have you been making dresses?

Ruth: Oh, I don't remember—over 30 years, I guess. I sewed dolls clothes when I was young. Later on, I made my kids' clothes.

Brendalee: Do you call them tear or teer?

Ruth: I don't even know. Well, you can't tear it no more because it goes either way. Well, my oldest daughter, she run for Miss. Cherokee. I don't know how many years ago. So, I started doing it.

Brendalee: Do, you think they are traditional Cherokee dresses?

Ruth: I really don't know. I can't say. Well, my great-grandma she had . . . . Back then, there were skirts, regular skirts. A long skirt with an apron and long-sleeve blouse. That's what they wore. Cotton, I guess. There wasn't much store to go to.

Brendalee: I remember when I was little, she had someone send material and measurements all the way from Germany.

Ruth: California. Texas. I make them and send them back. Louisiana.

Brendalee: You made ribbon shirts for Steve Reavis, Tommy Wildcat, and them, right? Lightfoot, Cherokee rapper?

Ruth: Uh, huh. I don't remember there were so many. I had two of them this morning. Somebody come got them.

Brendalee: She made my wedding dress. It was a Tear Dress. And my husband's shirt was a Ribbon Shirt. She wakes up crack of dawn. I can remember staying the night at her house and five o'clock in the morning, four o'clock in the morning, she'd be sewing away and then about noon, she would stop and watch her soaps. And then she would make quilts. She'd have a thing hanging from the ceiling and would handsew. Well, most of the time, us kids ran underneath it and got in trouble. Yeah, we had to stay out of there. I remember sitting around Granny's house and everybody would help put the little fringe on the shawls. We used to help with the dolls; we'd have a bag full of legs. (She laughed.)

Makes us feel proud that she is a Cherokee National Treasure.

—Ruth England and her granddaughter, Brendalee Lasiter
Interviewed by Shawna Morton Cain

edith catcher knight

continued from page 147

I graduated from Stilwell High School in 1957. I wanted to go to college. There was just no way. We didn't have the funds or a way to get over there and back. Another cousin and I tried to get them to let us stay at Sequoyah Boarding School and go to college, but they wouldn't let us. Later, I started working as a bookkeeper at Stilwell Foods in Stilwell, and they needed a lab to check for cleanliness of the machinery. So I got a chance to be a lab assistant. Claude Todd gave me the chance to do what I wanted to do. I would go to Northeastern State College, and Dr. George Clark used to come over, and he taught me a lot. I just really got some

continued on page 278

edith catcher knight

continued from page 277

good training, even though I had to go take the ACT test and all that. They taught me how to grow the microbes and identify them. So I just had my own little lab there. I'd go over to Fayetteville where they taught me everything about the canning part of it—how the cans were sealed and what it took to hermetically seal them. I learned a lot over there. I was there for 11 years, at Stilwell Foods.

That was about the time the mother of my husband, Owen, got sick. She had cancer. We couldn't afford for anyone to take care of her and didn't want to leave her by herself. So, I just dropped out of work and took care of her. After she died, I went back to work at Facet. I was there for about four years. I stayed home for a while and then went to work at Maryetta School. That was a good job. I retired in 2001. I didn't miss the work; I missed the connection with the people. But I enjoy the other things, like getting to go fishing when I can. I still like to sew, although I don't do as much fine sewing as I used to.

Mama made most of our clothes. We'd get flour in the 25-pound sack, and those sacks would have a design. She'd save enough of those—maybe she'd get enough of one kind—to make a dress. Well, when I was in high school, I learned how to sew. And that's where I get my love for sewing, I guess. When I was in high school, I'd have to buy me some material. When you lay a pattern out the way it shows you, you waste a lot of material, and Mama was always telling me, "No, you can't waste that material. You've got to be saving with that material." So, even if I make something now, I won't put it down like the instructions show me; I put it on to save material and come out with a big old piece of material I don't need.

I call them a tear (pronounced *"teer"*) dress, although a lot of people call them a tear dress, like tearing something. And you do a lot of tearing. I don't have a pattern. If I'm making a dress for an individual, I just cut newspaper to fit that person. If it is for someone out of the family I try to make the dresses to where they can fit as they grow a little bit; they can still wear the dress. I haven't made a whole lot of clothing for other people who are not in the family. But I have made some. I did make a dress for Chief Wilma Mankiller. I just build a dress to fit that person. Not having a pattern, if someone wants a dress, I'll take my newspaper and cut it, customized to that person. I like to make what I call my "shadow diamonds." That's my design. Most of them are whipped-stitched down. I make this like a bound button hole; each one of these diamonds has its own backing. I just wanted to be different. I picked diamonds because of tradition. If you look at almost everything that's Cherokee, there is a diamond in there. I always use seven buttons to represent the seven clans.

—Edith Catcher Knight
Interviewed by Shawna Morton Cain

thelma forrest

continued from page 151

North Carolina weave. You see more of it now—not the cane but the weave. So, that's how I got started with it—Chief Swimmer and John Ketcher.

I have woven honeysuckle, buck brush, white oak and river cane as far as natural materials. I have also woven commercial reed—both round and the flat reed. Commercial is what I choose to teach with. It is easier to teach, and it helps preserve the natural materials. It takes a while—some experience—before you can weave with the natural materials.

One of my favorite things to do is go and dig blood root. I never take too much. That is a no-no. But I really enjoy going out with other basket weavers and now, with my grandkids, to dig blood root. Blood root is one of our oldest dyes. We used it way back, and we still use it today. There is a certain way to gather it and a certain time to get it that is best, but that is knowledge that we pass to each other after we know that someone is a serious basket maker and someone who won't take too much. If we take too much, there won't be any left. It is already getting harder and harder to find because you can't get on certain land that we used to be able to get on. Sometimes, I will go back to a patch I used the year before to find that it is all dug up by someone. That is not good.

I like to teach basketry. I have taught a lot of people over the years because I like to share what I know and what has been taught to me. My grandkids are all either already weaving or learning how. It is important to me that they carry this knowledge on and keep it alive. Then, they can teach their children. I want to make sure that my descendants always keep the skill and knowledge of traditional basketry going. I have confidence they will. One big thing is to learn the cane right. Kendall has really gotten into it and the other kids, too. They go and we gather cane and honeysuckle. We deal with the cane, mostly. Laney, she goes. When we go, she goes. Darrell will just go, and he did a whole bunch of the blood root.

I like to do all of it. I like to gather it. Like when I go down to the Keetoowah, down to the old bridge, if I'm fishing, I'll have my knife and Kendall has a whole bucket full of knives in her car. She says, "What if somebody stops me! They'll take me to jail." She's got knives and saws, and I always have some in my car. I'll walk over there and cut a couple of switch cane, and I'll work on that while I'm fishing there at the river.

— Thelma Forrest
Interviewed by Shawna Morton Cain

nancy smith *continued from page 153*

they have made "quite a bit of them too" without her help. Smith believes she or her daughters have made ninety percent of the shells worn by women at the stomp dances at the Stokes Ceremonial Grounds near Vian in Sequoyah County. That makes her proud, she said.

She recalls being proud when she was named a Cherokee National Treasure in 1992, and proud someone knew she was helping preserve Cherokee culture by making turtle shell shackles.

— *Nancy Smith*

Interviewed by Will Chavez

wendell cochran *continued from page 155*

Mrs. Hagerstrand credits the costumier for making the first pattern for the tear dress. On the day the people in the costume shop began work on building the costumes for the show, there were only two existing dresses: the original trunk dress and the one currently worn by Virginia Stroud. No one had thought about drafting or cutting a pattern of the dress to make more for future Miss Cherokees to wear.... The prototype dress from the trunk was owned by Wynona Day, a Cherokee lady (who was) a member of the search committee appointed by Chief Keeler. I need to correct a misunderstanding of a fact, I have, for years, understood that the dress was miraculously "discovered" in a trunk that once belonged to some anonymous person in North Carolina. I have recently been told that the dress actually belonged to Wynona Day's grandmother or great-grandmother and that it had, in truth, been stored in a trunk. She had come across it by chance after she inherited her mother's belongings. She remembered having seen the dress and had retrieved it for the committee to examine. As far as everyone I have talked to know, that dress is still in the possession of the Day family. Wynona is now deceased. Her only heir is a son, and his whereabouts are unknown.

At the end of the season, the costumier took her notes for cutting the dress and returned to New York. The following year, I was hired as the costumier designer. I owned my own set of period-costume patterns for men's suits and American women's dresses and had taken a college course in how to draft patterns. I had never seen or heard of a tear dress. Marion taught me the rudiments of making a tear dress the way she had been instructed by the first costumier. She also showed me some of the tear dresses that had been made the previous season. They were not pretty.

My job as costumier was to make new costumes, and the director directed me to make more tear dresses for the cast. He wanted to use them in a dance number. So, I made tear dresses. It was a chore to use the examples I had at hand to try to figure out how to make tear dresses that looked good, fit well, and still keep the construction historically correct using only squares and rectangles. By trial and error, I discovered the tricks of constructing the Cherokee tear dress. I also picked a lot of seams out after the rest of the crew had gone home for the night in the process. I finally realized that the looks of the dress depended entirely on proportions of length and fullness to the body of the person wearing it.

That summer of 1970, Marian Hagerstrand, a high school girl named Cathy Cunningham, a Creek woman whose name I can't remember and who was also in the show, and I made a lot of new tear dresses. We gathered yards of ruffles, sewed miles of seams, and make innumerable buttonholes. By the time the drama opened, we had become the first and only professional tear dress experts in the Cherokee Nation and the world. Every other Cherokee tear dressmaker since that time owes the knowledge of the craft, in no small part, due to the efforts and labor of the four of us during those weeks in the costume shop at Tsa-La-Gi.

I have mingled fact with opinion and pray that you are able to distinguish the boundaries between the two. My feeling for the need for first-person documentation of our living crafts-people was intensified while I was composing this paper. I had forgotten some of the details of the not-so-distant past where I was involved in making culture and tradition. I certainly didn't appreciate my impact in creating precedence while I was doing it. I thought that all I was doing was making a living and doing what had to be done.

I have not taken credit for the creation of the tear dress, but after reviewing the sequence of dates and events, I must, in all modesty, place a few laurel leaves at my own feet. I certainly was instrumental in its perpetuation and some modifications.

I forgot to mention that the dresses Marion Hagerstand and I made at the drama were used over a period of many seasons because they were well-made. They were also borrowed by many individuals and groups to be used for learning and teaching how to make tear dresses. Women who worked in the costume shop at other times while we made tear dresses have used that experience to continue making tear dresses for others. I get a sense of real satisfaction when I see their work or am told that the dress someone is wearing was made by one of that select group of women.

I hope you find this as informative as you had hoped. Moreover, I worry that you will find a modicum of pleasure in reading as I vastly had in writing it.

—Wendell Cochran

Interviewed by Shawna Morton Cain

thomas muskrat *continued from page 157*

they gave to help put this on, to pay for everything."

The next meeting we came to, I was asked, "Tom, would you consider taking that money back to them?"

I said, "Sure, I'll take it back to them to ease your mind up."

(I was told,) "I don't think you can have a Pow Wow down here. It takes too much."

I stood up and said, "There will be a Bell Pow Wow down here."

They all left. We kept meeting and I got up and said, "I've got friends that I went to school with that I can call. They'll come down here and do it for nothing." I did! I called.

First guy I called? Got him. He said, "We'll help you. I'll start putting the word out right now. Give me the dates, time, we'll all be there."

And I said, "OK."

First Pow Wow we had was at Bell School football field. That was the biggest crowd this community ever seen! That was 29 years ago.

After our Pow Wow, there was a Lincoln pulled in right there. Little ol' short Indian guy got out; names Kenneth Anquoe from Tulsa. He said, "I'm looking for Thomas Muskrat."

I said, "That's me. What can I help you with?"

He said, "I need to visit with you." He said, "Next year. You are thinking about (an) annual Pow Wow at Bell?"

I said, "Well, we can make it annual. People really enjoyed theirselves. And people's coming by telling me what a great show they seen. No problem. No nothing. No Budweiser."

He said, "OK, where would you like to have your PowWow?"

I said, "At the (Bell) community building"

We went up there and he said, "You got a place picked out?"

I said, "Kenneth, I'm gonna leave that to you because you're a dancer. I know how it feels to dance. And it's the real way. Just a place to have (a) Pow Wow."

Well, he picked out a place there on the hillside. I said, "Kenneth, have you noticed this? It's on a hillside."

"Well, Tom, if they can't dance downhill, uphill, they don't need to be there. We're gonna put dancers out here."

I said, "OK!"

So Kenneth said, "Don't worry about the drum. I'll handle that part."

I said, "OK. That's your job. Get the drums here. Call in whoever you want. That's your job. The other job? I'll handle that."

So, next year it was bigger, more people. Next year, Kenneth come down and said, "I want you to jump in my shoes."

I said, "To do what?"

He said, "I want you to take over my position."

I said, "Kenneth, I can't do it. I can't even talk to five people without covering my face up." He said, "Don't worry about that. You do it! You're gonna have to do it!"

Man, he talked to me rough and scared me. I said, "Why are you doing this?"

He said, "I want you to take over for the other tribes. The other tribes are gonna look at you like their leader. If they call you to put on a Pow Wow, you do it."

Pretty soon, somebody calls me, says, "Have you seen your picture?"

I said, "Where?"

They said, "Billboard! Tulsa County."

And I said, "No! What's it all about?"

"You putting on Tulsa Pow Wow."

I said, "Dad gum, I didn't know nothin' about it!"

I called Kenneth and said, "How about all this stuff that's going on, I don't know nothin' about it."

"Oh, nobody hadn't contact you yet? Well, don't worry about it, they'll get ahold of ya. You're the arena director at the Tulsa Pow Wow."

I said, nuh uh, not me."

He said, "Yes sir. You watch. You're a natural leader. You can do it."

I said, "Kenneth, I just can't do it."

Well, I couldn't back out. I couldn't get out of it. Sure enough, I put the Pow Wow on in Tulsa. People coming up hugging me and shaking my hand, telling me, "You put on the greatest Pow Wow we've ever seen." From there on, it was every week, in New Mexico, Louisiana, New York, Colorado. I done that and then, every year put on Bell Pow Wow.

What Kenneth told me has come true just step by step. I can go to another tribe, I don't care where they are. I mean, they'll greet me and just treat me like a king. But, every time they holler help, I'm there. That's just like when he told me, "I'm gonna adopt you into our ways."

And so I went and I asked different people, my Elders. I went to my Elders and I told them. Now I'm getting adopted into Kiowa Tribe. They said, "Take it! That's the greatest honor you can receive."

—Thomas Muskrat

Interviewed by Shawna Morton Cain

hastings shade

continued from page 161

former chief of the Cherokee people, and all books were destroyed for some reason.

Hastings was always ready and willing to share his knowledge, which led him to create the "Turtle Island Liars Club." Giduwa people don't have a word or title for storytellers so they call us "liars" (*gagoga*). It isn't a mean-spirited title, but sort of a pun, a "play on words," and also an example of the dryness that hallmarks the Elders' humor. This is the reasoning behind Hastings' naming the group as a 'liars club' because of the stories that are told. But also, along with the stories are lectures of history and culture.

In the mid-1990s, Hastings noticed that nearly everywhere he went to do a presentation about his tribe, there were three others the institute usually invited as well. One day he invited Sammy Still, Woody Hansen, and me to travel with him and do presentations about the Cherokee people. Hastings would talk about history and culture, Sammy would talk and tell stories about crafts and sports, Woody would talk about wildlife safety, then I would come up last and tell stories. In this way, the group traveled across the country giving presentations as the Turtle Island Liars Club. Now and then, other people would be invited along to fill in if a member was absent, but the core of the club was Hastings, Sammy, Woody, and me. Hastings was always proud to say that we four had grown up in our culture. It was our way of life as children. We didn't just wake up one day and say we were going to do this or live this way. We were brought up being taught by Elders, and he, of course, was our Elder.

When Hastings passed on, his funeral was held at the Sequoyah High School gym in Tahlequah, Oklahoma. The place was nearly filled by people he had touched in one way or another. Sammy, Woody, and I stood at the back. When it came time to view his vessel for the last time, the line of folks was so long (that) we told Loretta that we'd wait to pay our respects later on at his resting place. A few days later, we three met at the cemetery where he was laid to rest. We told each other stories of him; we laughed and cried. We knew we had lost a large part of our lives, but not nearly as much as his family had, and we came away feeling the emptiness in our hearts.

Hastings Shade did a lot for his people, even before and after being in the office of Deputy Chief of the Cherokee Nation of Oklahoma—more so than I've mentioned here.

The world may never know just how much, but that was Hastings—never caring for the fame just as long as things got done.

One last observation: when Sammy, Woody, and I left the cemetery after saying our "see ya later," we were passing a small field not far from his grave site. There in the air above the field, Woody and I saw an eagle, a hawk, and a buzzard—flying in a circle. These three birds are never seen together. We figured it was Hastings sending one last lesson for us to always remember: the eagle representing the spirit, the hawk representing the warrior, and the buzzard representing medicine. I always saw these aspects in Hastings Shade.

—by Sequoyah Guess
Tradition Keeper/UKB
Turtle Island Liars Club/member
Interviewed by Pamela Jumper Thurman

jess oosahwee

continued from page 167

Although pow wow is not considered the Cherokee Way, it has become my way. While I was in Kansas, I got introduced to the pow wow by other Haskell students. Now I travel all during the spring, summer, and fall to attend pow wows. I have been honored by being asked to be head-man dancer at many pow wows. To me, the pow wow is a way of holding on to the Native American culture. As we travel, we learn more and more about other tribes. The respect I have for my people comes from my Cherokee family and the Cherokee culture and also from all the other tribes and their traditions I have come to know and respect. Veterans and elders are treated with highest respect, and I think this is an important thing for us to be teaching to our younger generation.

—Jess Oosahwee

jim buckhorn

continued from page 169

grinder or anything like that. I use a Bowie knife, a pocket knife, and an axe and a glass to shave the wood.

A lot of them sold here and there, in the United States. I've even sold one in Vietnam. It's a beautiful bow. Everything is all handmade, and they don't have that notch cut out for the arrow rest. See, on all the traditional bows that I make, you don't have a notch for your arrows to rest. To me that's modern if you notch it out. In the old days, they wouldn't notch (the bows) 'cause the arrow rested on the knuckle of your hand. That's why I got a lot of marks on my hand.

When they were riding on horseback, they had to use the index finger in order to hold that arrow, to keep it from falling off the bow. They released it when they shot. You don't do that because all they do now is just shoot 90 or 100 yards. When my grandpa was alive, it was 100 yards. What they are shooting right now it's at 90 yards.

That's all I did was Cornstalk Shoot and Bow Hunter Association in Tulsa. I shot six years in that. I'd just shoot bows

continued on page 282

jim buckhorn

continued from page 281

every Saturday and Sunday. My daughter shot, my wife shot, and we had trophies. I mean it would fill this room up. Man, we had a lot of them that we won. We'd bring six every weekend. We shot in five clubs and never went nowhere else. Never went to church. Always a bow in my hand.

Finally, one day, I said, "Well, we're going," 'cause it was the last day.

My wife said, "No, I already got the chicken cooked for dinner."

I said, "Uh, uh. Take it to church. We're going back to church!" Started back to church then. And I just forgot my bows and arrows and I quit. She couldn't believe it. Anyway, that's one thing I used to enjoy was shooting bows. That's every Saturday and Sunday. But, not anymore. I get tired and I want to just make my bows and sell them now. I also enjoy knowing my daughter is carrying it on. Yes, she is.

—Jim Buckhorn
Interviewed by Shawna Morton Cain

wynona "chicken" dreadfulwater

continued from page 173

company. She continues to show up every day that she feels good and she weaves. If restored, the building could be a historic treasure, a Sequoyah Weaver's museum. The looms are very old, yet perfectly intact and still working.

Wynona is the only consistent weaver in the family. She said that her daughter made wall hangings for a while but after she got a job, she didn't get to weave as much. "I still call her if I make a mistake. I have her come out and look to see what I've done wrong. I used to be able to weave a blanket in one day. Now it takes me about a week. It takes two days just to set the loom up, and if you miss threading a place, you can see it when you weave. There are 720 threads to be done and you have to thread it one loop at a time. When mama was living we had quite a few women wanting to learn to weave. Loretta and Hastings Shade came up here. Both of them wove on their blanket. We had some other people from Stilwell come here, but now, few people come. Mama wove until her death at ninety-three years of age."

Wynona received recognition as a Cherokee National Treasure in 2000 for her weaving skills. "I like to weave to pass the time, or if I get an order or need money, then I weave. If I felt better, I'd be here all of the time. If I have money to buy yarn, I go buy it. Herringbone pattern is easy for me and I've been trying to do diamond weave. I'm still learning, even at my age. Sometimes I lose count on diamond weave on the pedals, and then I make mistakes."

"I love coming up here to work. Red is my favorite color. I like to pick out the colors, but I don't think I'm always good at it. A lady from Mississippi came up and wanted an afghan in purple and gold. I didn't think that would look good, but it turned out okay. I've made them in Oklahoma University colors and in Oklahoma State University colors. Sometimes the Cherokee Nation buys them. I remember once that we got an order from somewhere in Texas for about one hundred saddle blankets. We made them!"

Wynona recalled that a news anchor from Channel 2 in Tulsa came out and spent the day. He filmed the weaving process. She laughed and said that her stepson called because he saw her on TV. Wynona has five children—Jackie, Madonna, Michael, LaDonna, and Shirlene.

Today, Wynona is one of two treasures still weaving. In fact, this art form is practiced by very few Cherokees. "Chicken," however, still has a weaver's eye. "Every time I go to the hospital, I see the colors in that Cherokee Seal and I think those are such pretty colors. I'd like to weave that but I don't know if I would know how to put them all together to make a blanket."

—Wynona "Chicken" Dreadfulwater
Interviewed by Pamela Jumper Thurman

anna sixkiller

continued from page 175

making baskets. She'd have her runners in the creek. It was really honeysuckle and sometimes split oak. She sat by the creek and make baskets. That's where my interest in basket making started. I'd stand by her side and watch her and watch her, (working) with flat reed as well as the round. She used honeysuckle and, mostly, buckbrush. And the split, if I'm not mistaken, was some kind of hickory. She sold them for five dollars or less.

We had several of her baskets. What we used baskets for was to carry stuff in. She didn't make her baskets to beautify the home. Then she gave Mom a basket which was kind of flat but it was a sifter. That's what we used to make *kvnzchi*. By the way, that was my job when I was growing up. I'd pound the hickory nuts, and then I pounded again in the *kanoni*. That was my job. And I didn't mind. I liked doing what I did. But that's how my basket making got started. I started making more and more baskets when I started working at the Heritage Center back in the early or middle '70s. From there, I entered in competitions at different places.

Under Chief Wilma Mankiller, they gave me "Master Craftsperson." I was in the Cultural Resource Center and one day, Dr. Morton came in and talked with me. He said, "We will open up

continued on page 283

anna sixkiller

continued from page 282

a different department and I want you in there. I want you to be the manager or the advisor."

I said, "What's it going to be?"

He said, "It's going to be called the Translation Department."

I was there, by myself, for several years, and then Margaret Raymond thought of an idea to contract some people. That's where David Crawler came in and John Ross and Phyllis Edwards.

I like doing what I do—looking at old documents and different things like that. When I first started at the Cultural Resource Center, we had some old documents. We read history on the old Cherokee Jailhouse that we were working in. I learned (the name of) the first marshall; his name was Samuel Sixkiller. They would write their business doings in Cherokee. I was reading a Cherokee document that was written back when he was the sheriff. My co-worker said, "A Sixkiller wrote this 100 years ago and a Sixkiller is reading the document that was written at that time. Isn't that something?"

I said, "Yeah, I guess so." But it didn't really click until later.

It is a good feeling to be able to read things in our Cherokee language which people want to know and to tell them what's on that letter. I like doing that and sometimes, when you read documents, it seems like you go back in that day and time. You can actually visit there, and when you come back, you seem to know more than you did when you went there.

— Anna Sixkiller

Interviewed by Shawna Morton Cain

jane osti

continued from page 177

to teach hundreds to find those two or three who have the passion to continue and pass it on. Of all those years that Anna taught, only a few of her students continued. Anna began our Cherokee family tree of potters here in Oklahoma. Some of her students—myself, her daughter, Victoria Mitchell Vazquez, and Crystal Hannah—are still teaching others. In fact, some of our students are now teaching. The tradition continues. I have had many students entering art shows locally and then go on to the big markets, like the Eiteljorg Museum, Santa Fe Art Market, etc., and some have won awards. A few of them have also started teaching classes. Some of my former students who have excelled are Stephen Wood, Linda Taylor, Karin Walkingstick, Ron Tanyan, and Lisa Rutherford, just to name a few. I need to mention that I was not their only teacher. A few of them had degrees in fine art, and I taught them the Cherokee way of coil building and firing.

My love for the old Cherokee pottery, the forms, and designs are ever present in my work. I work every day because it is what I do, what I love and what I have a passion for. I have been blessed to have lived most of my life in the arts, especially the Cherokee traditional arts, and to have known the people I've known and for them to be a part of my life. People like Anna Mitchell, Dorothy Ice, Bessie Russell, Bill Glass, and Lorene Drywater have inspired and enriched this journey.

Of all my children and grandchildren, my granddaughter, Lillie, is the one who has moved forward with pottery. Maybe it's just in her DNA; her fingers know how to touch the clay and make it go where it wants to go. I'm very proud of her and want to encourage her to keep doing pottery. She's also talented in music. Lillie has been entering the local art shows the last two years and she's won something every time and that encourages her. Competing and knowing that others think your work is good helps to motivate. Lillie was accepted into Santa Fe Indian Market 2015 and won a first-place award in the youth pottery category. She shared a booth with me. I started out sharing a booth with Anna. Anna opened those doors for all of us. Anna was the first Cherokee potter to be in Santa Fe Indian Market.

The Cherokee National Treasures/Mentoring Program is a project that began last year. The purpose of the program is to perpetuate the traditional arts and to provide income for our Treasures. Victoria Mitchell Vazquez, Anna's daughter and Cherokee Nation Councilor, has been instrumental in asking for funds to make this program stronger. I am a member of Cherokee National Treasure Advisory Committee and am very passionate about this program. Many of our arts in this program—arts such as loom weaving and mussel shell carving—are being taught by the last elders who have that particular knowledge. I really love the fact that the Treasures are getting paid to participate in this program. This income makes a difference for them. They can buy wood, propane, and other necessities not easily bought on limited incomes. I'm just very proud of this program

I will always be making pottery, doing some painting and sculpture. I am grateful to the Creator for all the blessings that this journey in art has brought to me. I will be passing it on, as it was passed to me. *Wado*

— Jane Osti

Interviewed by Pamela Jumper Thurman

durbin feeling

continued from page 179

East of Locust Grove about three miles, there's this place called Little Rock Community. There's a church. Every community usually had a church and a number of families there. That was the community (of) Little Rock. Just south of us was Snake Creek; just north of us was Standing Rock. Beyond that, there was New Jordan. But we're from the Little Rock Community. There was also an elementary school there. The community is still there; the church is still there. The buildings are

continued on page 284

durbin feeling

continued from page 283

still there. I know it consolidated with Locust Grove Schools.

All three of us went to what they call an Indian school, up North Central Oklahoma. Just right above Ponca City—South of Kansas City, half a mile from the state line—was a school called Chilocco. We just had a reunion and had about three hundred show up. In the past, there were more that used to show up—I think because of the economy—and it's getting to the point that those Chilocco alumni are getting old. Chilocco had students coming from the West Coast, East Coast, New York, up in Washington, Oregon, and up north from the Dakotas (and) Montana. My graduating class had 125. I guess for the record, I graduated with Wes Studie. It was the boarding school, and it began, I think, more than one hundred years ago—1889 or something like that. At the boarding school, there was a beautiful campus—maple trees and the lawn. There's an oval in the middle with some trees and a fish pond in the middle, and beyond, on the outside of the oval, there were classrooms, dormitories, dining hall. And even beyond those (buildings), there were other trades, like body and fender, they used to call it, where they fixed cars. Electricity, dry cleaning, agriculture, drafting, home economics, and other trades—(for) women as well.

In eleventh grade, I specialized in agriculture. I started in the sophomore year. The sophomore year, all the guys get a pig to raise. Every day you go out there and clean the stall and put new hay down and feed them—water and clean them and brush them and everything. Then you go to class. You raise that hog, and they give it to you at the end of the school year, and the money is yours. I started like that, and when school was out after the sophomore year, I stayed there and worked on what they called a plot. Just for the agriculture. I guess a plot means you had certain things to do during the summer. There's a lot of things to take care of around the farm and ranch. We did a lot of riding horses and bringing cattle in from the fields, to the corral and to the shoot and to the truck and sell them and stuff like that. It was a lot of fun. There was always something to do.

In athletics on weekends, there were activities that were a lot of fun. We'd go on hikes. We'd have ballgames, depending upon what season it was—softball in the summer and basketball intramural in the winter. A little place just to meet—the girls' gym. And inside that every Tuesday night, they had a dance. Not a formal dance, just where everybody could go in there and dance and play volleyball and things. It was a lot of fun.

You lived clean. You had details, kind of like in the military. But each person had something to do or was assigned something to do, like mop the floors, sweep the floors, dry the floors, wax them and buff them, clean the walls, or whatever needed to be. The dorms were slick. The floors were just glassy. Then our rooms (were) individual rooms. You had to line the drawers with newspaper. You had to polish your shoes in the evening. Line them up just right under the bed. You had to wash your clothes at a certain time and hang them up a certain distance apart, and (you) ironed and everything. Good training! I didn't have any problems when I went to the military because we did the same things in there. It was a good school!

I graduated while I was at Chilocco. Also, I took band, concert band, and marching band. Started when I was a freshman. By my junior year, I became a drum major and finished out my senior year, too. I played trombone—slide trombone. I wrestled for a while until I took agriculture. Agriculture took too much time from my schedule, so I had to quit wrestling. I played football. I played quarterback for a while, and then I was put into running back. It was good. In 1964, I graduated, and there was a Baptist group. It wasn't a church, but it was in one of the buildings in the campus.

I went out to Oklahoma University in 2001 while I was working with Cherokee Nation, and you know how programs go; financing and things like that happen. So I signed up at Northeastern State University. Dr. Terri Baker was an English teacher out there. She asked me to come over there, and I stayed there for a year. I left Cherokee Nation to go over there. I stayed there for ten years. It was the early '70s—1972, somewhere in there, I started teaching Cherokee language through Agnes Cowan's Bilingual Program, Title VII. I started setting up classes in communities. I would leave after work, and then go to Washington County, get home about midnight, come back to work and eat, 5 a.m. to Sallisaw or something. This is voluntary work I didn't have to do.

To me, our language is an art form because it's like this: there is a person that can draw stick figures, and there's one guy (who) can detail it. Our language is the same way. As an artist, it's art.

—Durbin Feeling
Interviewed by Shawna Cain

eddie morrison

continued from page 183

I did my first Santa Fe Indian Market while at IAIA. That was in 1990. I've been doing that show ever since. This last year (2015) was my 25th market.

My work depicts a variety of themes. Animals—particularly bears, eagles, and buffaloes—are a prevalent subject. I also carve human figures in traditional presentations, some wearing a wolf skin cape, a blanket, or feathers. I want to produce work that represents American Indian people with pride and dignity. My ideas and themes come from the philosophies of Indians about life, spirituality, respect for life, animals, and all that is around us and the Great Creator.

continued on page 285

eddie morrison *continued from page 284*

When I work with wood, I use a lot of red cedar because of the beautiful color variations. I just allow the gentle curves or unusual twists, found naturally in the wood, to appear in the finished pieces. Another material that I really like to work with is Kansas limestone. I collect that myself. This limestone contains fossils from a prehistoric sea that once covered much of North America. The fossils are often visible in the rough portions of the stone sculpture. Some of my pieces are fully carved; others have the figures emerging from a rough-hewn background on some of the stone or wood that I leave un-carved. I want my carving to bring out the beauty of the natural materials and capture a moment in time.

I'm always willing to share my story. People think that the life of an artist is glamorous, but it's really a journey of ups and downs. You have to have support. My wife, Faye, is my support. We met in high school; we were high school sweethearts. Then we went our separate ways and saw each other again years later and got back together. We've been together fifteen years now and she's my rock.

The life of an artist isn't easy. You have to stay with it. Over the years, I've seen a lot of great artists give up because they just couldn't stay with it. Maybe financial struggles stopped them, but if you love it, you're going to do it. Even with the ups and downs, you don't lose your abilities.

It's a passion within you, and it's a gift from the Creator. I still get a thrill to this day, thirty-eight years later, of being an artist. Even now, when I create a piece, I get excited. Sometimes, I'll create a piece and I just sit back and say to myself, "Did I do that?" It's rewarding.

I have great hope for the future of Cherokee art. The quality of young Cherokee artists out there is great. This past Cherokee Art Market, I saw some really good, up-and-coming young artists. It's good that the tribe is really supporting and helping artists now. The tribe is offering mentors and teaching opportunities. I've always tried to give my children, grandchildren, and great-grandchildren a piece of my art. I have one granddaughter, seven years old, who says that she wants to be an artist. I also have a couple of great-grandchildren who say they are interested. I hope they carry it on.

In 2014, I was honored to be recognized as a Cherokee National Treasurer. That feels like the pinnacle of my career. This year, the Tribal Council appointed me to serve on the Cherokee National Treasures Committee. It's a task I'll take very seriously, and I'll make every effort to do it well. I feel very humbled that my sculptures are in permanent collections throughout the country. I have a monument on the Chisholm Trail at the Kansas/Oklahoma border and a piece in the Department of Interior Building in Washington, D.C.

I just want to represent American Indian people with pride and dignity—respect for life, Animals, and all that is around us, and the Great Creator.

—Eddie Morrison

Interviewed by Pamela Jumper Thurman

Thank you to Jami Murphy for use of excerpts of her article published in the Cherokee Phoenix on November 7, 2014.

bill rabbit *continued from page 185*

"Work as hard as you can. Be true to yourself. Do the best you can do. But, if eventually you want to do it for a living, the more you can learn...."

I'm so fortunate; my daughter takes care of everything—the computers, the website, I mean all of this! If I had to do it, I'd be in trouble. I'd have to hire someone. I've had a lot of young people come up and say, "Well, I want to be an artist like you. What do I have to do?" I tell you, I'd need an hour and a half with all the particulars and all the things to watch out for. Like Bill (Glass) said, I've been stung. I've been hit. I've been kicked. But they only do it once! I would just encourage them to be the best they can. And then if they want to get serious, I would say to them, "Well, wait a while until you are able to get out there." 'Cause making a living with your art: it's hard. I've been doing it long enough, and I've been very blessed. God has taken care of me. Now I can sit back and rest a little bit and still make a fair living. I am Cherokee, a Christian, a good father, and a veteran who fought for his country. I hope that people always get enjoyment from my work when they look at it.

—Bill Rabbit

Excerpts from "Spirit Red" exhibition panel discussion
Fred Jones Museum, Oklahoma University

ed fields *continued from page 187*

It used to be hard to connect with students online at first. But, not now. I still used to get sort of nervous at first. I always get nervous at first. For years, I would get nervous when I came to class because I couldn't see them, and I didn't know how many was out there. And if you didn't know who was out there, it was kind of hard to figure out who they are and what they might need, you know. So I just talked. That is what I was doing—just talked in the language and in English—because they were English speakers trying to learn the language. Then I try to tell them (that) the words in Cherokee associate with other words and might come out a little different. If you understand the root words, then when you come across another word that is kind of in the same area, maybe it's about the same thing but (there is) a little different meaning to it. Like I say, *Jigotiha*,.like when I see something, then I say like *na ana*, tell a story like a bear *ugohena*. The root words is "go" in there cause that's the see. And the prefix tells who because "u" references the third person—so he, she or it. And the suffix is the past and the present tense 'cause they saw it. It could be that they say it just a while ago or way back when. Then I was trying

continued on page 286

ed fields

continued from page 285

to get them to understand the words so they can use it (Cherokee) one way or another, like when they are talking or giving it a trial run so to speak. I've heard some people email about when they went back to where they grew up at and they spoke to the speakers there and the speakers heard them talking a few words, and they were glad they were learning Cherokee. That was neat to know. And I heard some people who were retired teachers, who took the substitute teaching, used those Cherokee words with kids. So, it's kind of spreading Cherokee around.

Last session, we had a guy from Europe. He was born in Switzerland, and he was learning Cherokee. Through the years, we had a Hungarian-born person, a couple from Ireland (and) Denmark, and one from Venezuela and one from Tahiti. I guess they just got to know the language somewhere, and maybe there were Natives so they wanted to learn the language. Some are part Cherokee and some are not Cherokees at all. And some want to learn the language because they just want to learn. And then we have quite a few who have been with us since way back that are still sticking around just to keep up with—brush up on their Cherokee language. Some say they don't have anybody to talk Cherokee, too, so they come back to refresh their language.

I thought that was pretty good, really, adding language. When they are National Treasures, they are Cherokee, and in Cherokee, everything is supported by the language, whether that is the art or whatever you make is spoken by the person in the language. Because that's how we started out speaking the language. How a person lived, survived, did, and created, he spoke the language with it. So, I always feel that speaking the language is the base of everything. I guess the language should have been in there a long time ago. I'm glad it's there now. And language needs to be alive. Well, as long as they keep trying, it's going to stay with them. We picked up some new learners because we have the immersion school down here where the children learn. One of my students came a few years ago from Illinois, and he hadn't heard Cherokee before. And he took the classes and he learned to speak it. A lot of words he says is talk—like a real speaker does. Even if one can't commit themselves entirely to it, to use it off and on and a little bit at a time, it will add up some day. Just keep learning. Keep on going.

—Ed Fields
Interviewed by Shawna Morton Cain

vivian bush

continued from page 189

well if they didn't want somebody to go pick them, they saw this great big snake out there and all of this stuff. That's to keep people away. And people sold it back then, but it wasn't like it is now. Now what? About $40 a gallon? It's ridiculous. So is blackberries.

I done all the stuff all the other Indian kids do. You know, go swimming, go fishing, crawdad hunting and all that stuff. I'd run around the woods with my aunt because she liked to go hunting. We hunted squirrels. They'd make dumplings out of it and squirrel gravy. You'd go with her when she said, "Let's go squirrel hunting." When she says, "Go fishin'!" Ya go fishing. And when she'd want to go look for wild onions, poke salad, whatever? Well you'd tag along whether you want to or not. You know, I learned, like you say, the *kvnzchi*—how to make it and all that. And as time went along, I learned how to do homemade hominy. It's not easy.

As far as I can say, they are called, "shackles." You can call them *daksi*. I started making them because my aunt wouldn't make them for me anymore. She told me, "OK. just sit. You're on your own." I'd say I was about seventeen. That's when she quit making them. So, if I wanted them, it was up to me to make my own.

Sam Ed Bush nominated me (for Master Artisan in making turtle shackles), and I could have killed him! Sam Ed, uh huh. And then he'd get tickled and stuff. Yeah, and I didn't even know about it until he had done it! Then he tells me. He says, "You know what I did?" Yep, I still can make them (turtle shackles.) I don't do it as much as I did back then. But, like I said, I've taught a couple of people how to put them together. It is a lot of work! Yes, it is. But when you're younger, it don't matter to you. Because, hey, all night long doesn't bother me. But somewhere down the line, I guess it catches up to you. Like you say, the older you get, you got to slow down somewhere.

Some years are harder than other years because now so many people are getting turtles and selling them. At one time, I think that they said, you were only allowed to have seven, and if you were caught with more than seven in your possession? Well, trouble if you got caught. I mean the live ones. When I was doing mine, there was a guy asked me one time—'cause I had them under my spare tire in the truck so they wouldn't roam around—and he asked me, "What do you got back there?" I told him and he said, "What do you do with them?" I told him, and he said, "You want more?" He said, "I travel around a lot of places. I see them a lot." He said, "I can get you some if you want them."

I said, "OK." He did get them for me. I could go through and pick out the sizes. He didn't know no better, because he was a white man, about them little bitty ones. So I just picked out the ones that would work for making shackles. And then the smaller ones, I'd just go turn them loose. What he didn't know didn't hurt him.

I've made some for people, mainly just for people in the family. A few will ask. I say, "Well, furnish me the turtles." But of course, I had to clean them and everything. As long as they were used at the grounds, you know. Not just used here and there. Because I don't believe in trying to make money off of something like that because it's to do with religion. And then I wouldn't feel right to have them used here and there or wherever.

— Vivian Bush
Interviewed by Shawna Morton Cain

martha berry

continued from page 193

work I was learning from the how-to books was Plains beadwork. Because of twentieth-century Hollywood movies and pan-Indian influences, this work dominated the images seen by all people, including Cherokees.

I could find no classes in the old-style Cherokee beadwork, no books about it, and the Internet was not yet up and running. So, I collected photos of Cherokee beaded artifacts and taught myself to create beadwork like that in the pictures. With a grant from the Smithsonian Institution, I was able to examine some of the old work there and learn from the pieces I examined.

Now, twenty-five years later, I have learned much about materials and construction of authentic, early-nineteenth-century Cherokee and Southeastern Woodlands beadwork. Exquisitely made bandolier bags, belts, ceremonial sashes, moccasins, small purses, leggings, and knee bands were created in the Golden Era of Cherokee beadwork, c.1800-1840. Our Cherokee ancestors took ancient design and construction influences and blended them with then state-of-the-art materials purchased from European traders.

I work hard to use only materials that are authentic to that time period. Those include wool stroud cloth or broadcloth in navy blue or scarlet, linen or cotton lining fabric, silk ribbon, and fine wool yarn. I have learned the techniques necessary to create the beautiful curvilinear beaded designs like those found on the old pieces, even a rather difficult technique that was only used by Southeastern Woodlands beaders and only on ceremonial sashes.

There has been great interest in this beadwork among modern Cherokees, and many have taken classes and are beading regularly. They are winning awards in art shows and are selling their work. We are growing beaders, growing collectors, growing brokers (museums and galleries), and now find that we need to grow more teachers. Best of all, more and more Cherokees are wearing our old-style beadwork at stomp grounds and special functions. That pleases me a great deal.

I could never have done any of this without the constant support and generous help of my husband, Dave. He takes all the photos of my work, maintains my website, accompanies me to art shows and to teach classes, and does all the heavy lifting required. He is my courage.

Perhaps even more gratifying is the interest my two daughters have taken in preserving and perpetuating Cherokee culture. Although neither of them does the old-style beadwork (so far), Christina operates the All Things Cherokee website offering information on Cherokee history, genealogy, literature, art, and travel to hundreds of thousands of people on the Internet. Karen has taught herself to carve and paint gourds, and she is a wonderful finger weaver. She uses the old eighteenth- and-nineteenth century techniques, with beads interwoven in the work, and uses period authentic materials.

And yes, I feel closer to Mattie. I believe I have learned much about what made my Cherokee grandmothers tick, how they thought, what they felt. I hope they are as proud of me as I am of them.

—Martha Berry

margaret wilson

continued from page 195

So I have let him do that a few times. He thinks that is the best thing and tells his mother he is helping me quilt. A couple of my granddaughters have been interested but haven't gotten too far into them—cutting material out or anything. I'm pretty much the only quilter in the family. My sister does baby quilts and does a pretty job.

My mother's name is Sara Blossom, and she has also made a lot of quilts and has given many away. She has seven children—three boys and four girls. The last quilts she made—it was a few years ago—she said these will be the last quilts she will make, and she made us each a quilt. Now, she is not in very good health and has just quit quilting. She has a quilt top that she has made, and when I have time, I will quilt that for her and give it to her 'cause it is the last one she made. She is eighty-eight. Mom inspired me to sew, and even today, I can sit all day long cutting out pieces. I can do it all day long, but, of course, my eyes get tired. I just really enjoy doing this 'cause it is my art. Everybody that has my quilts gives me a good feeling that people like my work.

We grew up around Teresita Community and went to grade school there. It's been gone for years now. I went to high school at Oaks Mission High School. It's where I graduated. In high school I wasn't interested in quilting or anything like that. It was after I graduated that I was watching my mother. Seems like she was always quilting, and she had one of those old-fashioned treadmill sewing machines. It was a Singer sewing machine. I didn't make anything on it 'cause I didn't think I could do it. So I just started and picked up a needle and saw some material one day, and I just started from there. She would give me some material here and there and told me I could make a quilt. From there on, I thought I was picking it up on the way. After high school and about the age of nineteen is when I really started in, getting more interested in what she was doing and how to make a quilt and what we always used in the quilts she made. I don't think I ever finished one myself at nineteen, but the ones we quilted at church we did to raise money for the church. They would ask us if we would make a quilt for a quilt top, and of course, we charged a fee for doing the quilt. Then the church would get the money we would make, and it stayed in the church.

Now my quilts are here and there. It's a lot of work, and it's hard to put a price on your work 'cause it is hard to get what you want out of piece compared to the amount of work you put into it. I do get asked how long it takes to make a quilt a lot. This last quilt that I made? I think I worked on it maybe two months to make the top, because I knew the lady and already had it sold. I felt I was being rushed even though she told me to take my time doing it. After I got the quilt top finished, I timed myself this time, and it took me three weeks to quilt it, and it was a queen size. The pattern on it is a "Flower Garden." I do make a lot of Flower Garden quilt tops. I guess they are not the easiest ones to make, but to others they are. I just like making

continued on page 288

margaret wilson

continued from page 287

those kind of quilt tops. The hardest ones that people say to make is the "Double Wedding Ring," and I've made some Double Wedding Ring quilt tops. One is in England. The other one I made is "Trip Around the World," and it is in South Korea.

I'm working on a top right now, and don't think about what I'm going to do, then realize, "I've already made one of those!" Then I think, "I'm making it and can make whatever I want." So I have a lot of scrap pieces that are still good pieces that can be used on anything. The girl that bought the last quilt, she knows I'm a National Treasure and she tells everybody, "I tell them I buy my quilts from a Cherokee National Treasure."

I'm not the last one, because there are a lot of other quilters out there, and I'm just among the other ladies who can quilt and think to think about it. I don't think I am the last one. Not long ago, I saw a lady at Walmart was buying material to make a quilt.

—Margaret Wilson
Interviewed by Shawna Morton Cain

william cabbagehead

continued from page 197

dart makers only used one piece. "So his darts were always really big and fluffy. He set the standard. We tried to make our darts like his," he said.

As for his blowgun-shooting skills, McCarter said Cabbagehead was hard to beat though his friends would try. "He was the blowgun champion for the longest time."

McCarter believes Cabbagehead deserved the Cherokee National Treasure honor because he taught him and many others how to make blowguns and darts.

Current Diligwa villager Noel Tim Grayson said as a young man, he appreciated visiting with Cabbagehead because, "there was no telling what he was going to tell you. He would teach you something. That's why I liked talking to those guys because no matter what, they would tell you something, especially if they knew you were interested," Grayson said.

— by Will Chavez

victoria mitchell vazquez

continued from page 199

kiln. Sometimes, I've even wondered why I don't just use commercial clay. Instead, I keep digging and doing all of this hard work to make this traditional pot, but then when I electric fire it, I feel that it takes away a little from the tradition. That's why I feel that I'm a mixture of both traditional and contemporary.

I love to make traditional pieces similar to the Mound Builders and similar to the things I find in the many materials that I have researched. I certainly share the traditional ways when I teach my classes. I talk about Cherokee history related to our arts and industry. I talk about Cherokee history relating to how we lived. I also talk about why the art was lost when removal took place. I then talk about Mom and how she revived the art in the 1960s. I share that she was the only person, at that time, who was trying to make pottery as much like our ancestors as possible. I love both types of pottery—the traditional and the contemporary. In 1988, my mother was designated a Cherokee National Treasure for her pottery and for her efforts in keeping that tradition alive.

When I was named a Cherokee National Treasure in 2012, the very first thing that I felt was being so very proud that I was selected and that there are people who would think of me, as well as the other Treasures, as being special and unique to our crafts. There was just such pride in being named a National Treasure. But at the same time, I really feel like it is something that I share with Mom and Dad and their spirits knowing that I received this honor. It also changed me a little bit. I feel a responsibility even more so now to share and teach and guide and mentor others, especially other Cherokees. I feel that the designation of Cherokee National Treasure lends more credence to what I do as an artist and a teacher of pottery. I also feel a deep responsibility to really know what I'm talking about. I feel as though I am an ambassador for our people, for Oklahoma, for our tribe, and for what I've learned from my Mom—to share her knowledge and keep traditional pottery alive. It's such an honor to carry it forward.

In 2014, this sense of responsibility became even stronger, when I was elected to the Cherokee Tribal Council. As a councilor, I have made it my mission to ensure that the arts are recognized and perpetuated through teaching and mentorship. This is another way that I can carry forward my Mom's art, my art, and the art of other Cherokee National Treasures.

My daughter is Lori Dawn Howell. She and her husband live in Lincoln, Nebraska. She is a nurse and has three children—Carter, Kailey, and Elliot Hill. Perhaps one of them will carry forward the family art of traditional pottery. I certainly hope so.

— Victoria Mitchell Vazquez
Interviewed by Pamela Jumper Thurman

donald vann

continued from page 203

drawings" and then visit him again in a few weeks. "I did, and then I bummed a ride and went back over there, and he looked at them and said, 'It looks like you're ready to start painting.' He started me out on tempera, (watercolors), which was the big thing back in those days. He showed me a few techniques, and, of course, there was trial and error," Vann said.

"A little bit later I went back and showed him what I had done with the paint, and he said, 'You're doing good.' He sent me home with

continued on page 289

donald vann

continued from page 288

a couple of his originals and said, 'Take these home and study them.' He did not say they were mine; he just said (to) take them home and study them."

Vann added that Tiger coached him on understanding colors in his paintings and he was invited to Tiger's home for instruction. Vann and Tiger even collaborated on a large painting—using a drawing of a stickball game—that Tiger had prepared to paint. He said he knew Tiger for about three years before Tiger died.

"To me, Jerome was bigger than life, I tell you. He was one of the most awesome people I've ever met in my life. I'd like to think that I was the only person that Jerome had as a real student," he said. "When he died, a lot of people kind of looked at me to carry on what was going on at the time for Indian art. I went ahead and kept doing what I could do. For many years, people would say, 'It (Vann's work) looks like Jerome's work.' Not really, but you could see the style, and I was proud to say I was influenced by a great man like him."

Wheeler became Vann's agent and started selling his art—a mixture of Cherokee, Plains, and animal imagery—throughout the country.

In 1968, shortly before his high school graduation, he dropped out and voluntarily enlisted in the U.S. Army. He later earned a general education degree or GED. Vann served in Vietnam with the First Cavalry Aviation Division as a door gunner on a helicopter. His helicopter dropped off and extracted soldiers from the battlefield.

After he left the Army in 1973, he resumed his art career—painting the images of his Cherokee heritage. As the popularity of Native American art grew in the early 1970s, Vann's skills were in high demand, and he soon found himself—with a business partner—starting a publishing company called Nuwoduhi Galleries, later renamed Native American Images—in Austin, Texas. Before long, Vann's artwork was being displayed in galleries across the world and in the homes and offices of private collectors.

In the early 1990s, when movies like *Dances with Wolves* were popular, he said he painted tribal people from Plains tribes because that's what the public wanted. Eventually, as the public became more aware of other tribes and Native American culture, Vann said he began to paint more Cherokee-themed subjects. He includes Cherokee culture in his paintings and said he is glad he has lived the culture to enable him to use it in his artwork. He grew up listening to his elders about medicine and Cherokee little people and has also included little people, who are sacred to Cherokee people, in his art.

Vann says he is "sort of retired," but also understands that he can't retire from the Donald Vann Company. "I just work when I feel we need to put something new out there. I spend most of my time in the woods when I'm not working, but right now, we are working on some large pieces on canvas for other shows that we might enter later, and I do small pieces to keep my name out there," he said. "If I can make people see with their hearts and feel with their eyes, then I have succeeded."

—Donald Vann
Interviewed by Will Chavez

knokovtee scott

continued from page 207

I began to study jewelry making—silversmithimg. At that time, turquoise was sweeping the nation. It was the biggest fad in the Indian Market, and a lot of Indian people were earning their livings through silversmithing and cutting turquoise, making Southwestern Indian jewelry. While I was there, I started studying Hopi inlay and overlay and also Navajo tufa casting (and) turquoise cutting. I learned all these Southwestern Indian jewelry processes and while I was doing this, I become very curious about what type of jewelry the Cherokees and the Creeks made. When I returned to Oklahoma, I started studying the jewelry forms of the Southeastern Indians. That led me to the study of our ancient designs. As I started realizing how our ancient designs look very contemporary, that led me more into wanting to try my hand at making something in the line of traditional Cherokee and Creek jewelry.

When I first started looking into the design motifs, the ancient motifs, they were very mysterious to me because I didn't understand what they represented or what they meant. As I began studying them, I found out more about the traditional past—the Southeastern Ceremonial Complex cultre—that we have. It is very vast. These were the people who built the mounds throughout the Southeast. As I got more and more into it, I could see how the culture covered a great deal of ground—the Spiro area (and) the Caddoan People. At one time, we all shared the same basic culture, the Southeastern Ceremonial Complex.

Spiro was where my design work started. I began to research that and draw upon those designs. It's one of the places that has the most fantastic, elaborate shell work that's ever been found. The greatest concentration of it was found in Craig Mound. It was a treasure house of information. I have a lot of the Spiro designs in my work.

As I got more involved in researching and talking to other Indian people about (the meaning of) some of the motifs—like the whirlwind motif—I came to find out that this motif is called the Strength of Life design. This was told to me by Phillip Deer. The Strength of Life comes from things that you find in nature, like the whirlwind, the tornado, (or) the whirlpool. And it also represents the movement that the Indian people dance around the sacred fire in a spiraling motion. In the center of the ceremonial square, four logs represent the sacred fire that's kept burning continuously from ancient times. These four logs represent the four seasons (and) the four phases of a person's life—when he's an infant, a child, an adult, and an Elder.

Part of the enjoyment that I get out of my shell art is to see the person it eventually might sell to. Because a piece to me is almost like a child, I want to see it as it grows and maybe—when it is purchased by someone—where it's going so I can get to know that person, too, and find out who appreciates it and why they appreciate it.

continued on page 290

knokovtee scott

continued from page 289

I teach elementary Indian art. So basically, I have to teach the fundamentals of art. I have to teach basic shapes and basic designs. I use the traditional motifs in doing that, especially the circle, the square, the triangle. I teach these basic forms to the children and show them how to put them together into the different motifs. I can teach them the names of the motifs and what the designs represent. Therefore, my main curriculum is based on the study of Indian art. I feel this is so important because most of the Indian children there don't really have a background of their own traditional culture. What they know is what they see on television and in the movies. It's the same for little white children, too. They have a stereotypical view of what the Indian is. They all feel we lived in tipis and rode horses on the plains and hunted the buffalo. I'm trying to teach more about our traditional culture of the Southeastern Indian Woodland Period.

My definition is one that Enoch Kelly Haney gave at a Symposium at Northeastern one time. He said, "Indian art is that art done of an Indian subject matter by an Indian artist." I feel like that needs to be carried a little bit further in that Indian subject matter should be something that pertains to that particular Indian artist's tribe (and) tribal background because I want to see the shell work grow. It is the traditional art of the Creeks and the Cherokees.

As an artist, I'm always looking for a direction. I gain that direction from my heritage and from nature and those things that are around me. I've looked into it so hard, I've tried to find a true direction for myself, and I feel like I'm getting a lot of strength from those things from nature—from my heritage—and I think this is what's helping me to continue on and to put all this into shell work and to keep up this work.

—Knokovtee Scott
Edited by Pamela Jumper Thurman

Note: In 1988, the Tribal Council passed a resolution renaming the purple shell mussels found in the area the Mankiller Pearl Shell after then-Principal Chief Wilma Pearl Mankiller. This was likely due to the recognition brought to the shell and the art of Knokovtee Scott.

Copyright permission gained by Talia Myres, CNE for use of excerpts in the Cherokee National Treasures Book.

dennis sixkiller

continued from page 209

I really enjoy what I do. I can still speak Cherokee, and I like to speak to the Elders. It really is what I enjoy. My daughter can understand some Cherokee. I have a son who lives in Grove, and he understands some. My grandkids understand a little—a few words here and there. I was teaching my grandchildren Cherokee one time, and when we got through, my granddaughter said, "Papa, I have something very important to tell you," and I said "What is it?" And she said *"Agiyosi!"* That means, "I am hungry" in Cherokee.

Language is important to being Cherokee—not just acting like it, but really being who you are. People think they know who we are, but they really don't. Being Cherokee comes from the heart—inside out, not outside in. Cherokee is our first language, and without our language, we're very limited as to what we can do. So much of what we do has to be done in the language; otherwise it can't be done.

One example: my hobby is playing Cherokee marbles; I talk Cherokee to those guys. Now, though, maybe only two or three speak Cherokee. When I first began playing, all the players talked Cherokee. I try to teach some of them to keep my language skills going. In Tahlequah, not as many marble players speak Cherokee, but in Jay, there are more that speak it. My cousin and I used to speak Cherokee, and the others couldn't understand us, so that gave us an advantage in the game. Ha ha.

The language is gradually going away because our speakers are going away. It doesn't seem to be as important to our younger generation. We offer lots of classes, but not that many people attend, and it's mostly mixed bloods; not many full bloods attend. I honestly believe that our speakers think that as long they can speak, that is enough, but if they would learn how to read and write it, it would change their world like it did mine. We have a lot of documents that are written in Cherokee. If you can't speak it, then you can't understand what you're reading. That's why it's so important to me to teach people how to speak Cherokee. I go out into the communities to teach a two-hour class once a week, for ten weeks, twice a year. Other than that, I'm just teaching whoever wants to learn. I'll just keep on doing that.

—Dennis Sixkiller
Interviewed by Pamela Jumper Thurman

richard shade

continued from page 213

I made a lot of Black Locust bows. Probably Bois D'arc and Black Locust are the best for me. I make arrows out of Bois D'arc. I've made them out of Black Locust. They make good arrows. Basically the way I make them, you get a piece of Bois D'arc that has a fairly good ring growth in there that are about thirty-two inches, and I split the tree with an axe. You can split them any way with a wedge. When you get them into about 3/4-of-an-inch-square sections, you just split them and you'll have three 1/4-inch planks, and they may be a little crooked. Then you just go from there and sand them down, work them down, shave them down to arrow size. The closer you get to arrow size, you want to use sandpaper and a sharp knife. Take your time so you can get them as straight and smooth as you can. It takes time to make an arrow. It takes a lot of time. It will be a little crooked. So what you do is put it over heat and then bend it. Straighten it up with heat and it will stay straight. And get it the diameter you want it, anywhere from 5/16 to 11/32. Cut you a knot; that's where the string is going to go on it.

continued on page 291

richard shade

continued from page 290

Since we shoot a lot—targets and things—you can buy field points. Like at the archery shop, they glue right on there. That's the simplest way to do it. If you break them, it is no big deal. But the actual flint arrowhead you know, we didn't live back in the Stone Age, so we never used flint tips. But I put them on arrows! They look good.

I'll tell you what Mom said that her dad, Looney, and them used to do. Everybody had a little forge and shop out behind the house in the shed where they made their own metal stuff. They were all blacksmiths anyway, tinkering around with stuff. What Looney would do, if they find metal, they'd just heat it up and bend it, and he'd make a little practice tip. Really, actually like a little cone. He'd cut it out flat and roll it on some type of little template he had and just roll a sharp little cone. He (would) glue them to the sharpened point of the arrow, might put a barb on there. Because what he did was go down there and shoot fish with those in the creek right beside the house.

They might find a turkey feather or a chicken feather or whatever. Usually wild turkey is what they used and what they prefer. The wing feathers is what you want from the turkey because they are thicker and stronger. I've heard some tribes used eagle feathers, but that's kind of against the law now. What you want is a stiff feather that catches the wind and spirals that arrow. Some people think owl feathers are a real good feather but they are real soft. They don't catch the air to spin the arrow.

Dad's name was Carl Shade, and my mom's name was Linda Rattlinggourd. There's nine kids in our family. There's six girls and three boys, and I'm the second to the youngest. Growing up, I didn't know that much about bows. Dad never messed with bows. I don't know if his ancestors did. Mom just told me that her dad, Looney, had made bows and her brothers had made bows. But she did say that right back behind her place by Fourteen Mile Creek, they used to grow corn. Trees had all been cut down. She said those older men used to have Cornstalk Shoots around there. In the fall, they would have Cornstalk Shoots 200 or 300 yards from the creek. I wasn't born yet, so it had to be back in the 1930s.

She said it was usually men. Women and kids didn't hang around there. It was usually just older men and a few younger men. That's about all she knew about it. What I've heard other people say about it is it was kind of a gambling game. Somebody probably had a bottle of whiskey. It was something to do—a game. They had fun, I guess. I don't remember them shooting a lot of places back when. Buck Neugin, he used to grow corn. They used to shoot at his place. There wouldn't be a lot of them. A lot of people back then did things on the spur of the moment. They didn't have no time limit for anything. If they felt like they wanted to do it, they did it. At that time, I was young. Archery didn't really interest me. We'd play around out there. I wish I had paid more attention to some of those older guys and their equipment and watching them shoot. I did watch some how they shot. But I didn't pay enough attention back then. I was eight or nine.

I like to make a bow when it hits me.

—Richard Shade
Interviewed by Shawna Morton Cain

john ross

continued from page 215

children. We can hire the fluent speakers to teach the children our fading language. Our future depends on the young children. I am proud to serve our Cherokee Nation in promoting and building our Cherokee language. I have taught at a college level, presented our language in public forums, and created ways to learn our Cherokee language for Cherokees in the future. I want to thank Principal Chief Bill John Baker for awarding me as a Cherokee National Treasure in the Cherokee Language.

I want to be remembered as a public servant for most of my working career. But first, I want to be remembered as a Christian, that I took care of my family, and that I have integrity and work at my job.

I've come to realize that we are the last generation raised in the Cherokee language—that we are the ones whose parents spoke it and lived it. My parents and grandparents did not speak English, nor was there any need for it. The decline of our language is a direct consequence of centuries of government assimilation, and it deeply affects our children to the core today.

Little did I know that we would be working so hard to keep the Cherokee language alive. I did not know how quickly we would lose our Cherokee language, which is our culture. I grew up talking my language; it's my first language, which I took for granted. What I have in common with everyone that speaks the language is the concern for the loss of our language. When we speak our language, we have fun, we are always laughing. This is why it's important that our young children learn the language; they are our hope for the future, our hope for the survival of our language and our culture. We need to support our children, revitalize our language to restore dignity, identity and self-confidence in our future generations so they can succeed in life.

My mission in life is to promote, preserve, and perpetuate the Cherokee language and culture for future generations.

—John Ross
Interviewed by Will Chavez

betty christie frogg

continued from page 217

try so hard to teach people that want to learn Cherokee language. I cry now. But I didn't before.

See, I came from two different Cherokee worlds! I come from two different Cherokee worlds—Christian and traditional. The Christies have always been traditional—stomp dances, stomp-dance leaders. And my mom's side all come from Christian. Every man I can think of, starting with my great-great-grandfather, was a Baptist preacher. He was the Kingfisher of Kenwood. My grandfather always was devoted to the church, and he would take us to church every time we'd go visit. We went to church with him. And my grandmother always was there to cook the meals, you know. My grandparents on Mom's side were readers and writers of the Cherokee language—I guess because of the Cherokee Bible. While I would go to church with them growing up, I never heard English spoken in that church. Nobody spoke English. So, all of their readings were always out of, and in, the Cherokee New Testament. That's one thing I always wanted to do was learn how to read. And I didn't do that until several years ago.

Oh my gosh, I've always looked at baskets and wanted to learn how to make baskets. My grandparents would make baskets. But they didn't teach me. I just watched. Somehow or another, as I grew up, they didn't make baskets anymore. They didn't show anybody else how to make them. As I got older, I kept wanting to learn to make baskets. I love making baskets. I love the flat reed. It is relaxing to forget about everything else outside the door and just make baskets. I love it. A lot of people, when I teach them, they don't have the patience for it. Usually I tell them, I hope they have patience, because that's what it takes to make a basket. And a lot of people want to learn how to make a basket so they can make money. And that's O.K., but I think you have to have the love for what you're doing before you can make a good basket. I'm not saying people make ugly baskets or anything like that. I'm just saying you have to love what you do. It's like cooking. If you love cooking, people's going to love your food.

I do contemporary, and I do traditional. I've got traditional here. And I really enjoy making traditional baskets. And I'm a traditional person, but I am open to contemporary things. I love all the designs in them, traditional Cherokee designs. I think the traditional basket will stay. I think the traditional colors, the traditional way of gathering materials and splitting the white oak, splitting the river cane. I think that is going to stay. I don't think it's going anywhere.

— Betty Christie Frogg

Interviewed by Shawna Morton Cain

tonia hogner-weavel

continued from page 219

for him. When he would tell me how to reset the gusset, move the waistline, or expand the neckline, he would have to illustrate an example. I still have all those little scraps of paper with his scribbles. That is my tear-dress text book.

Sewing is tedious work and requires the ability to keep on task to do things correctly. I've ripped out many seams and once I learned to fix my mistakes, I began to see a better quality in my work. When I put seven pointed stars on tear dresses my hand goes across each piece five or so times before it's on the garment. After all these years it still takes me ten to twelve hours to complete a tear dress. Every dress I make is custom fitted to that individual.

The first embroidered leather coat I made changed my perspective about my work with a comment from my friend, Martha Berry. When I said, "There are only four historic, leathe embroidered Cherokee coats," she replied, "And now there are five. You will always be associated with that coat. Your DNA is all over it." That elevated my thinking and gave me the confidence to view myself as an artist.

I love weaving the past into modern garments. I try to incorporate hints of Cherokee culture that Cherokee people will recognize. I enjoy the freedom to create and bring into light the subtle yet powerful symbols and icons that directed our ancestors in their daily life. It gives me great satisfaction to keep the culture alive through clothing and textiles.

I have dedicated my time to researching historic Cherokee clothing and I still feel like there is so much more to learn. I may not be like former Cherokee National Treasures, especially those elders who grew up perhaps having to do their craft to keep food on the table. Mine came from the love of the craft. I was able to devote time and energy to studying. I wanted to learn all I could about Cherokee textiles so I'd have a rhetoric side and a creative side. I respect and honor women who came from the ground up in their art. I'm a different Cherokee National Treasure. I go to the store and buy fabric and use modern ways. It is still my creation and energy that brings my art to a modern way of looking at Cherokee National Treasures.

—Tonia Hogner-Weavel

david scott

continued from page 223

the language where it's easy because a lot people say it's a hard language to learn, but there's got to be a way. I don't think anybody has really studied our language in depth. Whatever these language people do, I don't think it's ever been done. If someone ever does that, maybe there is a way to teach it a whole lot easier than the way we're teaching it. We've come a long way with teaching, but we still have a long ways to go.

If you don't have the language, if it ceases to exist, there's no culture to pass down. People think that the bow making, basket making and this stuff is the culture, but it's not. It's a whole lot more. It's the way you think, the things that are passed down to you, the do's and don'ts—that's part of it. There's plenty more out there as far as the culture is concerned. That's what I tell people. I think language is the culture when it comes to Cherokees because that's where it's at, and the reason a lot of it is not passed down is I can't translate a lot of this stuff into English. There's a lot lost in the translation. I wish I could, but it's just impossible. There are things that are said in Cherokee that if you knew the language, you would understand 100 percent. If I tried to translate that into English, you probably wouldn't be able to understand half of it. To me that's where your culture comes from, and understanding that culture goes right into the arts.

The reason I know the Cherokee language is not an easy language to learn is my wife, (Sam Watts Scott), has been trying to learn it for several years now. She knows more than what she thinks she does. If it was easy, she would already know it, but it's not. The other thing is today it seems like to me we are teaching a slang type of Cherokee—you know where you say, *siyo*. It's *Osiyo*. That's the correct way to say it. They leave off the first sound of it, which isn't detrimental, but I try to teach her the correct way. I'm going to try to pass what is correct. That's my goal.

I can't say what's going to happen to the language. I do know if there's not an effort made, we're going to lose the language, and the old people used to say once you lose the language, you've got no identity. You're unique when you have your own language; you're a unique people when you have that language. The way they (elders) used to say it, "When you lose the language, you're going to be like the white people."

My father used to tell me all of the time if you're not careful, that's how you're going to end up. It didn't sink in, but today, as I grow older I can see there's no initiative to learn the language at all. I don't see it in the young people. I don't see it in the middle-aged people who don't speak the language. I just don't see the enthusiasm.

It's sad that they don't know the language. And that's the same with the culture. When the language goes, the culture is going to go. A lot is going to be lost when that language goes. From what I see today, that's where we're headed and at a quick pace, too.

— David Scott
Interviewed by Will Chavez

vivian garner cottrell

continued from page 227

of 4; either a 16- or 24-rib start (4-over-4-over-4-over-4 and 6-over-6-over-6-over-6).

Mom and I would weave together for twenty-five years, until her death in June 1997. I pay much tribute to her for her teachings. We not only shared a common interest, but we also shared a mother/daughter bond. My mother was my mentor.

Having retired from our CPS audit firm in June 2016, I will be teaching double weave, rivercane classes as part of the Cherokee National Treasures mentoring program later in the year.

— Vivian Garner Cottrell

perry vanbuskirk

continued from page 233

with a broom—sweep the dirt and stuff out. But it was a dirt floor. With him being right next to us, and then my aunts and uncles was all around us, too. We really was never subject to anything White because he never told us anything. That's why we know our heritage.

We was taught plants, how to take care of yourself. And I still use it, because when I get sick, very rarely do I go to the doctor. And people's like, "Man, you look healthy, and this and that." Well, I can tell you this: I don't take no man-made pills and stuff. That's the way I raised my family. And even like our kids, our kids don't think anything of it, because they are exposed to it every day.

My boy was the same way. He didn't know, say, the Indians done this or this is something that is a Cherokee culture, (a) way of life. He didn't even distinguish that, because we didn't say, "This is Indian" or "This is white." We just taught them all of this because we just wanted him to know his culture, whether he realized it or not. I tell my kids this all the time: "One of these days society is going to get to where we have to take care of ourselves. So, if you don't know how to make a bow (or) chip an arrow point or anything or know how to hunt and fish or anything like that, then you're actually gonna be sunk."

I truly believe if that time does come, people's gonna come looking for the Native American and say, "Show me this. Teach me this. Because I cannot survive without it." That was the stuff that I heard from my grandpa, my uncles, (and) from my mom.

I think we're the type that adapt real quick. We are an adaptable breed of people. We can actually almost adapt to anything that is out there. Even now, we adapted to the, let's say, "modern" way of living, but we still actually add our heritage, our lineage, and everything to it. Because we might just tweak it a little to make it work so much better. Because we kind of added our little bit of tweak to it, and it works so much better for us now.

continued on page 294

perry vanbuskirk

continued from page 293

It's just like planting. If you don't know how to plant it, the old-timers knew the time to plant. They knew where to plant. How much sun. And that's the things they look at. And people will go out and say, "I'm gonna make a garden right here," (and) break the ground up, and they don't look at, well, the soil might not be the right soil for it. It might be too shady. It might be too much sun. All of that kind of stuff. Sometimes they don't even take anything into consideration. Like with gathering—we just passed the wild-onion gathering. Next is the mushrooms. And that's just like through seasons, because mushrooms (and) wild onions are not here year-round. So, it's almost like you have to know when that season is. And it's almost like you have to be willing to do your part and put your effort into it. Because it's not going to be given to you, because when all them seasons are here, if you don't make the effort to go out and gather, then you've wasted your time.

My grandpa, he said, "If somebody gives you something or teaches you something, you teach someone else." He said, "Everything that I teach you it isn't mine. It isn't me. It is something that is being given and taught to me." Grandpa said, "All I'm doing is holding it until it is time; the time is right to pass it on to that next one that needs it or that wants it." He said, "The biggest thing is the one that wants it."

Just like my Uncle Scott (Rackliff), being that my grandpa was his dad. That verified exactly what he said. I went to him and I said, "Scott, I want you to show me how to make an arrowhead."

And he's sitting there, and he done it all the time. I'm at his house. He's just sitting there. He's chipping away and just kind of laughed. He said, "Why should I show you?"

I said, "Well, I just really want to learn."

He said, "OK." He just stopped and he looked at me and he said, "I'll teach you. But it's gonna cost you."

And I said, "OK, what's it gonna cost me?"

And he said, "Hmm, let me think." You know how Indians are." He said, "I tell you what it's gonna cost you. If I show you and teach you, you have to show and teach someone else. That's what it's gonna cost you." And I thought about that a minute and said, "Yeah, OK."

It's almost from that point on, through the years, that's why we did so many programs with these children. That's kind of the way I lived—by passing everything on. I don't walk around and say, "I'm Mr. Cherokee. I'm Mr. Know-It-All on that."

No, if you want to know what I know, come and ask me.

—Perry Vanbuskirk
Interviewed Shawna Morton Cain

lisa smith

continued from page 235

The fact that hers and her family's shackles have been sold to people throughout the country, even to a person in Hawaii, is something she is proud of. She "was flattered and honored" to be named a Cherokee National Treasure in 2011, after making turtle-shell shackles for about twenty years.

She works at W.W. Hastings Hospital in Tahlequah and said she sees a lot of fellow Cherokee National Treasures at her job. She likens the group of artists to "a big family" that sees each other once a year at the annual Cherokee National Treasure banquet in December. She understands that she stands among some great artists.

"I'm glad to be a part of it," she said.

—Lisa Smith
Interviewed by Will Chavez

kathy vanbuskirk

continued from page 237

(Heritage Center). I've taught teachers, college students, you know. I've gone to different places to teach people." She said that over the years, she has competed against some of her former students in area art shows, but she said she encourages them to keep working on their craft and enter their work in art shows. Her son, Chris, and daughter, Melissa, have learned to make their mother's baskets and have won their own awards at art shows.

"That makes me feel good. It means what I know is being carried on," she said.

— Kathy Vanbuskirk
Interviewed by Will Chavez

dan mink

continued from page 239

word 'branding.' I think 'identity' was a better word for it, in this case—'cultural identity' in a contemporary setting. I was excited to get to work here."

He believes you don't really have to be an artist to be a good graphic designer but it helps. When he has an idea, he said, it is quicker and easier for him to draw out his idea, scan it to his computer, and save it for later. He said if younger artists or youth who are interested in graphic arts came to him for advice, he said he would tell them to "stick with it" and "leave their pride at the door" because their work will be critiqued and criticized. He said you have to be able to take constructive criticism from your instructors in school who are trying to help you become a better designer and, later, from your work manager who might want a different design than you created. "My advice would be to listen, take lots of notes, and don't be afraid to just go out there and try," he said.

His inspirations are artists A.C. Blue Eagle and Jerome Tiger. They were the first Native artists he noticed who were creating Native art. He said he noticed—in Tiger's drawings—lines in people's faces and muscle structures were different and unique. "To me they were simple. I could see why he did what he did in my mind. I studied his technique."

Mink said he is interested in studying photography. He would also like to try making pottery and sculptures someday. "I always thought I could do well in that. (There is) something about three-dimensional art. You have a little more detail, especially in sculpture where you have to get the muscle tone right. With pottery, I just love everything they do."

He said he is most proud of the graphics he created for a seven Cherokee Clans poster in 2005, which often can be seen in tribal offices. He created a Southeastern-style border for the artwork he created for each clan. "It took off. I really didn't expect that kind of response from people."

Creating the main design for the Cherokee Nation Holiday has become something he looks forward to every year. He said he is pleased with the Southeastern-style designs he created in 2014 and 2015. The designs are used in advertising, for the holiday T-shirts, and the official holiday program. "I appreciate this administration allowing me to do what I was trained to do," he said. "I'm always up for a challenge."

—Daniel Mink
Interviewed by Will Chavez

roger cain

continued from page 243

The first art show I entered was at the Five Civilized Tribes Museum, and I placed second after Anna Mitchell. I didn't know what a big deal that was until after I got my ribbon and other artists told me who she was. That blew me away. Soon after, I met Anna and she talked so much about the importance of Cherokees' knowing and using our own Southeastern designs. It was the way Anna talked and encouraged me that made me want to represent as a Cherokee artist! A few years later, I was talking about river cane and dye to my grandma and grandpa and asked Grandpa Pumpkin to show me bloodroot. The very same day, I asked him if he knew anything about river cane. That day I learned a lot. That was 16 years ago. After that, I found out that Grandma Christie's family and Grandpa Pumpkin's family all made river-cane baskets a generation back. Lucky me: they both wanted to teach me their way. I am grateful for the gifts that my ancestors have given me.

I always liked drawing faces and just fell into mask making. I made my first gourd mask after I saw a Wendell Cochran booger mask made of gourd at my in-law's house. I had been studying about the Cherokee Booger Dance from books, and here is this local Cherokee artist who was making them. So, I tried it. I liked to make mine ugly. Elders were telling me the uglier and scarier, the better, when it came to making Booger Masks. And so I have been doing that. I always try to use natural dyes, hides, sinew, and such, to resemble the Cherokee masks from the late 1800s and before. Then, sometimes, I just like to get crazy and make some weird masks.

I like to blend contemporary and traditional ideas, styles, and mediums. I think it is important for Cherokee artists to use traditional materials because we are continuing that tradition of our culture. We have used these materials and designs for thousands of years in all sorts of forms and shapes—river cane, copper, wood, and stone-carving. I like to incorporate a contemporary twist, sometimes, just so I can express new ideas that are relevant to Cherokees today. For me, that is what Cherokee art is all about—bringing the old traditions in with the new to reflect our past and present as a people. It's a balance. We can't forget who we come from, and we can't stay stagnant. We Cherokees know how to roll with the flow.

— Roger Cain

robert lewis

continued from page 245

Robert reflected on one instance while performing. He said that it is greatly empowering to see an individual become involved with how he tells the stories.

"I once performed for an alternative school where the students had seen only the worst things others never see, things like abuse, alcoholism, broken homes with no one seeming to care for them. In the course of telling the story, I pulled out a student, and this person began to do all I had asked the others to do in telling the story, like talk, react, dance. I noticed the teacher left the classroom and brought back the principal and counselor; they both watched the performance. Afterwards, the teacher remarked on how I had brought forth such

continued on page 296

robert lewis

continued from page 295

performances from her normally reticent students, and then she mentioned how she had to go get the principal to watch what I was doing, and I said I had noticed her leaving, and then she said, 'I wanted the principal to see, but also I wanted the counselor to watch because you had chosen this one student to interact with the others.' That particular student had been at that school for six months, and it was the first time anyone heard him speaking, and I had that student speaking and dancing and laughing with the others.

"The student no longer felt like an outsider, and change followed with this one moment, where a year had gone by and the student was talking about attending further schooling in nursing and wanting to embrace life again. The teacher said it all could be traced back to that story that I had told.

I love my family; my father and mother and brothers have always been supportive in anything I have done. Having such a strong solid-core foundation has helped me become who I am. My two sons, Yazzie Lee (*Swee Mosai*) and *Ke'yah E-sil* are my pride and joy. They have always inspired me to do my best at whatever I reach for."

Robert works for the Cherokee Nation as a school and community specialist and conducts outreach classes and services in art, culture, and storytelling. As part of the Cherokee Nation cultural outreach program, he also travels the country to perform before a wide variety of native, school, college, museum, festival, and art market audiences. He is the winner of the Dreamkeepers Perry Aunko Indigenous Language Preservation Award and the Cherokee National History Society Seven Star Tradition Bearer Award.

—Robert Lewis
Interviewed by Will Chavez

shawna morton cain

continued from page 247

if I am going to take, I must give back. I must protect and assist the growth of the bloodroot if I expect to take from it. I must respect the river cane if I expect to take from it. And sure, that may sound kind of hokey. But, it is the truth.

In my short life span of weaving over the past few decades, I have seen it: I have seen native plant patches wiped out again and again, and I have watched people overharvest. That just isn't right and should be frowned upon by us all. I do speak out pretty loudly on this topic and teach about this respect for our plants to anyone I mentor or take on to teach traditional basketry. Then I watch! I watch to make sure what I said was heard. Too often, it just isn't. So, I teach less and less about how to gather and teach more and more about how to plant or keep a patch healthy.

To me, a basket that I make is a living thing. People ask me, "How do you 'keep' a basket?" as in how do you keep one from getting old and falling apart. It just depends. Like people, baskets that are living will get old. They will age over time. But, that basket has lived and has a lot of stories to tell. A lot of hands have touched it. For this reason, I use most of my baskets. All have different purposes. I always think of our traditional basketry as an art form that has prevailed all the trials and tribulations of the Cherokee people. Basketry and other traditional arts represent to me tradition and pride in those who came before us. It is amazing, and somehow comforting, to me to know that we continue that tradition today over a thousand years later.

Over the years, I have had many teachers, most of them Cherokees. Thelma was my first. Bessie Russell taught me a lot, too. Charlotte Coats taught me the flat, double-wall basket. (She laughed.) I hate to admit Victor Wildcat helped me because it will just make his head big. But, he did! He helped and taught me a lot when I later taught Native Studies at Stilwell High School in the 1990s. Anna Mitchell taught me to always represent! She would say, "Represent Cherokees well! Do good work and teach them about our own Southeastern Indian designs and traditions." I can say that I have had some of the best Cherokee teachers going! Can't name them all here but they know I acknowledge and respect them immensely.

I received National Treasure for river cane basketry. When I started way back in the mid-1970s, I used only commercial reed. It wasn't until almost twenty years later that I started learning about using natural materials. I have woven honeysuckle, buck brush, white oak, a little hickory, and some ash. Overall? My favorite is river cane.

I guess I started to tackle river cane when Roger, my husband, and I found out there weren't any Cherokees out there working with river cane basketry, except Thelma. Well, I can't say no one was working with cane here in Oklahoma. There just wasn't any evidence anyone could find of it. That is when Thelma Forrest and Aaron LeMaster, who then worked at the Cherokee Heritage Center, came out to visit us when we lived out at Chewey for a while. They encouraged us both so much that we felt that we needed to do it!

It took us a few years to really get it down—trial and error! Thelma would give me hints, my husband's Grandpa Pumpkin showed us how to split the cane once, and his grandma, Agnes Christie Pumpkin, made sure that she got her word in on the subject, too! She kept telling all of us, as she pointed to this big wash tub of water, "You have to put fire to it!" Later, we figured out that really hot water made all the difference in the world and Agnes was right. We laugh about that now. She knew what she was saying. We just couldn't understand yet.

That's how it works when traditional Cherokee Elders teach you something. It really is true that they often won't repeat something twice. So, you better be listening the first time! That is my experience, anyway. For me, being a Cherokee basket weaver and a Cherokee National Treasure has created some of the best memories and experiences of my life. I never would have gotten to know all these talented, outspoken, honorable leaders—traditional people. My life is richer for having known them.

continued on page 297

shawna morton cain

continued from page 296

Respecting our Elders is something that we Cherokees—all Indian people—talk so much about. But sometimes, I think we forget our Elders in this busy modern world. I know I wish I had my grandparents back so I could ask them questions I never asked or say things to them I never said. Taking the time to sit down and slow down that pace we are all so wrapped up in is important! Sitting all day and just talking and, especially listening, is something I have learned to appreciate by being around Cherokee Elders. When life is getting me down or I feel like things are unjust or wrong with the world, I try my hardest to remember the knowledge Elders have shared—often that life is too short to worry or mess with negativity. Whether that sounds corny or whatever, I don't care. It works for me.

—Shawna Morton Cain

noel timothy grayson

continued from page 249

And I made a bow not too long ago, just for my own self. I went out and I cut one of the sticks down around by my dad's old place. And I mean, I went "old school" on it just like when we was kids. Took the hacksaw to it, cut notches in it, put a string on it—just found a string. You know, we used to use my brother's shoe strings, his boots. Tied a string on it and checked it. It was a thirty-pound bow. Not bad, ain't it? Not bad for a stick—a stick and a string.

When you're looking at trees like that, you look at the bark. Whatever that bark is doing, when you split that wood, underneath it's going to do whatever that bark is—exactly the same thing. That tree right there. See how it's got that big gnarly spot right there? How that bark goes around it? When you split that wood, it's going to split underneath just like that. That's the tree I wouldn't cut. Now if it's already blown down, you know, knocked down? Yeah, I'll go ahead and cut it—because, I can use character wood. It's got character to it! That's part of being a bow maker is just knowing how to work it. We know we can take it and heat it and bend it and straighten it out if we want to. But, that's just character. Just like us, you know?

—Noel Grayson
Interviewed by Shawna Morton Cain

tommy wildcat

continued from page 253

Creating a musical production as a self-taught musician and flute maker has been an educational journey. But I love to share the music with people. All my songs are original compositions that are meant to honor our Cherokee values, including family, friends, and Elders. That's important to me that these songs have a special meaning.

In 2002, I won the national Native American Music Award for "Flutist of the Year," and I was proud to have earned national recognition for my artistry. But an even sweeter honor was given to me in 2013 when I was bestowed the title Cherokee National Treasure. I have always been grateful to follow in the footsteps of my father, who was named Cherokee National Treasure in 1995. I am so proud to have joined him. It is a true honor for me and my family. Along with earning a degree at Northeastern State University, being named a Cherokee National Treasure is the thing I am most proud of in my working career.

Being a Cherokee historian and culture specialist allows me the opportunity to share our American Indian heritage across the country. I have played and performed around the world, including at the National Museum of the American Indian in Washington, D.C. I have been truly blessed by my ancestors to do something I love for the last twenty-five years and, at the same time, to educate and entertain people.

—Tommy Wildcat

david comingdeer

continued from page 255

every man (or) boy was using a set of sticks I had made. Since then, I've seen my sticks at many grounds, and that brings me great satisfaction," he said.

"Another memorable moment was when I saw my son, Spencer, complete his first set of sticks. He had helped me finish many pairs, but he finally learned to make his own pair."

Comingdeer said making sticks and playing stickball is an important part of the Cherokee's cultural life. "The ball game comes from our tribal towns' ceremonial grounds. Sticks are a part of that tradition which makes us a tribal nation. Without our cultural life ways, we are not a tribe. To me, and others from the ceremonial grounds, our cultural life ways are of the utmost importance to keep our status as a federally recognized tribe. Our cultural sovereignty must balance our political sovereignty, because our political sovereignty cannot stand alone."

He said he would like for people to remember him and what he did to perpetuate the art of stick making. "I've made sticks for Cherokees, Muskogee Creeks, Seminoles, Choctaws, Chickasaws, Yuchis, and Ojibwa, and non-Native Americans," he said. "On behalf of my family, I thank all the Elders who have helped in raising my children to adulthood, with a strong cultural upbringing. Many of the folks that influenced me and my children have passed away, and we are doing our best to carry on what has been passed down to us."

Comingdeer resides in the community of Spade Mountain. He is of the Paint Clan and is a member of the Echota Ground at Park Hill where he is chief. He and his children have an active ceremonial life and spend much of their time traveling to ceremonial stomp dances across eastern Oklahoma.

—David Comingdeer
Interviewed by Jami Murphy

Index

Index

S

T

U

V

W

Y

THE HENNESSEY CLIPPER

Cultural heritage
SEAL OF THE CHEROKEE NATION
SEPT. 6. 1839

Do da da go hv i
until we see each other again